Russian Music Studies, No. 5

Malcolm Hamrick Brown, Series Editor

Professor of Music
Indiana University

Other Titles in This Series

A Book about
Stravinsky

A Book about Stravinsky

by
Boris Asaf'yev

translated by
Richard F. French

with an introduction by
Robert Craft

UMI RESEARCH PRESS
Ann Arbor, Michigan

Produced and distributed by
UMI Research Press
an imprint of
University Microfilms International
Ann Arbor, Michigan 48106

Library of Congress Cataloging in Publication Data

Asaf'ev, B. V. (Boris Vladimirovich), 1884-1949.
A book about Stravinsky.

(Studies in Russian music ; no. 5)
Translation of: Kniga o Stravinskom.
Includes index.
1. Stravinsky, Igor, 1882-1971.   I. Title. II. Series.
ML410.S932A83   780'.92'4 [B]   82-4810
ISBN 0-8357-1320-2   AACR2

Contents

Igor Stravinsky, c. 1930 (photo courtesy Robert Craft).

Foreword: Asaf'yev and Stravinsky

It has taken a centenary to bring out an English language edition of the one crucial book so far published about Igor Stravinsky. I refer to *Kniga o Stravinskom*[1]—*A Book about Stravinsky*—by Igor Glebov, *nom de plume* of Boris Vladimirovich Asaf'yev.[2] This brilliant interpretation of Stravinsky's music and its meaning for the twentieth century appeared in Leningrad in 1929 and was virtually banned on publication. Five years ago the volume was re-issued in the USSR, with the music examples corrected, and now Richard French has performed the great service of translating it.

After conducting concerts in Russia in the spring of 1928, Ernest Ansermet wrote to Stravinsky:

> There is no place where you are more loved and better understood than in Leningrad, at least among an elite, and notably by a man who is very close to your ideas and your tastes as well as to your music. Boris Asaf'yev is a marvelous human being, extremely sensitive and incredibly intelligent. Not only does he know you intellectually, but also has an intuition of you.[3]

This last statement does credit to Ansermet's own perspicacity, despite Stravinsky's curt answer: "You would think otherwise about Asaf'yev if you had been able to read him."[4] *A Book about Stravinsky* is a classic of criticism, the peer of that great work on Leonardo da Vinci by Asaf'yev's younger fellow-countryman, V.P. Zubov, which I mention because the strengths of both studies are in their insights rather than in their histories, and because both books continue to outlive more recent and exhaustive ones.

The fifty-year delay in the appearance of *A Book about Stravinsky* in this country is partly the fault of the composer himself. Asked for a blurb to promote a proposed English edition, he refused, explaining that any interest in Asaf'yev was misplaced. This attitude is understandable in a man who hated the communism and atheism of the new Russia that Asaf'yev represented and had described as having been preceded by "a millenium of credulous and naive faith." Philosophically the two men could hardly have been further apart: a Christian who believed in the divine nature of artistic inspiration versus a dialectical materialist who sought to explain artistic phenomena in terms of a constructivist social theory. Indeed, the party-line polemics with which the book commences make one wonder why it was placed on the Soviet index, except that Stravinsky himself, a White Russian reactionary in the official eye—in Asaf'yev's, one of the greatest composers who ever lived—was considered an unsuitable topic. Clearly, the subject of *Kniga o Stravinskom* began to read it with strong political and religious prejudices.

Stravinsky's animus against his disciple had other causes as well, perhaps dating back to the time when both men were pupils of Rimsky-Korsakov. This possibility seems to be borne out both by the book's complete absence of biographical information and by two or three asides accusing Stravinsky of arrogance in a way that suggests a personal history. In May 1914 Asaf'yev came to Paris for the premiere of *The Nightingale* armed with requests from Stravinsky's friends to admit the critic to rehearsals. But if a meeting took place then, no record of it has emerged, and, to Ansermet, Stravinsky denied ever having known Asaf'yev. Then, too, Arthur Lourié disapproved of this Soviet admirer: "I read Asaf'yev's last article with revulsion, and to think that at one time we almost spoke the same language!" (Letter to Stravinsky, April 14, 1925). Finally, the chapter on *Apollo,* the next-to-last composition that Asaf'yev discusses, is lacking in perspective, expresses fears that Stravinsky could be in danger of losing his way, and compares some of the music to that in Pugni's ballets. Naturally, this would have offended the composer, but it seems doubtful that he read this far. My explanation differs from these and is based on a trait of Stravinsky's character. He would tolerate no interpreter he could not control—hence his autobiography—and, in conducting, his preference for a mere craftsman over a Bernstein. Surely Stravinsky was annoyed that an infidel Marxist, living so far from the center and with only the rarest opportunities to hear the music, had penetrated it so profoundly—and it is inconceivable that Stravinsky did not realize that Asaf'yev understood him as no one else did, least of all the authors of the French and Italian monographs published at about the same time and written quite literally under the subject's nose.[5] After all, to be completely understood by anyone is threatening, and who, least of all Igor Stravinsky, wants an alter-ego?

In the spring of 1935, while Stravinsky was on a concert tour in the United States, his wife's sister, Lyudmila Beliankina, wrote to him from Sancellemoz that his young American friend, the pianist Beveridge Webster, while on a recent visit to the USSR, had procured a copy of the book. In it, she says, Asaf'yev dwells at length

> ... on *Noces, Soldat,* and *Mavra.* Up to this time I have not encountered such an interesting and intelligent critique of your music. I was especially struck by how subtly he evaluated *Mavra.* It is amazing that someone who has had no contact with you and no guidance from you understood your work so completely. He analyzed everything himself and he warmly and intelligently defends you against the academic circle in Russia.

Let me say at once that the *Mavra* essay is a revelation, convincing me, for one, that the work fails in performance only because it demands too much sophistication from its audiences. Being unacquainted with the sources, we in the West do not relate to the references, not only to such composers as Alyabev,[6] Varlamov,[7] and Verstovsky,[8] but also to Dargomyzhsky and Tchaikovsky.[9]

But Stravinsky had read *Kniga o Stravinskom* years before, having purchased the book through his publishers in Berlin on October 4, 1930. His 1935 Ecole Normale lecture on the Concerto for Two Solo pianos seems to owe something to Asaf'yev's discussion of the etymology of the word "concerto," and the composer's presentation of his aesthetics in his *Cronique de ma vie* might have been influenced by the Soviet musicologist. In any case, Stravinsky was well aware that Asaf'yev had already disavowed *A Book about Stravinsky* at the time he marked his copy of the book. The underscored lines, added question, exclamation, and check marks, and comments are so consistently deprecatory that when the margins are blank, as in the case of the chapter on *Renard,* the reader interprets the silences as signifying agreement, if not praise. Stravinsky entered a favorable word—"important"—in only one place, yet this could be taken as a clue to his recognition of the true value of the book, since, if not Asaf'yev, only Stravinsky himself could have written the passage to which the word refers:

> In instrumental music, pitches and rhythms are not used to compose sound complexes that have precise, emotional connotations. Nevertheless, the choice of material must be made, and that choice inevitably produces an inner logic of its own and a precise sonorous image . . . a unique complex of intonational "gestures" by which the character and pace of a piece are defined.

Except to correct mistakes in music examples, Stravinsky did not mark the book until the chapter on *The Nightingale*. He probably took exception to some conclusions concerning his three early ballets, but not, I think, to the charge that the unadventurous character of his music before *Fireworks* can be blamed on domination by Rimsky-Korsakov, who, says Asaf'yev,

> Walked behind his times. . . . Each new work of his represented . . . a *concession* to contemporary demands. . . . The pupil was of necessity behind his times.

Asaf'yev's analysis of *Firebird* is conventional, but he was quick to see the technical superiority of the 1919 Suite over the earlier one. In the *Sacre du printemps,* he seems to have been the first to notice the construction of the melodic ascent at the end, from bass A to treble A, A above the clef, then up through C, E, the pivotal F, and rapidly, in the last two measures, to F-sharp, G, G-sharp, A (the 32nd-note appoggiatura), and the ultimate A, five octaves above the first one. Needless to say, Asaf'yev regards the music as "tonal" and as resolving from dominant to tonic.[10] More recent studies do not even mention this melodic aspect of the passage, possibly because of distraction by the rhythmic and harmonic considerations. (I have added Stravinsky's bracketing of the measures to Asaf'yev's example, since these groupings remained the same even in the 1943 revision where downbeats and upbeats, bass notes and bass-part rests, trade places [see following example]). What must be emphasized is that at a time when it was still necessary to defend the *Sacre* against those who had "not enlarged their ideas about what is permissible in music," and to uphold "the originality that proceeds from organic and natural premises," Asaf'yev had grasped the logic, the substance, and the import of the work, proclaiming that Stravinsky's music is, "the child of the era that it has come to define."

For the Westerner, Asaf'yev's most valuable chapters are the ones devoted to the Russian-language theater pieces, *The Nightingale* not least among them. His analysis identifies not only the opera's specifically Russian features, such as the "Russian rococo" in the Nightingale's aria in Act I, but also those of Stravinsky's music in general. Thus the bell-like sounds that become part of the substance of *Noces* are already present in the texture of *The Nightingale,* in harp and string harmonics, in the timbres of piano and celesta, not to mention the actual bells in the Emperor's court at the beginning of Act II and the funeral gong in Act III. Asaf'yev, who knew that Stravinsky would have heard the great bell of the Nikolsky Sobor in his cradle, could not have been surprised by the continuing evocation of bells in the later music,[11] the tam-tams in the 1961 setting of Thomas Dekkar's *Prayer,* as well as in the *Introitus,* and the carillons and chimes in *Requiem Canticles.* The mention of this music performed for the composer's funeral in Venice, just before he was ferried to his grave, reminds me of his experiments with notations for the different speeds of the city's bells, since their rhythms absorbed him as much as their ring and the percussive articulation of mallet and clapper.[12]

Festive ritual, grotesquery, and the search for the primordial as well as for the new are integral elements of *The Nightingale* no less than of *Fireworks, Firebird, Petrushka* and *Le Sacre du printemps.* What is new, according to Asaf'yev, is the composer's "growing skepticism" and its "deepening effect on his vital instincts"—remarks, together with some others hinging on the "mature" attitude toward death in the New Russia, that provoke the first of Stravinsky's marginal grafitti:[13] "Very little has changed in this sense since I left Russia twenty years ago." Asaf'yev goes on that "the subject of death has always stimulated Russian composers to write deeply-felt music," and he includes the Stravinsky of *The Nightingale* in the statement. This seems like special pleading, since the idea of death has produced "deeply-felt music"from composers of all times and places. But Asaf'yev argues that "Life in Russia is so hard, many regard the gift of it as an unjust accident," a fact he relates to the hysterical reactions (peculiarly Russian, he says) of a Gogol, a Dostoevsky, a Tchaikovsky. Moreover, nightingales are messengers of Eros and, in Russia, wedding rites and funeral laments are closely related.

In any event, the Act III death scene gives Stravinsky's opera the human dimension and the depth it otherwise lacks. The struggle between the Nightingale and Death is the opera's dramatic and musical focus, the Nightingale's aria about the garden in the cemetery is the best and most moving music. The first two acts are mere and light satire at the expense of the "magisterial stupidity" of the Chinese Emperor and his courtiers, and of the Japanese and their Panasonic Nightingale. Moreover, after the Emperor's recovery, the opera is an anticlimax; his last words, instead of an affirmation of life, are a "puzzled interrogation," and the Fisherman's song is simply a colophon. When the Emperor's temperature returns to normal, Stravinsky's own "Nightingale fever"—to borrow Mandelstam's phrase—also disappears, but the emotions aroused by the music of the death scene linger on.

Apart from his stand against the new "mature" Russian attitude toward death, Stravinsky's criticisms of the chapter are picayune. Asaf'yev writes: "The voice of the Nightingale [is] first introduced instrumentally (an ornate improvisation)," and Stravinsky counters, "It is a cadenza and not an improvisation" (as if, traditionally, cadenzas were not improvised). "Kuzmin and Verlaine, Rimsky-Korsakov and Debussy" are among the influences on the opera, Asaf'yev states, and Stravinsky asks, "What is Rimsky-Korsakov doing in this company?" (to which the answer is "very little," yet Rimsky's influence on the music is undeniable). "In the symphonic poem, *Song of the Nightingale,* the middle section of the [opera's] entr'acte is made over into a new episode," Asaf'yev goes on, and Stravinsky rejoins: "As if no one ever noticed that in the opera this is sung."

In the next chapter, "Toward the New," the smaller works composed between 1913 and 1919 are examined—and illuminated. But Asaf'yev's usually reliable sense of Stravinsky's chronological development is contradicted in the conclusion that "the new style reaches maturity in *Noces,*" for we have since learned that much of the composition of that work antedates the *Berceuses du chat*[14] and *Trois Histoires pour enfants.* During World War I, Stravinsky was composing in different styles simultaneously, as is shown by the 1914-17 piano duets. On the other hand, Asaf'yev's remark that the piano accompaniment in *Chicker-Yacher* "suggests orchestral sonorities" reads like a prediction, since Stravinsky did score the piece, after *Kniga o Stravinskom* had been published.

In "Toward the New," Asaf'yev says that in Stravinsky's concluding chorus for *Khovanshchina,* "the ornate development of the archaic theme is incongruous," and that the composer "desires to be impudent at all costs." Since the piano-reduction hardly justifies these reactions, the remarks compound our curiosity to hear the piece—the orchestra score of which remained in Diaghilev's possession after the few performances in June 1913. I should also mention that Asaf'yev writes unenthusiastically about Stravinsky's orchestral *Chant funèbre* for Rimsky-Korsakov, a still earlier lost opus that, as the next step beyond *Fireworks,* continues to excite speculation and hope that the manuscript may be recovered.

In this same chapter, Asaf'yev enumerates the features of the new style, the exploitation of the responsorial principle, the rejection of the large orchestra, of tonic-dominant formulae, and of metrical regularity (or alternatively, the introduction of unequal time-intervals, of figurations with different numerators than those of the meter, and other devices—comparable to the enjambment, dislocated syntax, and so forth of the Russian poets of the time). Most essential, however, is Stravinsky's "new awareness of the functional relationship and interdependence of the various elements composing the texture of sounds." What this means simply, is that he has outgrown the rigmarole of academic composition and henceforth will follow only his own artistic logic.

Of Stravinsky's contemporaries, Asaf'yev alone seems to have recognized the importance of the Eight Easy Pieces (1915-17), and that they reveal the shrewd and incisive intellect of a great artist: "[This is music in which] no transplantation of the past can be found, but only contemporary life, with its cinematographic quality." Asaf'yev points out popular elements in each of the pieces that most of us would otherwise miss, in the Balalaika, for example, the abrupt interruptions and turns and the dynamics of the *chastushka*, and in the stretto movement of the Galop, "the sixth figure of the quadrille."

The essay on *Renard* is the only one, even to 1982, that does the work justice, though the shortcomings of the others can be blamed on the non-awareness of non-Russians that *Renard* represents the revival of "an authentic old Russian theater," long suppressed because of its blasphemy, mockery, and anti-clerical satire. *Renard*, a seventeen-minute romp that can be described as burlesque, masked buffoonery, mime, is enacted by clowns, actors, acrobats, dancers— anybody but singers. Based on gesture, it stands at the polar opposite of the narrative and descriptive tale of, for instance, Chaucer's Fox and Chanticleer. Stravinsky's singers impersonate the actors with shrieks and howls, measured speech, mock chant and prayer: the unctuous tone in which the fox, in nun's habit, confesses the rooster ("You have wedded, you have bedded, too many wives") is the most delectable lampoon of religious hypocrisy in music. "Laughter is life's real mirror," Asaf'yev says, "it's self-criticism."

As for word accentuation, Asaf'yev describes Stravinsky's aim as simply "to preserve the natural flow of the musical speech," which would be inconsistent, of course, with the association of every verbal accent with a point of musical emphasis. It follows, too, that the words must be independent of arbitrary metrical divisions. Near the end of *Renard*, with the arrival of the Cat and the Goat, the accents of the words adhere to the meter, but the dance conforms to a different beat, a counterpoint of accents. But of word-setting, more in connection with *Mavra*. The analysis of *Renard* concludes with an out-of-date defense of the work as "a deeply intellectual phenomenon" and the perennially pertinent observation that "this frightens many people."

Asaf'yev's "fertility" interpretation of *Noces* ignited a virtual explosion in Stravinsky, but for all his objections to the obtrusion of the mistaken thesis, he offers no clue to the right one, simply answering Asaf'yev's statement that the subject of *Noces* is "the confrontation of man and his instinct for procreation," with "I do not agree." Asaf'yev repeats his argument, "One must not forget that *Noces* is the embodiment of the ancient cult of fertility and reproduction," and Stravinsky rebukes him again: "Better to forget, because this has no bearing on it." Once more the critic reiterates that *Noces* is about "human beings standing face to face with the act of procreation," and Stravinsky objects, this time at greater length:

> I meant nothing of the kind: These statements, which I never expected from Asaf'yev, astound me. He has a great desire to find an orgiastic tendency that simply is not there.

Next to a remark about the work's "epic forcefulness and Euripidian rigor,"[15] the exasperated composer asks "What is all this deep-thinking nonsense? And

I, simpleton, was not aware of any of this." When Asaf'yev praises Stravinsky's economy, the compression into four short scenes, the composer jests: "*What? All of that into only four concise tableaux?*"

The sexual interpretation puts the composer so out of sorts that he chides his champion for using the diminutive "little berry"—"*Just plain berry,*" according to Stravinsky—and at a reference to the techniques and thought processes of Raphael and Velasquez, the composer snaps, "As if they were the same." When a tendency toward symphonism is detected, Stravinsky exclaims: "This is again your own improvisation, dear friend: Symphonism is not my intention." Seeing Bolshevism in a class-war reference to "unfortunates and captives," the composer wonders "Who?" and further vents his irritation in a rash of question marks. Asaf'yev's behavioristic analysis of Stravinsky's irony earns the comment from its subject: "A curtsy to Communists":

> It proceeds from pity and from envy . . . of people who, like children, can still find amusement in . . . toys because of the secret mechanisms that make them operate. The curious child breaks the toy open, but he does not uncover a secret thereby: the expert knows that there is no secret but simply a spring adapted to a form. He pities the child and wants to laugh.

Nevertheless, Asaf'yev's essay on *Noces* helps us to understand Russian wedding ritual as both tragic-ironic and grotesque, with threnody and buffoonery as its principal contrasting stylistic elements. On the one side are psalmodic chanting (the murmured "*Chesu, pochesu*") and the lamentations associated with the loss of virginity as well as the bereavement of the two mothers. On the other side are the paroxysms, the whooping and shouting—during the ballad of the little swan, for example—the rhythmically notated talk, the clapping, the basso falsetto. The antiphons and responses, of course, derive from peasant music as well as from the church.

That Asaf'yev does not elaborate on the traditions of matchmaking and other ritual is understandable, since he assumed his readers' familiarity with such matters. Nor did Stravinsky ever discuss these elements of the piece, no doubt having despaired of the work ever being understood in the West. Already in 1923 he had transcribed *Noces* for the pianola—which is to say, eliminated the voices, and he was to do the same with many of his Russian-text songs. By the time I knew Stravinsky, he was bored with folk-music and even more so with the question of its connections with his work. No doubt he interpreted, in a very different way than Asaf'yev intended, the latter's sage remark that "*Sacre* and *Noces,* two of Stravinsky's greatest achievements, are . . . tragedies of race, not tragedies of destiny."

Asaf'yev's observations on *Histoire du soldat* contain flagrant instances of his habit of introducing subjective interpretations, as when he writes of the opening March: "The soldier's head is full of random recollections—flashes of barracks life . . . " This is the more surprising since he has just said that

Stravinsky's musical thought is extra-personal, just as his music is extra-sensual (but not sensual-less...)...The best of his works are not "reflections" of inner life; rather, they incarnate the drive and appetites of life.... It is not the inner subjective experiences of people that fascinate him but the styles in which people display themselves.

Asaf'yev considers the "Little Concert," with its network of motives from all of the preceding numbers, as both the musical and dramatic centerpiece and a "synthetic, Lisztian-type" sonata-allegro, the first movement of a symphonic structure in which the Tango is the adagio, the Waltz the scherzo, and the Ragtime the finale. "Dance is the primary agent of form and movement in Stravinsky's art," Asaf'yev concludes, and, "the primary law of all life is rhythm, since all of our senses are rhythmic." In the Soldier's March, "despite the moments of silence, the rhythm is not silenced."

In the Tango, Stravinsky discovered the potentialities of an orchestra of percussion only, composing not just rhythm-lines for these instruments, but rhythm-harmonies as well, layers, or registers, of diffeent timbres and intensities. The "orchestra" of the Waltz suggests a band of street musicians, or a parody of one, through the ornamented, mock-virtuoso violin part. Here, and apropos the Ragtime, Asaf'yev remarks astutely on Stravinsky's "preference for sudden change, rather than long emotional intensifications and broad crescendi."

In the Chorale, "lines that have been moving toward the limit of individualized utterance" are brought together in tonic cadences that seem to be saying "Everything comes out well in the end." But the last one is a suspension, a 6/4 chord, and Stravinsky's ultimate irony, for the Devil soon leads the doomed Soldier below, to the accompaniment of hot jazz drums. Comparing the death of the Soldier to the "splendors of Isolde's last moments," Asaf'yev decides that the fate of Stravinsky's hero is "the more tragic, by virtue of its simplicity."

The *Pulcinella* chapter abounds in insights, both general ("The instruments are treated as characters in the comedy...the doubles of the figures on the stage") and specific ("The strings in the Toccata are used...to carry the movement from one *register* to another"). In the 1920s, however, when Asaf'yev wrote, it was not yet known that Stravinsky had not developed "fragments" in *Pulcinella* but, instead, arranged and orchestrated complete pieces, some by Pergolesi, seven (from the trio sonatas) by Domenico Gallo, and one by Count van Wassenaer. More thorough studies on *Pulcinella* have recently appeared.

Turning to *Mavra,* Asaf'yev says that "the whole composition is magnificent, and the melodic line is perfection," which did not stop Stravinsky from scolding him for attributing the "new level of intensity" in the Quartet to qualities of the deceased, for whom the singers repine. "The observation of a fourth-grade schoolboy," the composer writes, though it is one of many helpful evaluations of the musical means with which he delineates character. Thus

Parasha, whose prototype was Tchaikovsky's Larina, is portrayed by a gliding melody that avoids "disjunct intervals and temperamental rhythms," and the Hussar by bold entrances and "passionate cadences." Stravinsky's second outburst comes at the end of the analysis, after the statement, "The ingeniousness of reality finds a new and authentic musical utterance." "Only in this?" he demands. "Is it worthwhile, then, to give birth to a musical mouse?"

Mavra's melodic sources and genres, and its "musical speech" occupy a large and, for me, absorbing portion of the essay, but, then, I know nothing of Apollon Grigor'ev and Polezhaev, and was only vaguely aware that, like Stravinsky, Tchaikovsky, in *Onegin,* was attacked for his "misplaced accents, ungrammatical word-couplings, pauses in the wrong places, and metrical confusion." Asaf'yev's rebuttal is that "correctness" is not the issue:

> The central problem is to define the music of speech—speech that differs in style according to epoch, rank, society, the personality of the individual.... Speech... may be filled with interjections, exclamations, interrogations, declarations. The problem is to catch its whole excitement.... The critics have applied standards of written style and the pathos of theatrical speech, whereas *Onegin* [and *Mavra*] derive wholly from the music of the speech of the Russian middle class.... Words pour out in unbroken melodic lines, commas are ignored ... and emotional tone and its nuances take precedence over sense.

After the *Mavra* essay, *Kniga o Stravinskom* is less rewarding, both because the subject matter ceases to be Russian and because Stravinsky's 1920s, so-called international-style music quickly attracted a host of younger devotees, including a great many from the Western hemisphere, ready to pore over every note. Yet the final pages contain keen perceptions, both musical—"the reduction in the use of the dominant 7th in cadential formulas helps to unveil the tonic"—and dramaturgical:

> [Creon's] aria proclaims [the] inexorable decree of the oracle in a brilliant and authoritative tone, but... in such a way that, though [he] believes he is his own master, to the listener he is made to appear as a plaything... which has been set in motion and will go through its mechanical operations.

At the outset, Asaf'yev had distinguished two kinds of composer,

> the imitative and the evolving. The imitative preserves—or, at best, varies—what has been invented by others. The evolving always struggles to master new methods, new expressions.

One feels that if Boris Asaf'yev had lived as long as his great coeval, and not been the victim of Soviet mental misprision, he would have celebrated Stravinsky's glorious evolution through the music not only of the 30s and 40s, the Two-Piano Concerto and the Symphonies, but also that of the 50s and 60s, *Agon,* Movements, the Variations. No doubt he would have made the same pronouncement then that he did in his concluding remarks about *Les Noces:* "Our musical epoch is the epoch of Stravinsky."

ROBERT CRAFT

Notes

1. By Igor Glebov (Boris Asaf'yev), Triton, Leningrad, 1929, 398 pp., 257 music examples. Republished, Moscow 1977. Translated by Richard French. Ann Arbor, Michigan, 1982.

2. 1884-1949. Asaf'yev is better known as one of the villains in the persecution of Shostakovich. See *Testimony*, by S. Volkov.

3. Letter of April 10, 1928, in which Ansermet also reports that the *Sacre* and *Symphonies of Wind Instruments* were remarkably well played and received in Leningrad. He adds that Asaf'yev's brother and wife there desperately want to emigrate, and the conductor describes an incident when an icon, a gift entrusted to him from the composer's sister-in-law for his mother in France, was confiscated at the border. Ansermet was more successful in smuggling, *"Un ouvrage ancien"* presumably a Stravinsky manscript, between the pages of a score.

4. Stravinsky's library ca. 1924 contained a volume of Asaf'yev's essays on Russian composers, including Stravinsky.

5. This is not true of Herbert Fleischer's 1931 German monograph, published (1,000 copies) by the R.M.V. in Berlin. As Stravinsky wrote to F.W. Weber, September 29, 1931: "A month ago [Fleischer] wrote me a very kind letter in which he expresses ideas that do not concur in the least with that article of his in the *Berliner Tageblatt*. . . . That excerpt from his book had such a negative affect on me because of its complete misinterpretation of my intentions in, let's say, *Petrushka* and *Sacre;* I was utterly bewildered and depressed. And what *is* one to believe, what he wrote in his letter, or what, to my horror, I read about myself in the *Berliner Tageblatt* where, in his profound German-philosophical language, he characterizes my work as that of a thorough-going pessimist, a nihilist even, saying that I cannot believe—it is clear to him—in life beyond the grave, this and other arbitrary fantasies?"

6. A.A. Alyabev, 1787-1851.

7. A.E. Varlamov, 1801-1848.

8. A.N. Verstovsky, 1799-1862.

9. Recently, listening to *Perséphone* with George Balanchine, I was astonished to hear him exclaim "Tchaikovsky" and "Glinka" during melodies that to me seemed purely French.

10. In the 1943 score, the final bass note is not D but E. Asaf'yev seems to have used the 1913 4-hand score, but since the 64th-notes indicated for the flute are not found as shown here in any edition, I assume a misprint.

11. In a talk at the Cleveland Institute of Music in 1968, Victor Babin recalled a visit to Stravinsky in his Hollywood home during which the composer "showed me his *In Memoriam Dylan Thomas* . . . explaining to me how the four trombones sounded like funeral bells. . . . " (From *Victor Babin*, the Cleveland Institute of Music, 1982.)

12. One of the illustrations in Nathanial Spear's *A Treasury of Archeological Bells,* New York, 1978 is a photograph of a bell discovered in the 1950s in a Sarmatian (1st-2nd century A.D.) burial ground in the Dnepropetrovsky District of Stravinsky's ancestral Ukraine.

13. All of these are in Russian. The translations provided here are by Mme Lucia Davidova.

14. Stravinsky objects to the title *Berceuses de chat,* as Asaf'yev writes it: "Not lullabies *for* the cat but *by* him, . . . It makes a difference."

15. In the English text, "Aeschylean rigor."

Igor Stravinsky, from *A Book about Stravinsky,* Boris Asaf'yev, 1929 edition.

Translator's Note

Though Robert Craft states correctly that it took the Stravinsky centenary to bring Asaf'yev's book on Stravinsky to publication in English, my translation of it has existed for two decades. The story of the project is so unusual that it deserves a brief retelling.

When I was living in New York in the late 1950s, I decided to learn another foreign language, this time in an alphabet other than Latin. I toyed with the thought of Greek, abandoned that idea (I have since mended my ways), and chose Russian, the study of which I began in the Extension Division of New York University at Washington Square. I subsequently made a thorough review of the grammar with my NYU teacher, then known as Anna Michouroff, who ordered me back to Professor Aaron Pressman at NYU for literature and then for phonetics.

All this took four years. During that time I became more and more fascinated by the music of the language, and then by the almost unimaginable intricacies of the syntax which account for the very subtle differences of meaning that the Russian language can convey. Could one undertake, I asked myself, a project of translation that, besides reinforcing one's command of the written language, would thoroughly test one's ability to move from this highly inflected language into an English that—if the reader were not the wiser—might sound as if it were original? If so, what text could one use for such an experiment?

Spurred on by the preposterousness of these two questions, I found myself in the Slavonic Collection of the New York Public Library. There I came upon the Asaf'yev text. How? I no longer remember; it was just an accident. My wise friend Gustave Reese liked to irritate his colleagues and students by noting that most bibliographical tools are really unnecessary: what the good scholar needs is a good nose. Anyhow, I happened on the text, found out (with the help of suitable bibliographical aids) that only two other copies had been reported by libraries in the United States (Library of Congress and Harvard College Library), and satisfied myself that no English translation existed. I wrote out a call slip and waited for the book to arrive. When it came, I started to leaf through it, only to find that the pages had never been cut. In thirty years, no one had ever read it.

The work of translation took a year. Since then, the typescript has been in and out of the editorial offices of several respectable publishers, whose notes of rejection were virtually identical: it's a fine book, but it's out of date. I have in my head a basket full of the drafts I might have sent in reply: of course it's out of date, that is precisely its value. Through it one can view the critical response of a leading Russian intellectual and artist to this extraordinary musical phenomenon and thus learn something about Stravinsky and about the level, range, and nature of Russian culture in the 1920s that is necessarily absent from the hundreds of Western "interpretations" of Stravinsky's music, and which they ignore at their peril.

More than ten years ago, in an article for the *New York Review of Books,* Robert Craft mentioned in a footnote the existence of my translation; to this day I have no idea how he learned of it. But when Professor Malcolm Brown corresponded with him last year about the advisability of having this Asaf'yev appear in the UMI Russian Music Studies series, Craft was kind enough to advise Brown that my translation existed, and that he could probably get hold of it through the executors of my estate. That suggestion so unnerved a former student of mine then at Indiana University, Ted Gibboney, that he was moved to risk inquiring by telephone, in a suitable quasi-funereal voice, whether there was any truth to that rumor.

That is all there is to the story. I hope the recounting of it may encourage others to set forth without a road map, despite the risk of a premature demise; I also hope the book may encourage readers to think again about the methods, knowledge, and perspective appropriate and necessary to responsible critical writings on music. Mr. Craft rightly points out that the book has virtually no biographical information. My notes, which appear in brackets throughout the text, are thus meant only to clarify for modern Western readers references that might otherwise be obscure; I do not seek to burden this text, otherwise so free of voyeurism, with the apparatus of modern biographical scholarship. Asaf'yev's original footnotes have been translated in full and are included as notes at the end of each chapter.

The problem of transliteration from the Russian can be solved in three styles: rigid, flexible, and careless. I have chosen to be flexible, meaning that conventional spellings in English have been retained even if they constitute inconsistencies. The difficulties of translating texts of certain works—*Noces, Renard, Mavra*—I have found insuperable, however desirable might have been some other course. In these cases, the sound and the meaning are indissoluble. Anyone wanting to perform these works must know *exactly* what the Russian says—one can then decide whether to leave well enough alone or, if not, what style of English will convey the sound-sense of the Russian folk idiom. Most of the translations in print are useless or tasteless and violate the elementary canons of prosody to which Stravinsky was always so sensitive.

May I, finally, thank the staff of the Slavonic Division of the New York Public Library, the measure of whose professionalism is that to this day I doubt that any of them knows my name or has the slightest idea that this work is to appear in print. I particularly want to thank Victor Gepner, sergeant page of the Reading Room, under whose anxious and all-seeing eye I think I finally learned how properly to behave. I'm not sure.

RICHARD F. FRENCH

Yale University
New Haven, Connecticut

List of Names

Abert, Hermann (1871-1927)
German musicologist, among whose pupils were Friedrich Blume (1893-1975) and Gustav Fellerer (1902-)

Afanas'yev, Alexander Nikolaevich (1826-71)
Russian scholar and historian in the field of literature and folklore; compiler of *Russian Popular Fairy Tales* (1855-64), a collection of some 600 texts.

Aliabiev, Alexander Alexandrovich (1787-1851)
Russian composer; collector and harmonizer of folk melodies

Andersen, Hans Christian (1805-75)
Danish writer, master of the fairy tale

Ansermet, Ernest (1883-1969)
Swiss conductor, from 1915 principal conductor of the Diaghilev Ballets Russes

Arensky, Anton Stepanovich (1861-1906)
Russian composer, pianist, conductor, teacher

Balakirev, Mily Alexeevich (1837-1910)
Russian composer

Bal'mont, Konstantin Dmitrievich (1867-1942)
Russian poet, one of the early representatives of Russian symbolism

Belaiev, Mitrofan Petrovich (1836-1904)
Russian music publisher, whose Leipzig house published over 2,000 compositions by Russian composers

Borodin, Alexander Porfirievich (1833-87)
  Russian composer

Chekhov, Anton (1860-1904)
  Russian dramatist and writer of short stories

Cervantes (Saavedra), Miguel de (1547-1616)
  Spanish writer, whose masterpiece is *Don Quixote de la Mancha*

Cui, Cesar (Tsezar Antonovich) (1835-1918)
  Russian composer and critic, of French descent

Dal', Vladimir Ivanovich (1801-72)
  Russian author, lexicographer, ethnologist

Dargomyzhsky, Alexander Sergeevich (1813-69)
  Russian composer

Debussy, Achille-Claude (1862-1918)
  French composer

Dostoevsky, Fedor (1821-81)
  Russian novelist

Diaghilev, Sergei Pavlovich (1872-1929)
  Russian man of the theatre, organizer of the Diaghilev Ballets Russes

Dehn, Siegfried (1799-1858)
  German theorist, editor, teacher, and librarian, author of a treatise on harmony (Berlin, 1840), editor of Marpurg's treatise on fugue (Leipzig, 1858)

Dickens, Charles (1812-70)
  English novelist

Dukas, Paul (-Abraham) (1865-1935)
  French composer, from 1957 Professor of Composition at the Paris Conservatory

Glazunov, Alexander Konstantinovich (1865-1936)
  Russian composer, director of the St. Petersburg Conservatory (1905-30)

Glinka, Mikhail Ivanovich (1804-57)
Russian composer, father of the nineteenth-century Russian nationalist school

Gogol, Nikolai (1809-52)
Russian novelist and dramatist

Goncharov, Ivan Alexandrovich (1812-91)
Russian writer, author of the novel *Oblomov* (1859)

Gorodetsky, Sergei Mitrofanovich (1884-1967)
Russian poet

Grigor'ev, Apollon Alexandrovich (1822-64)
Russian literary critic and poet

Gurilev, Alexander Lvovich (1803-58)
Russian composer of songs and piano pieces

Ivanov, Andrei (ca. 1776-1848) and/or his son Alexander Ivanov (1806-58)
Russian classicist painters

Kochno, Boris (1904-)
Sometime personal secretary to Diaghilev, librettist, founder with Roland Petit of the Ballets des Champs-Elysées

Kuzmin, Mikhail (1875-1936)
Russian writer (translator of Bocaccio and Shakespeare), with ties to the Symbolists

Larosh, German (Laroche, Herman) (1845-1904)
Prolific Russian music critic, lifelong champion of Tchaikovsky

Leonardo da Vinci (1452-1519)
Italian artist and scientist

Leskov, Nikolai Semenovich (1831-95)
Russian writer, author of the novella *Lady Macbeth of the Mtsensk District*

Liadov, Anatol Konstantinovich (1855-1914)
Russian composer, teacher, conductor

Lopukhov, Fedor Vasil'evich (1886-1973)
Russian ballet dancer, choreographer, teacher

Maeterlinck, Maurice (1862-1949)
Belgian writer, author of *Pelléas and Melisande* (1892)

Maikov, Apollon Nikolaevich (1821-97)
Russian poet, many of whose works were set by Tchaikovsky and Rimsky-Korsakov

Mitusov, Stepan
Co-author with Stravinsky of the libretto of *The Nightingale*

Musorgsky, Modest Petrovich (1839-81)
Russian composer

Napravnik, Eduard Francevič (1839-1916)
Czech conductor and composer, eventually succeeding Balakirev as conductor of the St. Petersburg branch of the Russian Musical Society, composer of works for stage and orchestra

Nekrasov, Nikolai Alexseevich (1821-78)
Russian poet and literary figure, many of whose poems became folksongs during his lifetime. Cui, e.g., composed 21 Songs of Nekrasov, Op. 62

Ostrovsky, Alexander Nikolaevich (1823-86)
Russian dramatist, second only to Gogol and Chekhov in importance to the history of the Russian theater

Pergolesi, Giovanni Battista (1710-36)
Italian composer, a leading figure in the rise of comic opera in the eighteenth century

Polezhaev, Akexander Ivanovich (1804-38)
Russian poet, translator of Lamartine and Hugo

Prach, Ivan (ca. 1750-1818)
Russian musical folklorist, composer, and educator, of Czech origin, who compiled with N.A. L'vov (1751-1803) a *Collection of Russian Folksongs* (1790), whose contents were later utilized by Russian and Western composers.

Prokofiev, Sergei Sergeevich (1891-1953)
Russian composer and pianist, central figure in the development of twentieth-century music

Pushkin, Alexander Sergeevich (1799-1837)
Russian poet, novelist, dramatist, and short story writer, whose works had enormous appeal for Russian composers (cf. *New Grove* XV, 479)

Rabelais, François (1494-1544)
French satirist, humanist, physician, author of the satirical masterpieces *Gargantua* and *Pantagruel*

Reshetnikov, Fedor Mikhailovich (1841-71)
Russian writer

Rimsky-Korsakov, Nikolai Andreevich (1844-1908)
Russian composer and editor, teacher of Stravinsky

Romains, Jules (1885-1972)
French novelist, dramatist, poet

Rousseau, Theodore (1812-67)
French landscape painter, leader of the Barbizon school, important in the development of landscape painting from direct observation of nature

Scriabin, Alexander Nikolaevich (1872-1915)
Russian composer and pianist, explorer of musical timbres and symbolism

Serov, Alexander Nikolaevich (1820-71)
Russian composer and music critic

[Siloti] Ziloti, Alexander Il'ich (1863-1945)
Ukrainian pianist and conductor

Taneev, Sergei Ivanovich (1856-1915)
Russian composer, pianist, and theorist

Tchaikovsky, Peter Il'ich (1840-93)
Russian composer

Tolstoy, Lev Nikolaevich, Count (1828-1910)
Russian novelist, dramatist, philosopher, and social critic

Uspensky, Gleb Ivanovich (1843-1902)
>   Russian intellectual and writer

Varlamov, Alexander Egorovich (1801-48)
>   Russian composer, of Moldavian descent, whose songs were conceived in a popular, romantic vein

Verlaine, Paul (1844-96)
>   French lyric poet

Verstovsky, Alexei Nikolaevich (1797-1862)
>   Russian composer of operas and solo songs

Verdi, Giuseppe (1813-1901)
>   Italian composer, primarily of opera

Vrubel', Mikhail Alexandrovich (1856-1910)
>   Russian painter

Author's Note to the 1929 Edition

I first conceived this book on Stravinsky in 1924, at a time when the novelties of Western music were flooding our musical life and were being everywhere eagerly absorbed. As a next step, I began to examine the works more in detail and make a varied propaganda in their favor. Still later I collected my impressions into a series of analyses of separate pieces and groups of works. Thus, the book developed gradually as a series of study-variations on the theme of Stravinsky, each variation being a different approach to an understanding of his music, and each approach affording a fresh view of problems attending the creation of contemporary music. Because of the way it grew, the book is stylistically uneven: there are still traces of spirited polemic and lyrical enthusiasms. The book was finished early in the spring of 1926 and is being published in 1929. That is a long interval which has seen many changes. Even the author himself has changed. But I could find no warrant for suppressing the vestiges of those earlier emotions. I have, to be sure, added a few words about Stravinsky's latest works, but in a tone as near as possible to that of the original. For I did not want to destroy that quality of my remarks which derived from the immediate conditions under which they were born and took shape. Certainly now, three years later, having been abroad and having acquainted myself with the environment in which the work of Stravinsky is evolving, I should have written another book, different in arrangement and lighter in style. [The Opera Studio of Leningrad Conservatory was invited to the Salzburg Festival in 1928, with Asaf'yev as its artistic director. The Studio performed four works: *Bastien et Bastienne* (Mozart), *The Cave of Salamanca* (Paumgartner), *The Stone Guest* (Dargomyzhsky), and *Kashchey the Immortal* (Rimsky-Korsakov). Asaf'yev then went on to Paris to meet Prokofiev; they were photographed together aboard a steamer on Lake Geneva in September.—Trans.] But now other work beckons me.

Stravinsky's position among Western composers, of course, is not a menial one. The regalia of musical leadership rest in his hands. But a crisis, I fear, is approaching. Having gone into Europe even before the war, Stravinsky at once assumed the dominant position in Western European urban music, and the fertility of his imagination continued to impose new problems of content and form in each new work. The content, he brought out with him from his native land. The essence of this content, *industrialized* by him, is what secured and maintained his position as the darling of the European snobs. But he cannot forever be their darling. He may even find himself without a public, find that he has virtually exhausted the epoch and the musical culture that was so largely his own creation. Despite their great intellectual significance, his latest ballets are lacking in substance to a frightening degree [cf. Postscript—Trans.]. True, his considerable gifts have so far enabled him to make something of the subjects demanded by his social clientele, but in the end the clientele may be even stronger than the composer. The subjects he adopts are sufficiently out of the ordinary in theme and universal in import to place him well above any charges of Philistinism. But the dynamics and agogics of his music, its rhythms and timbres cannot for long take nourishment from the past. Their stimulus, when all is said and done, must be the contemporary city and its thoroughfares. If Stravinsky retreats within himself, like the Beethoven of the last quartets, then the disharmony between the composer and his environment can only be intensified. In a word, every sign indicates that the crisis is near. The minor French composers will gladly revolt against the Russian "Dictator of Taste," and for the sated international set of Paris, serious art is no longer necessary. The fate of all of Stravinsky's music, in the last analysis, will be determined not in the West but in the country where he was brought up—and will depend on how and to what extent his works are assimilated into our new creative life.

1 July 1929   IGOR GLEBOV
                                                            (Boris Asaf'yev)

By Way of Preface

I consider it my duty at the outset to make a few general statements not about the work as a whole (the fruit of long research and, owing to the difficulties involved, certainly not free of mistakes and oversights), but about its theme. I am writing a book about Stravinsky, as a prominent and extraordinary *phenomenon* in the European music of the first half of the twentieth century. As an investigator, I feel a deep interest in this phenomenon and I want to explain it, the more especially because I have reason to believe that in connection with my analysis of Stravinsky's work I may be able to make a few not entirely useless observations about musical materials and the contemporary forms that may embody them. This is a large undertaking, in which I am fortunately not alone. I shall proceed from a few general principles and premises which in turn come not from abstractions or rigid and outmoded canons, but from live observation. These principles and premises prescribe not a casual, routine appraisal of individual works, but an exposition that pursues a critical examination of the music finally to reach an estimate of it as a total phenomenon. It is procedural ease alone that invites me to organize the book by chapters in which I focus my remarks on a single work or a group of works in turn.

However, I do not look on the analysis of each work as an end in itself. I regard this as a method of perceiving the links in the chain, the separate facts that make up the total phenomenon under investigation, the separate organic manifestations of musical art as thought. I am not concerned with what kind of man Stravinsky is, with his opinions or ideas. I take only the *music* as evidence and write a book about it without any preconceived polemical goal: by praising the outstanding works of Stravinsky, for example, I have no wish to denigrate any other music or insult any other musician living or dead. I find it necessary to make this clear because we are not accustomed to bring our minds to bear on music free of the influence of personal taste or of the mood of the moment. To be moved to praise or to censure by the first impression of any piece is one thing; it is quite another to establish principles and orderly methods of thinking about music, or to understand the history of musical development and form an intelligent estimate of the events occurring in the course of it. The natural scientist or the physicist does not limit his research to a subject that he likes or that he finds beautiful; for him, this is elementary.

In endeavouring to work out methods of musical research and to discipline myself as a writer, I consciously strive to treat the subject in question with such respect that the reader may not even consider whether the composer was known to me personally or whether I was moved by his music. Toward this end, I try always to become so much at home in the language and style of any composer whose work I may be analyzing that at any time I can account for why he did such-and-such here, or something else there, and thereby explain a given phrase or mannerism. Personally, I should consider a test of my expertness that I should have written a good paper about a composer or music otherwise completely strange to me. This is not as easy as surrendering to the arrogance of personal taste, a disease that is widespread and the cause of annoying frustrations in writers on music who permit themselves to be influenced by the emotions and moods of the moment. My method, on the other hand, gives a gratifying measure of freedom, in that having insinuated myself into the subject and grasped the language and mannerisms of the composer from the inside, I am able to form judgments about his work from a variety of points of view.

Alas, we often misunderstand this, and regard judgments from different points of view as evidence of betrayal of one's "first love." This is an especially difficult matter in the case of operas and theatrical works in general. Often these works, which continue to charm and enchant one personally because they so intimately express the actual circumstances that evoked them, come at the same time to seem dated, like relics of the art and society of another era. Sometimes, also, music that is in itself very beautiful falls far short of exhausting the subject with which it deals. I have therefore tried, despite my addiction to the purely theatrical, to examine Stravinsky's theatrical works more closely from the point of view of music than of theater, without, of course, isolating the music from the entire musico-theatrical form.

Though polemical passages may exist in my work, they are not in essence its principal moments but rather the natural consequence of a purely personal impatience that what appears to me as striking, audacious, and obviously strong and organic is not immediately recognized as such by others. And although I know that every action has an equal reaction, and that with Stravinsky the reaction in any given case is particularly understandable and deeply natural, I nevertheless become excited and cannot contain myself. I retain these passages, because they are sincere and full of life. I have tried throughout to do my research honestly. I do not pretend at all to a cold and passionless scientism in a book on art. Genuine scientific works of real vitality are written with temperament and enthusiasm. I emphasize again that I am analyzing a *phenomenon* and not separate things, that my object is not merely to analyze Stravinsky's work but through it to make a much wider and more detailed investigation of the principles of musical thought in the twentieth century. A "Book about Contemporary Music": that is the goal that stood before me when I was working on this "Book about Stravinsky." I repeat again that I have not been interested in the composer as a person, or in his "life and works," but only in what he has done as the creative experience of a brilliant musician that defines an era.

The work of Stravinsky is instructive just because it is so many-sided. Stravinsky is a representative of European urban musical culture, a bold designer, a master of his craft. In his work there is no trace either of emotionalizing dilettantism and philosophizing erotic individualism, or of abstract, scholastic academicism. But at the same time Stravinsky, whose music, to quote the neat phrase of Alfredo Casella, appeared before the young generation of European musicians like a "dazzling beacon, dispersing the gloom before it," is bound up to the depths of his being with the Great Russian melos, with peasant folk art, vocal as well as instrumental. He took out with him into the West the rhythms, intonations, and formal principles of the Russian "music of the oral tradition," but little by little he shook off the whole veneer of Russian pre-revolutionary musical Philistinism. From 1910 on (the year of the production of *Firebird*), recognized in Paris as he was rejected by the old-fashioned theater of his native land (not one of his ballets was performed here before the revolution), Stravinsky assumed for Europe, and in particular for France, the rank that Lully, Gluck, and Cherubini had held before him: that of the great universalist composer. For us Russians, Stravinsky had long ceased to be familiar in person, but his work was and has remained an outstanding phenomenon. To build a barrier between ourselves and him means to revert musically to the Muscovy of the seventeenth century. And if some of our composers and musical ideologists nevertheless have nothing to do with him, acting as if he were Nikon [(1605-81) Patriarch of Moscow from 1652, whose reforms provoked the schism of the Old Believers (Raskolniki)—Trans.] and they dissenters, I personally see nothing good in this for them except the confession of their own foibles, or, at best, artistic night-blindness, which would be commendable were they otherwise strong and audacious souls for whom the provincial old-world existence had fully sufficed.

In 1916, forced by sympathy for Stravinsky, Prokofiev and Miaskovsky to part company with one of the most respectable metropolitan journals, I began seriously and earnestly to study the works of Stravinsky. The work ran into delays. By 1922-23, when I had come to know *Renard*, then *Histoire du soldat*, *Pulcinella*, and finally *Les Noces*, I was struck with wonder at the colossal stature that Stravinsky had attained. He had become a European master, one who had surmounted every foreign and alien influence and the whole legacy of school and locale. He had quickly liberated himself from Debussy and impressionism and had easily rid himself of the homespun aesthetic and chauvinistic academicism of official St. Petersburg, and had converted the simple harmony textbook into a "symbol of truth." As if this were not enough, Stravinsky had made himself a master of native Russian art, not just a clever stylist who knows how to conceal quotations, not just a native ethnographer who is unable to assimilate materials and make artistic use of them, but a master of the speech of Russian. In this sense, Stravinsky had become the Pushkin of Russian music. And only in this sense? The universalism of Stravinsky, his capacity to make any material his own, his clear intellect, free, of course, of all rationalistic organicism, his sober, ironical sensualism, the rich robustness of his grotesque (wholly different from that of Gogol and Dostoevsky)—in all these qualities he resembles Pushkin. The *Renard* of Stravinsky and many pages of his songs and pribautki yield nothing to the "Tale of the Pope and his Workman Balda," in my view the most perfect tale of Pushkin. Stravinsky's characteristic dread of Philistinism and of pure Russian bluster are "original" qualities, yet at the same time his eagerness to embrace the healthy manifestations of life right down to the most ordinary intonations of house and street music, his trenchant critical faculty, his skillful selection of materials and conversion of them into artistic form, without loss of characteristic organic and vital qualities—in these respects he also resembles Pushkin. I cite these analogies not to insist on them but only to offer them as examples.

Stravinsky's music is obedient to the tempi and rhythm of contemporary life, and especially to the rhythm of our times: the rhythm of work, of machines, and also of films. From this rhythm there is no escape. Academicism and romanticism, classicism and emotionalism—all "isms," including even modernism, fall under its hypnotic spell. This does not mean that they will not again awaken, but they will not be the same: the rhythm of our practical times will have left its impression.

Evidence of the ways in which European music is obedient to the rhythms and tempi of work may be found in three fundamental trends. First, there has been a noticeable disappearance of a self-satisfied, personal lyricism, and in its place have appeared tempi and sentiments now tinged with pessimism (the significance of the individual before the vastness of the universe), now sharply grotesque,[1] now dedicated wholly to the solidarity of the popular masses and to the sympathies and sensations of extra-personal life.

From this last there follows Stravinsky's inclination to portray in his music the moods of festival occasions. His instrumental style, also, owes much to the movements of people, to dance movements, to the rhythms of percussion instruments, and to intonations connected with the collective experiences of crowds.

Second, the relation of the contemporary composer to his materials has greatly changed: the spontaneous use of raw materials, not otherwise worked out in a constructivist sense, has disappeared. The composer now selects materials and expressive devices specifically to conform to his plans and goals, at the same time observing the principle of the greatest economy and rhythmic rigor. And the material so selected will be organized in such fashion that everything characteristic and essential will be disclosed, every detail will contribute to the final end without any digression, however charming.

The third trend places increasing emphasis on rhythm as a basic principle of musical design and on the evolution of percussive intonations as the "collective" disciplining the total organization of musical energies. Deductive, rationalized formal schemes must undergo thorough tests of their resiliency. The musical thought is important, and not the mold into which it is poured. Therefore it is impossible to write music imitating the "experiments of the great" and built upon formal skeletons. Metrical regularity, a relic of the era of musical dependence (the poetical yoke), loses its supremacy. As even the marches of Stravinsky show, their gait, though it has an obvious rhythmic basis, demands a delicate equilibrium of rhythmic energies quite different from mere regularity of step. Rhythm is the fundamental of contemporary music, for the essence of our industrial epoch is such that neither salon nor stage nor the charms of concert-hall virtuosity can keep music from being permeated with the pulsations of the rhythm and tempi of work, with which the streets of our cities and our whole life are now saturated.

But a rhythm separated from live intonations is abstract.

I often use the term "intonation," and I therefore state that I mean thereby the totality of sounds from whatever source, not only the *audible* music but the whole phenomena of sound, actually or potentially audible as music. To intone, means to define a system of sound-relationships. Everything I have to say in this book will be by way of analysis and even, in places, simple description of the intonations of Stravinsky. Like any critical analysis of a living phenomenon, this musical analysis cannot be exhaustive, for the works under consideration are alive and moving, constantly widening and deepening the analytical range. The coming years will perhaps open my eyes and ears to much that now passes unnoticed by either. In view of the inevitability of intonational analysis in the chapters that follow and also for the purposes of possible future use, I deem it necessary at the very beginning of this book to give my views on the intonational sphere within which Stravinsky's music is contained.

This sphere is extremely large: the melos of the Russian countryside and the melody of the Russian cities form its base, around which are found later European deposits. The Russian melos is the living speech of Stravinsky, his native language, and not just material from which he takes quotations. As a representative of European urban culture, Stravinsky does not busy himself with the romantic idealization of folklore, having gone far beyond that stage and having also overcome the great influence that the work of Musorgsky once had on him. From all this there follows the important fact that at the time of his mighty influence on the whole of European musical culture, Stravinsky's intonational sphere had come to include the general European musical language itself and had joined this with the Russian melos which, thus, for Europe had ceased to be some sort of exotic monster and was realizing itself in an organically developing complex of musical intonations.[2]

It is usually said that Paris, having spoiled Stravinsky, went on completely to subjugate him. This is a very rash assertion. One need only study any score of the master without preconceptions to see clearly that the pupil has conquered his teachers. I reiterate that Stravinsky early outgrew the influence of Rimsky-Korsakov as he later outgrew Debussy and even more recently the jazz band, although he has utilized the best of each of them for his own purposes in his own way. As I have already pointed out, both Lully and Gluck did the same thing in France, and Bach did it, too, taking from each culture contemporary with him that which was of greatest musical value and then holding dominion over all of it. To debate whether Igor Stravinsky is a Russian or a French composer is to no avail. One might as well debate whether Gluck was German or French (Bach, too: and what about his close bond with Italian culture?), whether Handel was German or English, or whether this or that was really the mother country of Bach or Beethoven. Indeed, one of the most valuable aspects of music in Europe is the strength of its force as a unifying factor. If anyone who wants to study Stravinsky's music thinks he can usefully do so with the technical resources of the pre-aviation and pre-automobile (or, in some cases, even pre-railroad) era, and if the virile rhythms of Stravinsky's music say nothing, and if its intonations seem almost demoralizing, then before debating such matters, he would do better to heed a useful historical truth. Every creation of a great artist is always in some way a protest and reaction against the Philistinism of his own epoch. Such also is the music of Stravinsky, and of course the Parisian Philistines did not love him for it—after all Stravinsky was no Meyerbeer, who was admired by such people as Berlioz and Heine!

Even if Stravinsky's recent ascent to the pinnacle of the synthetic instrumental style of contemporary urbanism cannot conceal his long isolation from his native soil, its social elements, and political history, nevertheless all his music is deserving of careful and attentive study, lest some Pharisee-Beckmesser, posing as Cicero or (even worse) Cato, do him injury [i.e., by being doctrinaire and censorious—Trans.]. The bagatelles of Stravinsky are more valuable than any number of sonatas and symphonies "without parallel fifths": by sheer intellect he has created his versatile technique, and for just that reason the technique is not a mechanical repetition of common practices. Those who write by the older principles say that Stravinsky has no technique, that anyone can write like Stravinsky. The question arises: why is Stravinsky the only one to do so? Is it that all the Philistines are too modest, that they do not dare to be adventurous, that in the whole world there can be only one universal sauce-box? No, the truth is in fact much more simple. There are two techniques: the imitative, and the evolving. The imitative preserves—or, at best, varies—what has been invented by others. The evolving, on the other hand, always struggles to master new methods, new expressions. In the final analysis, technique is the ability to do what one wants: but to do what one wants, one cannot want patience. Everyone must learn his own technique out of his own experience. All the arguments about the "rules of new music" come back to this simple fact. I am at a loss to understand why, for example, we now refer to the language of Beethoven as "classical," when he, in his own time, was moving well ahead of his contemporaries and was using a language new to that epoch. And for this, of course, he was himself abused. It is one thing to esteem the heroic tone of Beethoven's music; it is quite another thing to hear the language in which he expresses himself as his contemporaries heard it. The first we think natural, the second we naturally do not think of. Each epoch has its own language and its own means of expression. If we can still sense the intensity and strength of Beethoven's music, then it is just because Beethoven refused to imitate the imitators of his own time and go on repeating eighteenth century practices, knowing full well that Bach and Mozart had already completed the work they had to do.

With respect to the alleged triviality of Stravinsky's work I can only say: look carefully at Mozart and see how he used the "street" and "house" music of his time. Still others are disturbed by the theatricality of Stravinsky's music and the absence of the attributes of pure symphonism. In order to look at Stravinsky's materials with the same eyes that Beethoven used when he criticized Mozart for his choice of subjects [allegedly, e.g., that of Don Giovanni, which he considered scandalous—Trans.], one would have to be another Beethoven. He and he alone had the right to do so. To criticize Stravinsky for the theatrical bias of his work is like criticizing Shakespeare because he wrote theatrical plays instead of philosophical treatises. The theater is the great field of our times. It would have been ridiculous for composers to have avoided it, especially at a moment when it offered almost the only opportunity for development.

Nevertheless, it is not easy to comprehend Stravinsky's art, and for all my interest in the subject and although I have undertaken this book fully convinced of the need to write it, at the same time I fully recognize the difficulty and, in many respects, the impracticability of the task. In the present instance the difficulty is compounded by the fact that Stravinsky's music is the child of the very era that it comes to define. It defines its era not so much by being ahead of it as by setting itself problems of form and craftsmanship that demand the greatest intellectual mastery. It is one thing to see in perspective the art of the past, which has been known and subsequently studied by many generations. It is quite another thing in one's own time to be sensitive to that which distinguishes itself by inevitability and integrity from the fraudulent and vulgar remainder.

Those critics who want to malign, always have it easy. What they do not or cannot understand, what they do not or cannot hear, they repudiate as extravagant and bad for society. It is less risky to denigrate contemporary art than to be similarly critical of the familiar past. The critic can abuse the new with more self-assurance and impudence, he can inspire respect for himself as the defender of the little man against charlatans, as the protagonist of the familiar, accessible, and accepted. And he seems to have eternity on his side, because the members of the passive public want to feel that what they like, should have existed from the beginning of time and should go on to the end of the world. They forget, in such cases, their own mortality. I have always felt that to repudiate something because it was new or unfamiliar was an especially simple thing to do, almost as easy as offering a condescending handshake to an acquaintance. No need to think, no need to disturb oneself. The critic is the supreme authority, he is installed over the composers, and the less he himself hears, the more severely he addresses himself to the proper observance of the rules. If his severity reveals the arrogance of an empty self-conceit, his malignment betrays even more importantly a lack of artistic imagination and of direct contact with works of art. For whosoever has found out from personal experience of any kind or degree what in fact the creative process in music is, what it means to define and construct musical ideas, what it means to form these primary materials into an extended work and give it coherence and proportion, he will not stand off and lightly make ironical remarks about the incomprehensibility of music. Rather will he try first of all to come to the defense of the composer and to elucidate how and why he uses new and unusual means of expression. A critic of the breed of Beckmesser does quite the opposite: he is afraid to point out to the imitator that he is restating old ideas, or that life has simply passed him by (both of these things are already obvious). But he is not afraid to poke fun at every novelty, because he cares not about the creative process, or about music, but only about his cherished right to judge and censure. The only music that he knows, he has learned from the imitators: everything is smooth, clear, completely explainable, set in a familiar frame. What could be better? Only, alas, these pieces are not creative work, but mere lessons in penmanship.

The musical environment of the present is, on the whole, deeply unfair to Stravinsky. But worse than being unfair (which is its privilege), it is not even curious. That is the real hurt. If the penchant for Stravinsky's works were stronger, all the slanders would automatically fade away. Or at least people would stop believing them, as is beginning to be the case now with some of our young. Why, up to now, has there been so little curiosity about Stravinsky? Does the reason lie in the music, or is there some other cause? Certainly not in the music, because none of them knew any of it until recently, and now they know only a little, and that superficially. The reason is rather that until fresh energies have invaded the field of music and assimilated the latest accomplishments, the reactionaries will continue to profit by the present situation, speaking about everything contemporary with detestation, complacently viewing music as a mechanical art whose rules are laid down by precept, and haughtily and maliciously pronouncing judgments on everything unfamiliar, not unlike demagogues. I have set down my thoughts on what appears to me to be the abnormal superficiality of the current attitude toward Stravinsky not for the sake of empty polemic, but to point out how hard it is to encourage familiarity with his work under conditions where the simplest desire to describe the observations, views, and estimates resulting from one's work on the music of this composer is viewed as an attempt to degrade other musicians and musical figures.

In conclusion, a few additional words about the character of this book. It will probably be called formalist, because at the present time there is abroad a welter of ideas about formalism, formal method, formal analysis, etc. Without going further into the matter here, I want only to say that in musical research it is never possible completely to avoid what seem to be "moments of narrow specialization." The very conception of the art has its formal aspect, since the material that the composer uses is itself a conjunction of sound elements or a system of sound relationships formulated by careful selection from the limitless area of acoustical phenomena. Those people who are disposed to regard all discussion of "forms" with great disdain do not suspect that they cannot apprehend any music at all except by perceiving at least minimally the formal premises underlying the organization of sound. All this comes so naturally to them that they take no notice of it. Any piece of music is by definition a system of intonations apprehensible by virtue of an intellectual element whose presence reveals itself through form. Form in music is no abstract scheme into which materials are poured like wine into a crater. Form is the end result of the complicated process by which associations of sound elements crystallize themselves in our consciousness. The properties of the material itself condition the form, but the selection and disposition of the musical ingredients is a function of the composer's organizational thought. In the end, form is the concrete expression of the composer's mentality. Contemporary musical scholarship is being drawn more and more strongly to the study of the *process* of formal organization in music as well as to the analysis of the intellectual element in musical creation.[3] Does that mean that the emotional element, the so-called "content" of music, is being swept aside? Certainly not. What is rejected is the sharp antithesis of content and form. Form is not a mere collection of technical tricks and devices. To hold otherwise is simply to deny the organic evolution of music and its significance as an art and to revert to the naive ideas about the freedom of emotional inspiration being restrained by the rules. Every system of thought, after all, is just a shrewd guess about the properties of matter and their use. Music is no exception. The material at the composer's disposal contains its own potential for growth and prescribes the organization of the texture of sounds. It is the composer's mentality which selects and conjugates the material, and this mentality cannot, of course, be disassociated from the qualities of the intellectual environment that surrounds it.

Therefore, the formal side of music is neither a narrow technical area nor a sterile aesthetic superstructure. Progress in this field is always the result of the evolution of musical mentality and leaves a train of ever new possibilities of expression. One may, if one wishes, be indignant over the excessive intellectualism of musical creativity at certain epochs, but to regard the evidence of the intellect's work (form: what it is, how it is achieved) as mere technical refinement is, in my opinion, to confess ignorance of the evolution of music and shamefully to degrade it as a phenomenon. My book on Stravinsky pretends to be nothing more than an attempt to describe his formal processes by observing and analyzing the textures of sound that make up his work. These textures I have always heard in motion, as a constant modulation of elements that attract and repel each other in various degrees and ways. Those general observations that I make from time to time derive from correspondences that I find between Stravinsky's artistic experience and the experiences of other predecessors and contemporaries—correspondences that relate his personal experience to the complex evolution of musical culture, affirm the integrity of his work, and place it within the evolutionary stream. Digressions into the field of musical content, and analogies with extra-musical phenomena were also inevitable in the process of developing my research, and I make rather wide use of them. If they do not constitute the principal part of my work, they are absolutely essential to the complex of its ideas.

Notes

1. The grotesque itself may be sharply critical of society for what it is doing to the power and integrity of the individual, or it may be pure skepticism. In the one case, Prokofiev and Hindemith; in the other, Krenek and, if you please, Alban Berg.

2. Now, however, Stravinsky is trying extremely hard to free his musical language of certain of its specifically Russian qualities.

3. I must add that contemporary musical scholarship's concern with the examination of form as a living process is in sharp contrast to the academic concept of it as a dead architectural scheme perceptible as a variation of a familiar and rigid pattern.

1

Early Stravinsky

Later historians will probably find much more character and originality in the works of Stravinsky's first period than we can see today. If we pass from the youthful and unique Symphony in E♭, first performed in St. Petersburg, April 22, 1908, to *Firebird* (Paris, June 1910) and then to *Petrushka* (Paris, June 1911), Stravinsky's development seems extraordinarily rapid and intense. Neither then, in its own time, nor now can the impression made by the Symphony be compared with that made by *Firebird* or *Petrushka*. The Symphony was and has remained a comparatively fresh work on a level with other school symphonies of that period which revealed mastery of the compositional methods of the favorite teachers, including Glazunov. A few details of the scherzo and occasional passages in the first and last movements shows signs of indubitable talent and reveal a happy mastery of orchestral resources and an ability to allocate materials suitably according to instrumental timbres. [See ex. 2, note 1.] But the material itself is not original, and the music seems little more than the product of a good pupil.[1] [See ex. 1, note 1.]

There is nothing frightening—no evidence here of treason to school and tradition or infidelity to precept. Of the grotesque there is almost no sign (again: just a bit in the scherzo), and the decorous attire of the Symphony hides all but just a trace of the dangerous "illiteracy" of Musorgsky. No one could conceivably imagine that three years later there would come *Petrushka*, a score whose stunning, explosive impact would instantly make enemies of some of Stravinsky's old friends. Even after *Firebird* they continued to believe in his basic meekness and servility, in spite of his pardonable inclination toward the then fashionable impressionism whose major thirds and whole-tone scale implied a repudiation of Tchaikovsky. They "explained" *Petrushka* by saying that it was (of all things) flattery of Paris, and from then on such a "friendly" explanation became canonical. It was used in the criticism of every new work of Stravinsky, and even its multiple repetitions did not make its users aware of its triviality. True, Paris, Diaghilev, Benois had "caused" *Petrushka,* but not in the sense that the enemies of Stravinsky tried to convey: they had evoked the latent powers of the young artist and opened up a new world before him. Paris was for

Stravinsky what it had been for the Gluck of *Iphigenia in Aulis;* and I might add, not only for Gluck. At first, Stravinsky, like any good pupil, had followed in the footsteps of his teachers, i.e. in the direction of a modestly streamlined impressionism. Then he had joined forces with the more advanced French, and in *Firebird* he had presented a synthesis of his total experience to date. In *Petrushka* he began for the first time to speak as an independent, in his own brilliant, rich language. And the development of his gifts in the period between the first and second ballets is even more rapid than the development that had occurred between the Symphony in E_b and *Firebird*.

I recall my impressions of other first performances of Stravinsky. The charming, stylistically secure suite for voice and orchestra *Le Faune et la Bergère,* which stands midway between the elegant arioso style of Rimsky-Korsakov and the then current fashion, seemed to me, when it was first played in 1908, a work of one of Rimsky's gifted pupils that gave evidence of a special gift for instrumental color but not of a very independent personality.[2] One must not forget or lose perspective: this was the last year of Rimsky-Korsakov's life and the year of our first acquaintance with the magic of the overture and processional from *The Golden Cockerel.* Rimsky-Korsakov walked behind his times, and each new work of his in turn represented the *concession* of a genius to contemporary demands. In the eighteen years that have passed since his death, the progress that he nourished has ceased. New forces have arisen. The so-called School of Rimsky-Korsakov has become conservative. Therefore, if in 1908 *Le Faune et la Bergère,* for all its merits, seemed no more than the work of a gifted pupil, there is nothing surprising in this, since the pupil was of necessity behind his times.

It is obvious now that, though it has lost its bloom, the poem of *Le Faune et la Bergère* is still fragrant of Pushkin's playfully ironic sensuality, the music is composed with taste and refinement, and the orchestral design is fascinating. Of course the music is on a higher level than that of the youthful Symphony, in which the composer kept trying on different masks in search of his own, as if he were trying to prove that he was technically secure, that his voice leading was beyond reproach, that he could assimilate any style and master any influence. And yet his inability to break clear of early influences remains: the intonations and formal methods of Rimsky-Korsakov, and more especially of Glazunov, still largely obscure the occasional flashes of personal style. I have a somewhat happier memory of the Fantastic Scherzo, finished in 1908 and in 1917 given a scenario, transformed into the ballet *Les Abeilles,* and staged at the Paris Opera. [Cf. Eric Walter White: *Stravinsky* (Berkeley: 1966), p. 142. Choreography by Leo Staats, scenario inspired by an episode from Maeterlinck's *La Vie des Abeilles,* performed January 10, 1917.—Trans.]

Again there is a masterful control of the orchestra, but the materials and most of the formal devices are not yet Stravinsky's own. The occasional echoes of Wagner are amusing. In general, in comparison with the Symphony (where the Russian intonations of the "Belaiev" school are dominant), there is a much greater use of the palette of impressionistic colors and the more elegant impressionistic devices.[3] The work seems too long: the material is too lacking in potential energy to justify the lengths to which the composer has drawn it out. The best and most original work of 1908, in terms of depth of resonance and successful realization of the potentialities of the musical materials, is *Fireworks,* the short fantasy for large orchestra. Among the orchestral works of Stravinsky's first period, *Fireworks* has to this day preserved its aroma of novelty, wit, and delicacy and its character as a genuinely original handling of the rich impressionistic materials. It has air and movement, and one senses the dynamic of Stravinsky: here the composer does not "sit" for long on one complex of intonations, as he did in the Symphony and the Fantastic Scherzo. A characteristic (for Stravinsky) "revolving" ostinato figure sets the music going. In the middle section (lento) occurs the "magic formula" of Dukas (flutes and violin harmonics). The allegretto has a melody with Stravinsky's favorite sequence of tones [see ex. 3].

Example 3

Fireworks also shows Stravinsky's liking for high registers, for music "without bass," suspended in air. The lifeless and banal figurations of the Fantastic Scherzo give way to a mobile ornamentation. There are no traces of the "Russian" intonations of the Symphony in this score. I find personally attractive the work's festive quality so characteristic of Stravinsky's music.

One must also mention the beautiful *Funeral Chant* for orchestra (1908) occasioned by the death of Rimsky-Korsakov, and the two distinctive orchestrations of the *Flea Songs of Musorgsky and Beethoven* (1909) made by Stravinsky for the concerts of Siloti [Alexander Ilich Ziloti [sic] (1863-1945), Ukrainian pianist and conductor, who directed his own concerts from 1903 in St. Petersburg (and taught at the Juillard School in New York from 1924 to 1942).—Trans.] The four etudes for piano (1908) are not remarkable. They are largely written in the Russian salon style current at that time. The etudes are distinguished by tasteful harmony, neatness of ornament, and occasional rhythmic discontinuities, but there is little else to foretell the future inventor of new piano intonations: the works are really more dead than alive. Their lyric pathos—especially that of the first (c minor)—yields little pleasure, and it shows further what direction Stravinsky's talent might have taken if fortune had not helped him to find himself and set him on the right course.

The works for voice and piano of 1907-8 are all interesting, but perhaps the best is the charming Franco-Russian Pastoral (*vocalise* without words). Its fragility of line and delicacy of texture suggest two later vocal works of Stravinsky that are in a somewhat different style and of a more highly refined expressive character: *Forget-me-not* and *The Dove* (both 1911) to verses of Bal'mont. Particularly beautiful is the melodic design of *Forget-me-not*, which resembles that of *Nightingale* and shows Stravinsky's typical juxtaposition of major and minor thirds [see ex. 4].

Example 4

The Dove also shows Stravinsky's characteristic liking for lines moving by seconds and thirds within a narrow range [see ex. 5].

Example 5

This already points toward the Japanese Lyrics (1912-13). In 1907 and 1908 Stravinsky had already completed the two magnificent songs *Spring* and *Song of the Dew*, music full of Great Russian emotional sensitivity. The style is not yet fully formed, there are still concessions to the melodic mannerisms and harmonic sweetness of Rimsky-Korsakov, but the influence of Musorgsky is sharper and more direct, and one has the impression that Stravinsky achieves a genuinely personal sonority. I remember that these two works made a very strong impression at the time: it seemed that an epoch of stylization had come to an end, that a polished and traditional folk style had yielded to a new refraction of the national musical language, to a new and distinctive musical style. Today these pieces tend to sound passé—beside the clear intonations of *Les Noces,* even conventional and unctuous. But nevertheless, the charm of an earlier freshness and the feeling that here the composer was discovering his proper direction make them still exciting and worthy of occasional re-hearing.

The *Two Poems of Paul Verlaine* for bass and pianoforte (1910) have always seemed strangely and disagreeably lacking in authenticity. The melodic lines move without freedom, the harmonic backgrounds are too derivative, too imitative of impressionism, the intonations are more dead than alive. The first song *(Un Grand sommeil noir)* just manages to convey the burden of genuine sorrow, but I find no genuine sentiment in the second, *La Lune blanche,* with its paysage à la Debussy. Besides, the vocal line sounds even more gloomy and false in Russian translation. These two pieces could better be considered as offerings from a shy pupil to his beloved Paris. Even so, they do him no credit; they contain nothing stupid or in bad taste, but they seem clearly on the wrong path.

I pass now to *Firebird.* Here Stravinsky has really grasped a golden pen, and the whole score sparkles with an iridescent radiance, with the brilliancy of precious stones. To be sure, the music is uneven, it lacks formal and stylistic coherence, and there are annoying confusions and discontinuities. But all this is not grave. The work as a whole is a synthesis of all the elements which had exerted themselves on Stravinsky—a synthesis not in the sense of passive submission, but rather as the assertion of active sovereignty over lesson and precept. Every page of the score exhibits the power the young composer now has to project his own and others' ideas so that the music sounds like a personal refraction of his total experience, Russian and French. *Firebird* abounds in musical riches: the composer seems virtually stunned by the treasure of sounds he has discovered and hastens to thread the largest possible number of these dazzling instrumental colors into a necklace of brilliant sonorities. Sonorous abundance is in fact almost a burden to the music of the ballet, which is not devoid of its static moments. Now, of course, our ears have ceased to be astonished and no longer crave the colorful splendors of this paysage, of this musical *nature morte.* Apparently the composer was aware of this eventuality, because in 1919 he made a completely new adaptation of the suite from *Firebird* for small orchestra.[4] The new suite includes: Introduction, Dance of the Firebird, Round Dance of the Princesses, Infernal Dance of King Kashchey, Lullaby, and Finale. Although it does not, unfortunately, incorporate from the earier suite the charming scherzo Game of the Golden Apples, happily it does include the Lullaby, from the symphonic point of view the most deeply felt passage of the ballet. The orchestration of the lullaby remains unchanged, because the sonorities of the earlier version could not have been excelled. The other changes have, in my opinion, resulted in a gain of expressivity. There is a special theatricality contributed by a certain added richness of timbre, which puts one in mind of the examples offered by certain impressionists (Debussy excepted), even though the opulence of Stravinsky's profligate, almost "Byzantine" figuration was far more advanced than that of any of the models. The marvelous Infernal Dance is particularly improved, having assumed for the first time its real orchestral character. The earlier version was "arranged" for orchestra and with the echoes of Balakirev in its "minor" moments seemed half-way between *Islamey* and *Tamara* and equally derivative of both. Now it has become a composition for orchestra in the fullest sense.[5]

The music of *Firebird* explores the world of three fairy-tales. First, the ponderous gloom of the kingdom of Kashchey, a realm of oppression and servitude. Stravinsky magnificently conveys the peal of the tocsin, magic, terrifying, instinctively warning of peril. The Infernal Dance, a wicked and savage dance of servitude (and the center of the choreographic action of the ballet) is a brilliant musical expression of enslaved energy, raging for freedom, unable to break its bonds.

The second world is that of the Firebird, on the one hand a whirlwind of dazzling color, on the other a realm of hypnotic and lyric enchantment, whose lullaby is the best symphonic moment of the ballet. Here the langorous melodic line is given to the oboe, around whose basic motive Stravinsky weaves a delicate and limpid texture.

The third world is that of the captive princesses and the hero who sets them free. The figure of the hero is not interesting: he is the typical juvenile lead of Russian opera and ballet, lacking definition of character, existing only as a necessary link in the chain of action. On the other hand, the fragile music of the princesses is captivating, the character of its figurations and textures placing it among the most elegant pages of the score. My memory of the sonorities is still vivid. They have something of the magic of the fantasies of Vrubel' and the luminescence of his color, together with the intimacy and delicacy of the Persian miniature and the opulent decoration of carpeting. I have already pointed out that coloristic extravagance does not suffice to carry the ballet, which lacks formal clarity and rigor. On the other hand, this is less the fault of the composer than of those who designed the scenario. The episodes are not connected organically—the whole is a casual agglomeration of individually beautiful and effective units. The action is spasmodic, the rhythms and tempi unsteady. All this has its effect on the music, and even there, all is not well: the expansive and magnificently decorative frescoed style does not always blend with the technique of the miniature, with its tiny design and delicately elegant ornamentation. But freshness, fire, and force of imagination, and prodigality and flair of invention carry the day and disarm all criticism!

Though its effect is even more stunning, the score of *Petrushka* is entirely different from that of *Firebird*. With *Petrushka* Stravinsky finally reaches a fulfillment, with it he steps firmly out in front of his generation. All those who did not wish to be counted among the "living dead" realized that a great event had taken place, that Russian music had really made a new and unprecedented conquest. As many times as I have returned to a study of the music of *Petrushka* and its significance, so often have I been unable to add anything to my original impressions. As before, I still maintain that all the rumors that have been started about *Petrushka*'s superficial slickness and lack of coherence arise from simple ignorance. Stravinsky was more sensitive than ever before to the elements of mass motion, he evoked the special sonorous brilliance of native Russian instrumental intonations, he released the energy of the diatonic Russian melos in all its breadth and fullness, he declared the supremacy of mode as a free, independent principle no longer obedient to the dictates of major and minor and suitable only for stylization and archaic coloration. He destroyed the prerogatives of old-fashioned song and a lazy ethnography. He found among the most menial and everyday sources a music authentically Russian, and he gave it artistic shape without deforming or disguising its nature and origins. He chose to turn his back on the complacent cultivation of outmoded style, and face instead the living musical practice, the living musical language of the cities and countrysides, the rhythms and intonations that are produced and defined by the daily intercourse of successive generations. This deliberate choice to create from life necessarily gave the composer a greatly deepened awareness. The grotesqueness and incisiveness of *Petrushka*'s music is perceptible just because one is aware at the same time of the deep seriousness of Petrushka's plight. The surface of the music is all mask, all color and design of high festivity. But never in the literature of Russian pantomime and ballet have the basic misery, wretchedness, and humiliation of the world of "masks"—of the universal Petrushka—been conveyed in music so terrible, so excruciatingly realistic. Never have the howlings of impotent despair been so drowned in the hubbub of an indifferent public. The death of Petrushka—one single line of music—is as eloquent as many tens of pages of symphonic poems. In writing *Petrushka,* Stravinsky finally acquired the mastery of concise, concrete, intensive musical speech, toward which he had beeen moving in his earlier works (excepting the Symphony and the Etudes). Therefore, in comparison with the score of *Firebird, Petrushka* is more skillful and more laconic—not because of differences in instrumentation, but because Stravinsky's use of instruments took a new direction. Where his aim in orchestrating *Firebird* had been to use the instrumental color as decoration, here he strives purely for expression. Color has yielded precedence to characterization of and by timbre. The instruments themselves become figures of the drama (a development pointing directly to *Soldat*). The luxuriant paysage of the fairy-tale has given way to a rich, almost "Flemish" style, and the potential of basic Russian musical materials has been released in the actuality of a living musical speech.

The music of *Petrushka* is brim full of life. It is saturated—and this presupposes Stravinsky's extraordinary powers of observation—it is saturated with the rhythms and gestures of motion that are themselves concrete communications (and not mere descriptions) of the states of mind of individuals and crowds as they are conveyed by bodily expressiveness and physical motion. In this respect, the score has a striking plasticity. It is not the immobilized plasticity of sculpture, but the plasticity of a stream of living human beings, of pantomime. Springing as it does from pantomime and dance, Stravinsky's music always embodies motion, dynamics, characterization, muscular expression. It is through these qualities, and not by seeking to understand sounds in the abstract, that one penetrates to the "content" and "soul" of this music. Everything then becomes clear, understandable, simple. Like the music of Sergei Prokofiev, this music was a product of robust social health, and a counterbalance to the sterile aestheticism, refined exaltation, and convulsive lyricism of Scriabinism, and to the erotic intoxication that had captured almost universal attention. Of course, Scriabin, who rose head and shoulders above those immediately around him, dreamed of going even higher, whence no one could follow. That made a clearing of the atmosphere all the more necessary. The music of *Petrushka* was the first herald of the "new life," but Stravinsky did not stop there.

He could not stop, because he had begun to conceive music in a different way. No longer was he charmed by the fantasy of native poetry, by romance, poetic contemplation, and stylization. All this had disappeared. In place of pattern, color, refinement of design and harmony, modulation, tonal plan, etc., the activating forces now became life, strength, love, air, light, motion, play, and dance. Expressive subtlety and intensity take precedence over a rationale of architectonics. The revolution in Stravinsky's thought may be most clearly seen in the fact that for him form had finally ceased to be an independent scheme imposed upon ideas. On the contrary, it is the musical ideas that now create the form. To be sure, the fact that the score of *Petrushka* is composed as a sequence of episodic impressions from life, having as their only connection the drama being played out by the puppets, marks it as impressionistic theater, but at the same time it is dynamic, expressive, and even revolutionary by reference to the whole period of Russian theater music that had immediately preceded it. Of course the faithful followers of Rimsky-Korsakov were indignant, but to no avail. Before those applauding the eternal validity of the petrified canons of voice-leading, the voice of the courageous artist declares: the character and manner of voice-leading, and of every technical device, are defined by the expressive demands of the given situation. Rules are no longer their own justification. The composer is now free to choose any device to present or develop his ideas, and the appropriateness of his choice is determined solely by the integrity of the composer's thought and not by any display of academic formulae that frustrate inner necessity. In *Petrushka* Stravinsky forcefully confirmed his creative course and once and for all cut himself off from the possibility of returning to the composition of music by prescription. He could do it, but he might not. The design of the score has been altered almost beyond recognition. Lines have come to life and blossomed. In place of the old patterns of figuration disposed in a vertical-columnular arrangement, there is a free rhythmical play of a variety of motives and sound complexes. The bar-line has lost its tyrannical hold and has reverted to its original purpose: a coordinator of moments in time that does not in any way predetermine the bounds of lines. The arrangement and whole aspect of the score are conditioned only by the energy of the material and its potential for motion and development. The old academic technique was made to order for the weak: it enabled them, without the need for thought, to write down notes under other notes. The new organic technique is only for the strong; it recognizes no "eternal" rules. I repeat, this technique derives solely from the character and mentality of the composer. If the composer's mentality is chaotic, then no more can be done about that than could be done were the composer a writer or a poet. To deny to music the possiblity of the organic development of its inner premises, means to deny the existence of a musical mentality or to refuse to recognize its rationality, and thus to reduce musical creation to the level of a method for adding one voice to another and moving both according to canons laid down in advance and immutable. What an absurdity! Certainly, to think in "free forms" is more difficult than to embroider a design drawn on a canvas by one's elders, but the continuing life of music depends on the progress of the musical mentality and not on the repetition of acquired habits. That is the legacy of *Petrushka* to musical circles, and that is why the work is so significant not only for us but also for the leading circles of European musicians. In order to give music the capability and the strength to express a new living content, in order to give it back its basic energies, one had first to pull out by the roots the choking weeds of academic dogma that had flourished in a culture of security and prosperity and self-satisfied Philistinism. That Stravinsky did, and he thereby opened the way directly to *Sacre*.

From the point of view of construction, the music of *Petrushka* is extraordinarily simple, but rhythmically it is elastic and capricious. The first movement of the first scene gains coherence from the rondo-like recurrence—or, more accurately, rotation—of a few basic motives. The music of *Petrushka* conveys remarkably well the festive roar and hubbub of masses of people and gives the impression that a stream of living creatures is continuously in motion, now hidden in the background of a picturesque episode, now pouring out into the foreground. The music of the magician forms the center of the first scene. The magic of its beginning arrests the action, immobilizes it by the power of its strange, unreal, cold intonations. The finale of the scene is the dance of the Puppets, the Russian Dance. This is an iron-disciplined, mechanically precise play of motives stamped out in clear relief, whose captive energies give the sensation of the strain of great thrust. (Stravinsky is always successful with this kind of piece: see the Infernal Dance of *Firebird* and many passages in *Sacre* and *Noces.*) This Russian Dance is the core of *Petrushka:* its sonorities already have that bite, that toccata-like character, that peculiarly dry coloration that becomes the particular treasure of *Noces,* where the dominant sound is that of percussion instruments and the percussive intonations of the piano.

The second scene, Petrushka's cell, is in essence a monologue developed in pantomime. The raging and wailing of the love-struck Petrushka are conveyed by the capricious alternation of passages organized in strict rhythm with others improvised in fragile, convulsive cadenzas. Again the captive force bursting for liberty, again the expression of the strain of life's struggle, again the sensation of thrust—the striving to reach free space, to break through the rhythmic fetters. I emphasize the existence of such passages in Stravinsky's music, passages characterized by what I call the dynamosymphonic factor. Did not this pre-revolutionary psychic excitation and nervous impetuosity bespeak both a demand for emotional release, and the absence of it?[6]

The sharp sonorities and irregular rhythms of this second scene form a musical background whose trembling mobility is from time to time punctuated by short, "fanfare" motives.

After a nervously convulsive introduction, the third scene (the Moor's cell) settles down into the quiet and monotone of the Moor's Dance, a grotesque repesentation of Eastern voluptuousness. With the appearance of the ballerina there follows a number of amusing dance episodes, among them the grotesque pas-de-deux based on motives of the most ordinary provenance. The waltz, in which Stravinsky makes witty use of the humor of instrumental timbres (notably that of the bassoon at the beginning), is the prototype of the droll waltzes to appear later in *Soldat,* the Octet, and the Little Suite. A great deal of humor also derives from the unexpected interruptions of the waltz by fanciful turns, motives, and odd patterns in unusual registers at unexpected and seemingly inappropriate moments. The result is an amusingly disruptive "annotation" of the basic metrical order.

The finale of this scene is an agitated and convulsive "dogfight" of the rivals, the Moor and Petrushka, a grotesque "battle" symphony recalling that equally remarkable grotesque battle of the mice and the toy soldiers in the *Nutcracker* of Tchaikovsky.

In the fourth scene, the music is transposed from the sphere of intimate drama into the open air of the Carnival. From the point of view of length, development of the action, and musical saturation, this section forms the major part of the ballet and almost half of its total duration. At its center lie a series of genre-like dance episodes. Large choreographic actions such as this are customarily built as suites, as chains of dances and "pas d'action" providing a variety of rhythm and color. This suite is preceded by an orchestral introduction: a rich, bright music of festive gaiety, hubbub, and excitement which sets the tone for everything that follows. The orchestra glitters, sparkles, jingles, overflows with tones of rich well-being that are to contrast sharply with the abrupt instrusion of combat and hatred that leads to the denouement.

But first, the festivities are stretched to their dynamic limits. The initial episode of the suite is the Dance of the Nursemaids, whose fantastic rustlings now and then throw off a motive of the street song *Vdol' po Peterskoi.*[7] It is interesting to see how Stravinsky sets these Russian tunes: he does not start with the melody, which he need only harmonize, but with a distinctive background or a clear, concise rhythmic formula. One or more motives then appear and cut through the background of sound. But it is not the motives that control the dance: they enter only now and then and sound almost improvised. The initiative of the dance itself is found in the rhythms of the background, which may be a steady ringing, or a drone, or (as in the Dance of the Coachmen) a heavy stamping.[8] The episode of the Peasant and the Bear follows: the high register of the clarinet with the solo tuba against a deep background of intermittent bassoons and horns. Later, after the introductory episode returns, the strings are given a new motive, provocative, frenetic ("moemu nravu ne prepyatstvui"), ornamented with glissandi, also a variation of one of the most familiar melodies [see ex. 6].

Example 6

Enter the merchant and two gypsies. The gypsies dance, followed by the coachmen and grooms. Their dance is a savage and wild attack that stamps the earth with heavy tread. This is the dynamic center of the action of *Petrushka*. Stravinsky obtains from his orchestra a sonority of drones combined with heavy clangs of bells that sounds almost elemental. The rhythm is one of colossal tension, and no less colossal hardness and firmness. Against this striking background the dance motive is projected, inflexible, brutishly despotic [see ex. 7].

Example 7

It never appears complete but is assembled gradually, piece by piece, so that the zenith of tension, violence, and festivity is reached in the full fortissimo of the climactic canon. After the power of this outburst, the grotesque humorousness of the following episode (the maskers) is welcome dynamic relief. The revolving figurations (a device first used by Stravinsky in *Fireworks* and often found elsewhere in his works) rain down a shower of spinning musical tops that form a pattern of little whirlpools of sound. Out of this texture emerges a new rhythmic figure and the theme of the devil (a masker) characterized by wide jumps back and forth between high and low registers (trumpets and trombones) [see ex. 8]. It recalls the Red Jacket from the *Sorochintsy Fair* of Musorgsky.

Example 8

The infectious hurly-burly intensifies and turns into a dance of mad intoxication. The sharp, shrill fanfare of trumpets breaks it off: pursued by the Moor, Petrushka runs out of the puppet theater. Thus, the climax of the fight coincides with the moment of highest orgiastic excitement of the crowd and moves the action to a new plane. The Moor kills Petrushka. The crowd freezes before the figure of the dying puppet.[9] The orchestra depicts his final tremors in a marvelously tense and deeply felt passage.

The motive of the Showman, an echo of the music that introduces the scene, and the shrill fanfare of a Petrushka come to life again, bring the action to a close.

The score of *Petrushka,* quite apart from the scenario, is plastically and dynamically a striking and distinctive whole: a fantastic tale based on a theme drawn from life. The scenic stylization tends to constrict the dynamic range and qualify the imaginativeness of the music, which can be heard to better advantage in concert performance. In *Petrushka,* despite obvious concessions to the scenario, Stravinsky the musical illustrator and decorator finally becomes Stravinsky the symphonist. In *Sacre,* he gives the theater the entirely new problem of the "symphonization" of action, a concept that has not yet been suitably formulated.

Notes

1. The planning of the first movement is not interesting. Musical motion is rescued from
    monotony only by the delicacy of the orchestration and the rhythmically resourceful
    variation and foreshortening of the principal theme. Here is how the theme goes (I select a few
    passages in order):

Example 1

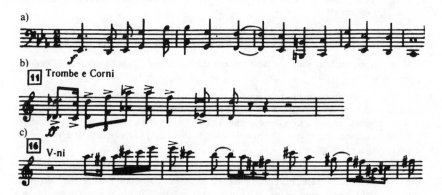

With the exception of the scherzo, the movements of the symphony (and especially the
largo) have generally anemic themes. Essentially, the themes do not lack beauty, but they
have such an indifferent formation that one can do with them anything one wants at any time:
everything goes well together and sounds successful. The score has the familiar "Belaiev" look
with respect to its vertical aspect, doublings, the disposition of imitative entries, the
calculation of instrumental balances, etc. The separate instruments have almost no expressive
individuality. The music is made by instruments, but the instruments do not create the music
out of their own characters. This is also the impression left by one of the last works of
Stravinsky's early period, the Fantastic Scherzo, a more original and advanced piece, about
which more later. The design is abstract, rationalized, not yet an organic expressive element.
The student character of the Symphony is relieved only by occasional revelations of
Stravinsky's instinct for orchestral color and by flashes of an original mentality in the scherzo,
where the orchestral sound flows in a shimmer of delicate hues. The pallid largo is
distinguished for the example it provides of a stylistic anomaly—when the solo bassoon, in a
single measure of transition [page 103 of the full score], "sings" a short, intensive-sounding
phrase in the instrument's highest register [see ex. 2]. This is a typical example of how
"correctness" of voice-leading and the "quantitative" factor in instrumentation (since the
bassoon can play these notes, that means they can be written) may have nothing to do with—
may even defeat—the dynamic, inner necessity of the musical flow. The intensity of this
phrase is alien to the whole structure of the music in this place.

Example 2

2.   It now seems to me that *Le Faune et la Bergère* occupies a place in Stravinsky's creative work corresponding to that of *Ruslan and Ludmila* [the first major poem (1820) of Pushkin (1799-1837)—Trans.] in Pushkin's. I do not draw a qualitative parallel but refer to the significance of the works within the evolution of each artist's development. Marvelous grace of writing and play of irony!

3.   Basically there is still the harmony of *Kashchey the Immortal,* and a clear and delicate melodic design modeled on the intimate lyricism of Rimsky-Korsakov.

4.   Nevertheless, the first suite was and remains the richest collection of elegant and brilliant episodes from *Firebird.*

5.   The instrumentation of the new suite is economical: 2 flutes, 2 oboes (English horn), 2 clarinets, 2 bassoons, 4 horns (F), 2 trumpets (C), 3 trombones and tuba, kettledrums, bass drum, cymbals, triangle, xylophone, piano, and strings. The treatment of the piano to suggest the celesta is very instructive. The practicability of this score, I repeat, has not destroyed the poetic value of the music.

6.   Thrust in architecture is the manifestation of the dynamic principle in immobility. The concept of thrust in music, of course, still needs argument and proof. But the sensation of the presence of thrust in music is for me beyond doubt, especially in works where the energy of a melos that has been constrained by an iron rhythm breaks or gushes out, like water trying to flood. Movement in music is a current whose flow is determined by the interaction of thrust and rhythmic control. In the absence of thrust there is only slack; the rhythm cannot support itself. In the absence of rhythmic disciplines there is chaos, flood, formlessness.

7.   Then *Akh, vy, seni moi, seni.*

8.   I call attention to the mastery and inventiveness with which Stravinsky varies the instrumental lines and develops the rhythms of the motives in this first dance. The score is completely alive: there is not one dull moment. And yet all the glitter and brilliance constantly refer back to two basic premises: the opening and closing of the accordion "box" (primarily a rhythmic formula), and certain physical gestures of favorite Russian dances.

9.   Petrushka falls with a broken skull; in the orchestra, against a background of cymbals tremolo, the piccolo "expires", and a tambourine falls jangling to the floor.

2

The Rite of Spring

Scenes of Pagan Russia. Two Parts: The Adoration of the Earth; Sacrifice. Composed 1912-1913

The first performance of *Sacre* in Paris in May 1913, marks a date in history. The influence of this audacious work on the whole of contemporary music is still unreckoned. The work is the beginning of that style of Stravinsky which now appears as his "middle period"—a period that comes into being after *Firebird* and *Petrushka* and lasts until the "new style" of the later instrumental works. *Sacre* and *Noces* occupy positions in the history of Russian music comparable in significance to that of *Ruslan* [i.e. the *Ruslan* of Pushkin— Trans.]. Like *Ruslan*, they mark the beginning of a Renaissance whose products will ultimately be seen and appreciated for what they really are. I believe that *Noces* represents the completion of the work that was begun in *Sacre*. To be sure, *Noces* contains much that is new and not found in *Sacre*, but at the same time the celebration of the cult of fertility and propagation in the sphere of the cantata contains and fulfills what was projected instrumentally in *Sacre:* the celebration of the pagan cult of the earth. Both works are dominated by the forces of regeneration, by their violence and their evil. In *Sacre*, the forces are more elemental, being directly linked to the renewal of nature and the ceremony of the rising of the sap. In *Noces*, they are diffused into the complications of the marriage rite, but without a loss of intensity. The Eros of *Ruslan*, as an artistic idea, is apparently inexhaustible: it yet knows no limit to the varied means that may give it expression.

Part I: *The Adoration of the Earth*

The work begins with an orchestral introduction (lento, quarter - 50, tempo rubato). The theme of the bassoon, accompanied by the horn, opens the Ritual Action of Vernal Regeneration [see ex. 9].

Example 9

Ritual Action of Vernal Regeneration

The clarinets leave a train of parallel fourths in triplets. A new theme enters in the English horn [see ex. 10]. Thus, on the first page of the score we have the materials basic to the construction of the whole introduction: the pastoral themes that form the principal melodic lines, counterpoints branching out from them, and a bass that moves in parallel fourths and forms an essentially static, drone-like harmonic background. In the next section, the "twittering" of the oboe (then flutes) accompanies a sharper definition of the pastoral subject given to the E♭ clarinet. The texture comes more alive, blossoms out, becomes filled with new voices. The triplet figure remains the principal unifying element of the rhythmic design [see ex. 11].

Example 10

Example 11

The clarinet melody in this example plays an important role later on.

Variations of these melodic elements and new offshoots from them compose a stream of sound whose aspect is forever changing, and this is the "substance" out of which form emerges. It is difficult to describe this kind of form because one must describe an aspect of movement itself, a texture ceaselessly changing, growing, expanding and contracting, in which the flow and ebb of sonorities produce a constant alteration of colors and densities. It is as if the texture breathes, now filling itself with air and expanding, now exhaling and reducing its substance to a single line. To describe the form as a series of periods and phrases consisting of so-and-so many measures, has no relevance to the process of growth and says nothing about it. The adherents of visual music and visual musical architectonics can do nothing more than declare: Long live the eight-bar phrase and conventional voice-leading: all the rest is no music at all. But criteria based on certain proper phrase lengths and on chords composed of certain forever acceptable intervals, cannot be used to measure the introduction to *Sacre.* When the exact sciences come upon phenomena that cannot be satisfactorily explained by conventional means, hypotheses are altered and methods are reviewed. In music, however, it is not the antiquated rules that are repudiated, but only the music that does not fit them.

The "form" of this introduction to *Sacre* must be understood as a musical texture in process of growth. The sensation of growth is achieved, as I have said, by two means: by varying the densities of the texture, and by introducing new melodies as offshoots of the old. For example, consider the new melodic material given the oboe over the wavy figuration of the alto flute [see ex. 12].

Example 12

Here there are two lines. The lower, an inversion of the dominant seventh on d, is derived from an earlier passage. The upper forms the archaic series: f^1, $b\flat^1$, c^2, $e\flat^2$, f^2. The two outer pitches—f^2 above and d^1 below—are pivotal points from which depend sounds functionally related to each. That is the way the texture should be heard, and not vertically, with the resulting clashes of major and minor thirds.

The E♭ clarinet plays a variation of the upper line an octave higher and continues on as a kind of upper pedal, while the dominant on d, having disappeared from the flute, finds its resolution in the heavy triplets of the contrabassoons that form another dominant on e. These are the two outer limits of the musical sound-area within which the clarinet plays a variation of one of the earlier themes. Then the English horn adds its pastoral timbre with a variation of another theme. The whistling of the flutes, cutting through the texture, begins to add its own new counterpoint. The sound becomes alive with the flutter-twitter of flutes, oboes, and clarinet. The muted trumpet grasps the melody and, with the oboe, sounds it clearly forth. The glissandi of viola harmonics, the trills of the solo violin, the arpeggios of clarinets and flutes—everything contributes to the flowering of a bright and rich sound. Abruptly, the continuous development is broken off: the introduction returns to its beginning, and the tense bassoon melody (now a half tone lower) recalls for a moment the mood of the opening. The trill of the clarinet and the violin motive (from the next dance) imply an impending change: the symphony of nature's vernal regeneration gives way to human revelry, dance, play. The transition is masterful.

The Auguries of Spring. Dance of the Adolescents

In the introduction, the prevailing intonations were those closely allied to the dynamics of breathing. Wind instruments predominated. Now the quivering chords of the strings, supported by the rich sound of eight horns, establish the background of a simple rhythmic tread, while the English horn chirrs with the peevish bassoon, the trumpet breaks into insolent cries, and the flutes sound lively whistles.[1] [See ex. 13, note 1.]. After the "neutral" coloration of the introduction, the flat key and major chords sound brilliant and colorful, like the gay clothing of youngsters on holiday. The "tweakings" of celli and violins pizzicato, the "screechings" of piccolo and clarinets energize the basic rhythm. The whole composition is sharply etched, garish [see ex. 14]. Using this same melodic idea, the passage proceeds directly to the Dance of the Adolescents, announced by a new and beautiful horn melody [see ex. 15].

Example 14

Example 15

At first there is no impression of heavy stamping: the texture is transparent, the colors clearly differentiated, the whole character mechanical, puppet-like, without lyricism. There is a gentle patter of chirrs, rustles, and squeaks (compare the Dance of the Nursemaids in *Petrushka*). One has the impression that the music does not really move or flow but just goes round and round, like a wheel on its axis. As a matter of fact, it resembles the style of country performers who, when they play dance music, weave a perpetual pattern of design around a central thematic pivot; and a pattern of diverse colors it is, set off against the monotone of the rhythmic support. In addition to the material just mentioned, Stravinsky inserts into the texture a favorite device of syncopation: the "propulsive" sevenths and ninths in the bass [see ex. 16] which break the snap and tapping of the regular beat and provide a charm that suggests the famous Dance of the Coachmen in *Petrushka*. The horns thereupon begin to imitate the mouth-organ [see ex. 17].

Example 16

Example 17

If I am not mistaken, the first person to make striking use of this material was Tchaikovsky in his *Children's Album (The Peasant Plays the Mouth-Organ)* [Op. 39, no. 12, 1878—Trans.].

Pages 22-27 of the score, beginning with the change to the tonality of C major, give an especially brilliant picture of how dynamic growth is achieved by adding layer upon layer of new musical materials that appear dismembered in a variety of ways but often derive from the two-measure phrases of folkdance improvisation. There is not, and there cannot be, a final cadence. The wheel simply stops—and gives place to motion of another kind.

The Abduction

Here there is resemblance in design and rhythm to the "maskers and mummers" of *Petrushka,* not in a literal sense, but as an extension of the same methods and a development from the same premises. But this music is more astringent and severe, for the action here is not far removed from the elemental manifestations of primitive instincts. The "runaway" theme (flutes, E♭ clarinet, and D trumpet, over trumpets, horns, and chirring strings) serves as a kind of signal for the action to begin [see ex. 18].

Example 18

The sinuous and muscular sevenths in the bass try to embrace the wild outbursts above. The trail left by the ascending fanfares of the trombones (alternating A major and C major) yields to the war cry of the horns, to which the first subject is then added. This is the initial conception, and without interruption or break Stravinsky develops the passage by repeating it and extending it, finally reaching an even higher degree of tension in the war cry of the horns at the level d^2, a^1. A powerful, resolute motive is inserted into the texture [see ex. 19] to restrain the motion by the pressure of its weight. The "runaway" theme tries to do just that, but each time it is stopped by a weighty sforzando. The Abduction is one of the most brilliantly terse and plastic conceptions of Stravinsky. The E♭ trills of the violins and flutes bring us back again to the "flat" tonal coloration.

Example 19

The Rounds of Spring

This section begins with an idyllic theme in the clarinets (that sound like shepherds' pipes) set against the trills of flutes: it is the invitation, the gathering for the round dance (slow tempo, quarter note - 108). The dance proper is massive, restrained, rooted in the earth (the heavy stress on the E♭ minor tonic and the cumbersome motion of the fifths) [see ex. 20].

Example 20

The passage is gradually laced with clarinet and oboe themes, piccolo tracery, and the archaic melodic fragment (strings, then horns [see ex. 21] whose upper and lower octaves are paralleled by lines beginning, respectively, a major third below and a perfect fifth above. Stravinsky often uses this method of thickening the texture organically—which, from the point of view of orthodox harmonic doctrine, is, of course, absurd. But orthodox harmony is just one particularization—or, more precisely, one fractional, transitory episode among many possibilities of developing and phrasing a line, or joining several lines together. In the case under consideration, the competency of orthodox harmony is at an end, and it has no right to veto a method of filling in a texture by means of "shadows" above or below. Having pointed this out here, I shall allude to it again only in rare and special cases.

The cumbersome motion changes to a sharp vivo (quarter note - 160) and to a figure resembling the "runaway" theme of The Abduction, whose course is also impeded by interruptive accentuations (chords sff). The return of the tranquil opening brings the round dance to a close without further development, and carries the action into a new movement sharply contrasting with what has gone before.

Example 21

Dance of the Rival Cities

The texture is severe, heavy; the tempo is fast (molto allegro, quarter note - 160). The basic dynamic premise of this dance is the conflict between the fast tempo and the weight of the massive layers of sound, in which the tempo is always trying to overcome the inertia of the sounds. The element of struggle is also conveyed by the collisions of dissonant sonorities: four lines apparently move in pairs, but the principal melody is not exactly reproduced at the octave nor is it shadowed at a constant distance. In the following example I give the opening measures of the dance. First the tuba sevenths and the heavy tread of trombones and kettledrums, then the principal theme with cross relations of major and minor thirds (horns), followed by its diatonic, archaic version (trumpets, violins, violas), but omitting the surrounding texture [see ex. 22].

The rest of the dance consists of variations, juxtapositions, and collisions of the diatonic and altered versions of this basic material. Through the harshness and severity of the confrontations, Stravinsky conveys the impression of elemental force, concentrated in itself and not yet differentiated into the fluency, elasticity, and suppleness of human movement.

Example 22

The whole first half of *Sacre* forms a massif of rough, uncouth sounds. On its lower slopes are the dances and the limpid symphonies of Spring. Above, towards the ridgeline, the terrain becomes hard, powerful, masculine; still higher, the vegetation is stunted, and the boulders are covered with moss.

The Dance of the Rival Cities already gives the impression of the massive severity of a great boulder. In orchestrating the four-line melodic fragment (measures 3-4 [ex. 22]), Stravinsky treats the four horns somewhat as Tchaikovsky handled the four violins in the finale of the Sixth Symphony: the lines are made to sound parallel without being so written. But this solution does not alter the essence of the conception: a very strict execution of the technical principle I have already mentioned—that of doubling a melody by its shadow or its reflection. The two outer voices always remain a minor third (tenth) apart, while the middle voices are separated by a major third (in its inverted form of a minor sixth). As a result of this arrangement, Stravinsky can make a chromatic confrontation of two pairs of lines (upper and lower), in which pairs of major and minor thirds will sound in each chord but will exchange positions almost every time. While the upper pair forms a major third, the lower pair forms a minor third, and the converse. If we designate the major third as "a" and the minor third as "b," then their relationship is illustrated thus:

that is, each interval formed by the said pairs of voices may be found next in the opposite register, as if it had been transposed there [see ex. 23].

Example 23

After several appearances of this material, a second theme enters, first in an ornate version, and then in its clear, archaic form [see ex. 24] with two pedal points: clarinet trills on c^2 and a^1, and basses and cellos pizzicato F♯, B, D♯, G♯. With the return of the first melody [ex. 22] over a pedal point, a new tonic is established.

This is the central moment. It leads to the return of the second theme [ex. 24], but at the fourth above. On the whole, the correlation of sections and melodies in this part of *Sacre* is strictly classical, despite the tonal, linear, and rhythmic complications. This is especially clear in the different appearances of the second melody, which is first presented in the Mixolydian and Ionian modes on G and C, and then in the Mixolydian mode on F. At the very end of this section, a new, weighty theme is heard (tubas in octaves, punctuated by shocks of the bass drum) [see ex. 25] and the movement passes on, without interruption or change of pace, to the sinister grandeur of the Procession of the Sage which is the final dance of the suite.

Example 24

Example 25

Procession of the Sage

As I have already pointed out, in the majority of Russian musico-choreographic works, the suite is the principal device ordering the design and action, and *Sacre* is no exception in this respect. Let us recall the ordering of the movements:

    I.   Symphonic Introduction (lento)
    II.   The Dances
          1.   The Auguries of Spring; Dance of the Adolescents (quarter note-56)
          2.   The Abduction (presto)
          3.   The Rounds of Spring (tranquillo, sostenuto pesante; vivo; tranquillo)
          4.   Dance of the Rival Cities (molto allegro)
          5.   Procession of the Sage
    III.   Final Action (finale)

The Adoration of the Earth and the Dance of the Earth

Therefore, the Adoration of the Earth and the Dance of the Earth, which follow the procession, complete the suite and form the finale of the first part. The movements provide a sequence of contrasting rhythms, melodies, and tempi, but from The Auguries of Spring to The Procession, the texture gradually becomes fuller and more encumbered. Indeed, it is by the very cumbersomeness of the materials that Stravinsky is able to evoke an image of pagan life in distant antiquity, of man inseparable from and dependent on the earth that nourishes him (the Greek goddess Demeter). Arranged as it is in massive, hard complexes, the material makes its heaviness increasingly felt, so that one is even led to wonder what colossal forces must be expended merely to propel the sounds.

Around the theme of the Procession and over the roar of percussion, Stravinsky weaves an impenetrable network of fragmentary rhythms and intonations. For a moment, the action freezes (Adoration of the Earth): nothing is heard but the sound of little throbbings (basses, kettledrums, and contrabassoon) against a background of bassoon chords. Silence reigns. The stirring chord, which ranges from the deep C of the basses to the airy transparency of the passionless violin harmonics, only deepens the effect. With the bass drum crescendo, the tam-tam roll, the glissandi of strings, and the whirling, upward run of flutes, clarinets, and horns, the spell is broken. The heavy mass quivers—and begins the violent Dance of the Earth, which is the final action of the first part. This dance is of elemental primitiveness and solidity: there are no melodic formations, only a cumbrous figuration suspended naked over a whole-tone bass. It is not melody that reigns here, but ponderous rhythms in a combination like the following [see ex. 26], now and then interrupted by the shock of accents in different parts of the measure, glissandi, trills, and other such "decoration." This dance has nothing in common with our notion of the ancient Dionysiac orgies: here there is no light and supple whirl of the Maenades, but a heavy mass that not only makes no attempt to free itself from earth, but actually lusts to blend with earth, to become earth itself. This is the orgy of earth-worship, the Spring dance of hope, the trampling of the grain. The music does not and cannot overcome the heaviness of the dance—indeed, it reinforces the total effect of massiveness and concentrated energy.

Example 26

Part Two: *The Sacrifice*

The worship of the earth is closely connected with ancestor worship. The music of Part Two is not so much concerned with the externals of primitive Slavic man's attitude toward nature, as it is with his subconscious, emotional attitudes: the sense of mystery, horror, and panic in the face of the unknown to which he has for so long made so many sacrifices as propitiation. The final, closing dance of the doomed maiden has been conceived not as character portraiture or as genre painting but as pure symphonic movement—as, indeed, has almost all the music of the second half of *Sacre*.

Introduction, Mysterious Circle of the Adolescents, Glorification of the Chosen One, Evocation of the Ancestors, Ritual Action of the Ancestors, and finally the Sacrificial Dance—these are the phases through which the action passes. But the superficial "subjects" of such action are not important, and neither are the conventions of pictorialism, imagery, narrative, tone-painting, and the like. I repeat, here the music expresses the confrontation of man and the phenomenon of Spring's renewal—man, prior to the creation of a personal God, hardly aware of his own separateness from nature, still half embedded in her. The opening pages of the second part convey the mystery and panic of nature's night as it is felt by adolescent maidens, for it is precisely through them that the strain of nature's growth and vernal renewal can be sensed with particular delicacy and directness [see ex. 27].

The beginning of the introduction has sustained notes in the horns (the d minor triad as subdominant of a minor, followed by the dominant seventh of a minor). Over these tones, like shadows, hover the airy outlines of violin harmonics, and through the shadows move the fantastic harmonies of flutes and clarinets.

The violins (harmonics) sketch the profile of the maidens' dance [see ex. 28].

The atmosphere is one of fumbling, groping, as if it were snow, or semi-darkness. Stravinsky, whose music embodies to a masterful degree human gestures and bodily movements, shows himself here a senstive poet and symphonist in the realm of the subconscious, that area of feeling where the

Example 27

Example 28

palpable and the tangible disappear, and where man, in a gloomy, shadowed world devoid of objects, moves timidly and with the caution of uncertainty and fear.

In the second part of the introduction, the sustained chords of the horns vanish: the music begins to rustle, to quiver with convulsive motions (see parallel passages in *The Queen of Spades*), with transparent "glassy" runs in the flutes, with dry, cracking pizzicati. Part of this is Tchaikovsky, part Debussy, and part Maeterlinck—an odd combination. But Stravinsky is already far removed from the surface exquisiteness and refinement of the expressionistic palette. He has taken from Debussy only what is most vital: the nuances of light and *plein air,* and also his depth and intimacy—exactly the things that the imitators of impressionism could not understand and could not copy.[2] Stravinsky is concerned not with casual detail but with underlying mood and condition.

The theme of the maidens is sketched again, higher, more distant, like an alluring echo of reality. Beneath the flute harmonics, horns sound it again softly, almost gropingly [see ex. 29]. This is one of the most poetic moments not only of *Sacre* but in all of Stravinsky. Four measures of transition lead to a further development of the same idea.

Example 29

Mysterious Circles of the Adolescents

Over the cellos pizzicato, the violas have the same theme in a six-voice harmonization that is produced by shadowing the basic melody with lines functionally related to it and moving by parallel or contrary motion [see ex. 30]. The simultaneous sound of major and minor versions of the same triad conveys a sensation of shimmering luminescence. The trills of clarinets and violins blaze up like little flares. Beneath, the alto flute has a new theme [see ex. 31].

Example 30

Example 31

The pace of the music quickens slightly. The clarinets take up this motive and play it in parallel major sevenths. Next the oboes and bassoons take it, then the violins and celli: the flames are ready to break out. Again a change of pace (tempo primo), again an atmosphere of caution and fear, ornamented by wails of flutes. There now ensues a number of easily recognized repetitions of the basic melody in a variety of tints and shades that reinforce the atmosphere of somnolence, half-slumber, rustling. Trumpet and horn calls intersect the motion and stop it. The orchestra rises to a sharp sforzando, and after a short pause there is one terrifying transitional measure of 11/4—the strokes of fate, beaten out by four kettledrums, bass drums, and strings. Minus the last measure, the episode as a whole conveys the magic, the fascination, and the web of panic from which the maidens cannot escape. I like to apply the appellation "Symphony of Silence" to this remarkable passage of great poetry, charm, and sensitivity.

Glorification of the Chosen One

A wild, violent outburst of long pent-up energy (vivo, quarter note - 144). It is as if hammers are beating out the rhythms, and after each stroke there is the hiss of flames to which the sharp whistle of the flutes adds an element of raging force. The basic formula of rhythms and intonations is the following [see ex. 32].

Example 32

In connection with this dance, or rite, of glorification, I must add a few words about one of the important principles of construction that will often appear in Stravinsky's later works. I refer to the principle of "metrical differentiation"—or, more precisely, the decomposition of metrical uniformity with a view to reconstituting the accent by means of easily identifiable rhythmic groupings. In this episode there are fifty-eight measures, most of these of unequal duration. They are arranged in the following way.

Section I

$$\left(\tfrac{5}{8} \times 2\right) : \tfrac{9}{8} : \tfrac{5}{8} : \tfrac{7}{8} : \tfrac{3}{8} : \tfrac{2}{4} : \tfrac{7}{4} : \tfrac{3}{4} : \tfrac{7}{4} : \tfrac{3}{4} : \tfrac{2}{8} : \tfrac{7}{4} : \tfrac{6}{4} : \tfrac{5}{8} : \tfrac{9}{8} : \left(\tfrac{5}{8} \times 2\right) : \tfrac{7}{8} : \tfrac{5}{8} :$$

Section II

$$\tfrac{3}{8} : \tfrac{3}{4} : \tfrac{3}{8} : \tfrac{4}{4} : \tfrac{3}{8} : \left(\tfrac{3}{4} \times 2\right) : \tfrac{5}{4} : \left(\tfrac{3}{4} \times 3\right) : \tfrac{2}{4} : \tfrac{5}{4} : \tfrac{6}{4} : \tfrac{5\,\overline{7}\,6}{4} : \left(\tfrac{5}{4} \times 2\right) : \tfrac{3}{4} : \tfrac{6}{4} : \tfrac{2}{4} :$$

$$: \left(\tfrac{3}{4} \times 2\right) : \tfrac{2}{4} : \tfrac{3}{4}$$

Section III

$$\left(\tfrac{5}{8} \times 2\right) : \tfrac{9}{8} : \tfrac{5}{8} : \tfrac{7}{8} : \tfrac{5}{8} : \tfrac{6}{8} : \tfrac{5}{8} : \tfrac{9}{8} : \left(\tfrac{5}{8} \times 2\right) : \tfrac{7}{8} : \tfrac{5}{8}.$$

It appears at first glance that the passage is a sequence of single measures whose durations change almost without interruption. But let us look more closely. The 5/8 motive, the principal rhythmo-intonational formula of the dance, marks the starting-point, serves as principal building block, and acts as cadential formula. This pattern contains the primary rhythmic and intonational accent, and the other groupings resemble it—or contrast with it. As a single measure of 5/8, the formula is stated seven times in the first section. But is also enters into the make-up of four other measures. Therefore, out of the total of twenty measures there are eleven that contain part or all of the basic group. Assuming that the duration of the eighth note remains constant throughout, it can be seen that this section of the dance is very tightly knit.

Let us look at the second section. It has twenty-five measures. The original formula is not present, but there are other materials that are just as closely knit. Without adducing musical examples, let us designate the two musical elements as ab (two measures) and cd. Then the construction follows the plan: 2ab : abb : c : 4b : 5c : 3cd, plus two measures of transition. We shall find the key to the passage's coherence by observing how cleverly Stravinsky inserts element c between abb and 4b. The third section has thirteen measures and ten statements of the original formula. I have not yet mentioned the brass fanfares that are also used as connectives [see ex. 33]. I have also arbitrarily identified the basic formula as a single measure. But we might consider this basic material as consisting of three measures, two identical ones and a third repeating the intial harmony [ex. 32]; and if we then consider the ways in which the elements of the basic material have been developed (lengthened, shortened, rearranged, etc.), we shall find the construction of the first and third sections even more coherent and organic. Let us designate the intial three-measure group as A, the

Example 33

connecting fanfare and accompanying rhythmic beats as B, and variations of the first three-measure phrase as Av. Then the first and third sections have the following arrangements: in the first (A : Av) plus (B : Av) plus Av, and in the third (B) plus A : Av[3]

Evocation of the Ancestors

This seems to me to be the least interesting passage of the whole work. The imaginative conception seems to have changed, to have become pale and colorless. Following each of the five commands of basses, celli, kettledrum, horn, and bass clarinet, the orchestra plays variations on the following psalm-like, almost choral material [see ex. 34].

Example 34

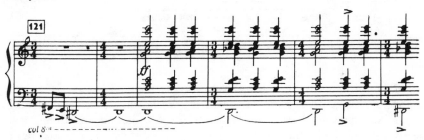

Ritual Action of the Ancestors

The Ritual Action of the Ancestors, to which the preceding Evocation passes without pause, contains intonational patterns that are sharply drawn and distinctive in both color and design. Slow tempo (quarter note - 50). The rhythm is quadruple, slow, regular. The horns and pizzicato celli and basses, later reinforced by the other strings pizzicato and the bass drum, proceed in quarternotes, while the kettledrums and tambourine follow them on the eighths between the quarters. Set off against this background of heavy pulsation is the quasi-improvisational dialogue of English horn and alto flute [see ex. 35]. With the entrance of the alto flute over bassoons, English horn, and

Example 35

viola, the color darkens; the atmosphere becomes sinister, autumnal, usurping and compelling attention. Over this same background, made even more somber by the horns, muted trumpets and bass trumpet begin the lament [see ex. 36].

Example 36

The rustling of muted strings joins itself to the cold sound of the flutes. Suddenly the texture becomes filled with magic: the flutes continue, but it is as if the autumnal cold, with its connotation of withering and decay, were suddenly touched by the breath of Spring: gurgles of clarinets, twitterings of piccolos and flutes, muted trumpets, strings sul ponticello, the dry, muffled peals of muted trumpets and trombones moving down in fourths over the strings pizzicato and the oscillating bassoons.[4] In the midst of this texture, the oboes and horns intone the lament again. This leads to the introduction of new material no less distinctive in sound, after which the "hollow"-sounding peals become even more expressive [see ex. 37].

The color again becomes dark, sinister, suggesting otherworldly apparitions. Stravinsky is always successful with music of this kind and mood. I think of the last breath of Petrushka, the entr'acte and chorus of ghosts (evoking the conscience of the dying Emperor) in the third act of *Nightingale,* and of episodes in *Firebird.* Stravinsky's sonorities are often characterized by the use of dry pizzicato, or the cold, muted rustlings of strings. I always imagine that

Example 37

there may be in such passages some sort of subconscious connection with the old cult of the Raskolniki [the Old Believers—Trans.]: with the "wooden" sounds of primitive drums deep in the forest, with gloom, darkness, servitude, and the whole atmosphere that so often attended rites celebrating the possibility of the survival of the dead. An atavistic transmutation of the dreams of ancient Egypt? A late manifestation of a primitive animism and ancestor worship? It matters not what unknown impulses fire the imagination, if the results have artistic validity and sharpen and deepen our sensitivities.

Important and essential elements of Stravinsky's music are terrifying and unusual sounds that can be described by such terms as "winds of autumn," "breaths of cold air," "muffled crashes," "slippery, noiseless rustlings," "muted peals," "the twinklings of silent flames." The passages that these terms describe counterbalance the other light, bright, rich colors and moods of his music. At their best, such analogies are bound to remain approximations only, but their use is unavoidable if one is to translate the language of music into a language of concepts and ideas. I might have found other terms more exact, but the most that I want to point out is that awareness of such areas of sounds, whatever may be its biological or psycho-physiological basis, lends an added dimension to our perception of music: it makes us alert and attentive, it forces us to hear in depth (much as we see in depth), it makes us more sensitive to all sound, to the sounds of quietude and even of silence itself. All that enriches our experience of life. My use of the term "otherworldly apparitions," for example, was an attempt to make the listener's ear aware of the undercurrent of sound in silence, much as the trained eye might see details of a landscape that would appear barren to the uninitiated.

The next section of the Ritual Action is even more heavily saturated with the peals, rustlings, and percussive shocks that surround the incantation, this time in the horns. The tension then fades away, and the music returns to the opening dialogue, this time led off by bass trumpet and alto flute and developed by clarinet and bass clarinet over a steady pulsation of strings pizzicato and percussion [see ex. 38].

Example 38

It is striking that Stravinsky here continues to develop the psychologically "expressive" sonorities of woodwind instruments, notably those of clarinet and bassoon, thereby following in the footsteps of Tchaikovsky. Many analogous examples may be found in *The Queen of Spades* (the monologue of the Countess, and other episodes), in the scherzo of the sixth Symphony, in *Iolanthe, Manfred,* and *Nutcracker* (the "characteristic" appearances of the bass clarinet in the variation of the fairy in the second act.) Obviously, the fact that Stravinsky uses woodwinds to express a succession of moods allied with the sensations of fear, cold, old age, dying, death, decay, and decomposition— this is not fortuitous, because we are dealing here not with Stravinsky's imitation of procedures used successfully by others, but with his attempt to deepen and develop what seem to him to be the connotations of the sounds.

The concluding section of the Ritual Action is informative in this respect. I shall have occasion to return to this theme in the chapter on *Nightingale.* Here I shall merely point out that Tchaikovsky's skepticism (his disbelief in another world, in a life beyond the grave) evoked in him a great sensitivity to death and to all ideas connected with death. The element of the grotesque in his music arises from this skepticism: he valued the creative, active individual at the same time that he was aware of the fantastic absurdity of the artist's life which led only to emptiness and to the annihilation of the very clever human machine. The intimations of "panic" and the "other-worldly apparitions" in *Sacre* (and in *Firebird* and *Nightingale* also) arise from different sources, but they are to an equal degree bound up with the grotesque and with an ironical attitude toward life. The difference is perhaps that Tchaikovsky's grotesque is nearer to Dostoevsky's, and Stravinsky's to Pushkin's. But have we not in both cases the characteristic Russian attitude that denies religiosity and intimations of unreality at the same time that it is frightened and horrified by the prospect of the void? After a millenium of credulous and naive faith and in the absence of any period of Reformation in this country, how could it be otherwise? It was impossible for the Russian artistic conscience suddenly to divest itself of layers of atavistic garments and courageously embrace life, like Brünnhilde in *Siegfried.* But there is reason to hope for such an act from Stravinsky, because he has in so many ways felt the joys of life for life's sake, the sensations of existing in the stream of life. He has made such contacts not only through his sensitivity to nature (as in the tale of the dying Chinese emperor and his recovery), but also through the intensity of his identification with the crowd, with the mass of people, and through his enthusiasm for "play," for expending a seemingly limitless amount of basic energy. I have in mind the mass scenes of *Petrushka* and the Red Table in *Noces,* comparable in its pagan expressiveness to the Feast in *Ruslan.* Since I have mentioned Tchaikovsky, let us not forget the bright pages of *The Sleeping Beauty,* or the finales of most of the Symphonies, or the great mastery with which Tchaikovsky gives musical expression to games, festivals, people, the masses (the first act of *The Sorceress*).

In the second half of *Sacre,* all parts of the action are carefully joined together, one leads to the other, each is preparation for the next. Here, at the end of the Ritual Action, clarinet dialogue carries us into the Sacrificial Dance, the final stage of the tragedy of a humanity still unaware of its power over nature and the elements. I am reminded of the figure of Iphigenia.

The fact that in *Sacre* the climax of the whole action is conveyed not by speech or by song but solely by dance is an element which greatly enhances the passionate intensity of the whole situation. The exaltation and fanatic enthusiasm of this dance (quite apart from its particular context) are marvelously expressive of the ecstasy and nervous animation of any individual whose fate turns on the accomplishment of a great deed, even at the risk of life itself. Even if we reject the entire set of archaic premises on which *Sacre* is based, two themes remain: personal sacrifice, and the impossibility of separating personal life from the life of the masses. These two ideas are the ineluctable conclusion of the whole sequence of dances and events. The music itself, quite apart from the props, costumes, or rites, communicates this also. For the music contains no stylization, no superficial descriptive details, no references to epoch, life, genre, paysage, etc. There is only the sound itself, and at the same time an attempt to minimize as far as possible any formal, stylistic, or emotional referents—in short, all the elements that stand in the way of the direct communicativeness of music's basic qualities, with rhythms as the only control.

The rhythm and the sound complexes—or, more accurately, the rhythm (as the basis of construction) and the sound material organized by it, are presented naked, without mediating factors: ornament, theme, melodic formation, harmony in the conventional sense do not have any independent importance. Take any passage: the controlling factors are *rhythmic* (transposition, displacement, inversion, diminution) and *dynamic* (expansion and compression of sound complexes and lines, accumulation and dissipation of materials), both of which contribute to the *energy* of tension and discharge. The nature and character of the material itself indicate the techniques and procedures to be used in any given case, and of course all scholasticism and routine that prescribe development according to sacrosanct and rational "rules" are swept aside. Basic to the motion of this music is the principle of improvisation: a series of impulses, or shocks, provoking a series of reactions, each reaction encompassing a broader range and utilizing a greater variety of materials. The sound complexes, lines, and timbres are first combined horizontally or vertically to show certain facets of their identity or dissimilarity, and each such combination immediately implies the development of a new combination. Instead of regular accents on the first beats of measures that are equal in length, Stravinsky writes a series of unequal measures that are grouped according to accent, according to the strength of attraction of certain intonational points of support. Lines may take melodic form, or they may not. Melody is only one particular case, one embodiment, of linearity, whose basic form here is expressed as a series of rhythmic impulses, supported by "percussion" instruments. The various groupings of the percussion instruments are therefore very carefully worked out, with due consideration to differentiation of range, intensity, and degree of mobility. In *Noces* and *Soldat* Stravinsky brings the use of percussion to the very highest level and thereby returns music itself to its origins and redeems riches that had been lost in the oblivion of the passing centuries.

But even in the area of pure melody—that is, in intonational formations whose shape, intensity, and mobility are constrained by the requirements of *singability,* by the dynamics of breathing, and by the uninterrupted flow of sound and pure harmonies (i.e., without the admixture of noise)—even in this area Stravinsky plants something new, again by first loosening old earth. The cultivation of melody from time immemorial, as it has come down to us by oral tradition, demonstrates that that tradition had long outgrown the crude restraints of an harmonic music that dictates the assimilation of all the voices to the one which carries the principal melody.

For Stravinsky, therefore, Russian folk music was not just something to which he could apply principles of development that were alien to the material itself (no matter how often this may have occurred): the folk music actually became a part of his organically developing language. His taste and technical facility made it unnatural for him to foist onto this music characteristics that were alien to it—on the contrary: by letting the folk art reveal its own qualities, vitality, and forms, he found the key to its proper artistic transmutation.

I have dwelt on such matters because without examining them, one cannot come to an understanding of Stravinsky's creative work. No mechanical division of the texture of melodies into periods, clauses, phrases, or motives will reveal its structure; on the contrary, one must observe the motions and interrelationships of similar and dissimilar motivic formations, groupings, degrees of the scale as they are stated, repeated, and combined into different *melodic situations.* I call such formations of tones *popevki,* and similar formations in instrumental music *naigryshi* (that is, in those cases where the popevki have an obvious instrumental character, often even with ornaments). But the question of terminology is not the only point, although I consider popevka a very useful term by virtue of the range of its applicability. The point is the principle: the dynamic view of music sees the melodic texture as a fabric that is alive with melodic cells (popevki) which are constantly changing position and aspect. My study of the versatile and improvisational nature of folksong and of the evolution of European musical polyphony has led me to this conception. Since I find in the later works of Stravinsky (notably *Renard* and *Noces*) confirmation of these very princples, I cannot but be persuaded that Stravinsky's creations are rooted in tradition and are themselves an organic development of that tradition, however much his methods may seem perversions of convention to our more conservative contemporaries. People who fear to abandon the accepted doctrines always begin by abusing the unfamiliar out of an instinct for self-preservation. By so doing, they lend support to a Philistinism which, fearful of tradition's overthrow, consciously encourages scholasticism and the preservation of outmoded beliefs. All this is well understood and perhaps even good, because all art that is new and young must temper itself in battle with the old. And above all the battle must be continued, because otherwise music will cease to be the area in which the thoughts and feelings of contemporary man find their most expressive outlet.

Before analyzing the concluding Sacrificial Dance, I have taken the time to explain the basic properties and premises of the style of Stravinsky's middle period (beginning with *Sacre*), because the final dance itself and a few other passages (including the introduction) were counted at the time among Stravinsky's most inaccessible and most frightening achievements. We can now see that the introduction and the final dance provide the most important clues to understanding the later works, and I have made this digression, before examining the final dance, in order to lay the groundwork of our understanding. I might have devoted a separate chapter to the matter (i.e., the bases of Stravinsky's style) following this one, but why do so when the subject could be just as well treated here? We shall see that the bases of Stravinsky's later style— of *Nightingale, Renard, Soldat, Noces,* and the so-called "new instrumental style"—are just those I have referred to, which derive from the dynamics of music, from the relation of rhythm to stress and sound complexes, and from the principles of Stravinsky's melodic design. Naturally the principles of construction become more important and more pervasive in the purely instrumental works written during the composer's temporary abstention from the theater.

Sacrificial Dance

Its most striking characteristic is the unequal measure—even more striking here than in the Glorification of the Chosen One. At first one sees only a motley of unequal metrical feet. With the eighth note - 126 remaining constant, the first twelve measures, for example, go as follows:

$$\frac{3 + 5 + 3 + 4 + 5 + 3 + 4 + 3 + 3 + 5 + 4 + 3}{16}$$

But the disorder is only visual. If one goes beyond the first impression, then one can soon see the logic of the design and establish the various sections of the movement. They are five, in number. I shall refer to them by the rehearsal numbers in the small score, and by pages in the piano four-hand reduction:

I: #142 - #149, 29 measures (pps. 73-74)

II: #149 - #167, 82 measures (pps. 74-79)

III: #167 - #174, 29 measures (pps. 80-81)

IV: #174 - #186, 53 measures (pps. 81-85)

V: #186 - end, 60 measures (pps 85-89)

The last section recapitulates the first and the third, and is based on identical material. I shall now try to explain the course of the music as a purely dynamic process and to stake out the path of this process without reference to analysis of the elements of sound as such (that is, the harmonic and rhythmic groupings and their instrumentation.)

One can designate the following two sound complexes as the bases, the points of departure of the dance: Elements A and B [see ex. 39].

Example 39

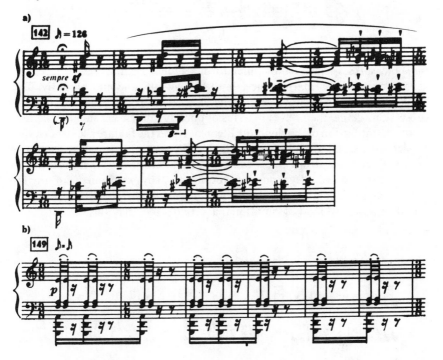

The dance begins with a statement and two repetitions of Element A, reaching a high point in measures 10 and 11. If we regard the first three measures (beneath the ligature) as the concentrated essence of Element A, then in the total of twenty-nine measures, this Element makes seven appearances. I use the term "appearance" and not "repetition," because each time there is some slight variation—some slight permutational or quantitative change. Element B in the example given [ex. 39], appears only in its original aspects, since its components undergo constant rhythmic displacement. Over it, there sounds the important popevka (first in the trombone), Element C [see ex. 40].

There is a surprisingly extended development of correlations between Element B and the ejaculatory fanfare (Element C), with a steady increase in tension. This second section of the dance has two clear subsections. The first encompasses fifty-nine measures, the last ten of which serve as its termination, with Element B spread wide throughout the orchestra in the chord D, A, f, b♭, e♭^{1}, f♯^{1}, a^1 (basically a thirteenth). The second subsection encompasses twenty-

Example 40

three measures, the last ten of which form a similar terminal passage. Neither subsection has a formal cadence; both are cut off, and end abruptly. This abrupt termination of movement is one of Stravinsky's favorite devices. Both subsections define themselves in terms of pure dynamics. Tension is generated by the juxtaposition of the rhythmic Element B and the fanfare Element C, with displacements and variations of both. The displacements are usually of two kinds: (1) from the strong to a weak beat of the measure, so that the center of gravity is shifted and a "syncopation" results; or (2) by extension or contraction of the individual components. Let us take, for example, the rhythmic Element B and consider the kind of variation that it undergoes in both subsections [see ex. 41].

Example 41

When the fanfares that intersect this line are superimposed onto it, there can result a number of highly expressive interrupted rhythms and cross accents.

The third section of the dance repeats the first, a half-tone lower, and with the same abrupt termination.

The fourth section (sostenuto, quarter note - 126) introduces new material:

a.   The rhythmic complex that acts as a basso ostinato [see ex. 42]

b.   A march-like popevka, utilized as a melodic element over this background, and then extended and transposed [see ex. 43]

The brass instruments (trumpets, horns, and trombones glissando) and percussion (kettledrums, tam-tam, bass drum) take the principal role in the development. The wild, martial character of this episode is a magnificent contrast to the convulsive ecstasy of the first part of the dance. But despite its contrasting nature, the section seems to have been perfectly prepared by the fanfare Element C that figured in the second section. Into the center of all this, and interrupting its course, there is wedged a fragment of the opening theme of

Example 42

Example 43

the dance, beginning with a measure of 5/16. This is a clever application of the rondo principle: the "refrain" appears both as connectives and as aide-mémoire and gives the movement an inner drama, so that the whole episode cannot sound separate and independent. The bold and absolutely exact execution of this interruption, even on the piano, makes a stunning effect. This section of fifty-three measures concludes with a further development of its original material over the remaining twenty-two measures. However, after the interruption, the march does not simply repeat itself but is developed with a great increase in dynamic tension. Not only does the rhythmic formula of the basso ostinato appear in the bass register—it begins to sound throughout the whole range of the orchestra. For example, while the strings, clarinets, and flutes carry the march-like motive, the following little phrases break out like streaks of lightning [see ex. 44].

The texture becomes further complicated by the horns imitating the march-like themes, with trombones glissando, trumpets roaring, and the din of percussion answering with peals of thunder the lightning zigzags of D trumpet and piccolo.

The fifth and concluding section of the dance is a further intensification of the material of the first section (the principal idea being presented here a fourth lower, that is, on the dominant of the original pitch). The intensification expresses itself in a number of details: the ascent to the first climax (e^2) takes not ten measures but fourteen; there is a larger number of phrases and abrupt terminations, as well as sharp contrasts of ff and p. After the first climax (e^2), there is another phrase climaxing at e^3. When this second climax becomes more commonplace by repetition, it turns out to be a point of departure for yet a higher climax at f^3. This pitch is first touched upon, and then repeated several times until the sound of it becomes habitual. Then at the very last moment there

Example 44

is one final quick ascent: g^2, c^3, e^3, f^3, followed by a short pause, a violent blow, the clash of tremolo strings on $f\#^3$ and g^3, and the upward flight of the flute to $g\#^3$. The flutes and strings leap to a^3 and a^4, and the dance terminates with the deep blow of the tonic D. The path has been followed, the summit reached, and by more decisive and quicker steps at the end than was the case in the more gradual early progress from a to a^1, then to e^2, a^2, e^3, f^3, etc. One must remember that each leap forward is followed by a step backward. The climax at e^2 subsides to c^2, that at a^2 and b^2 falls back to g^2, and the upward moves from g^2 to c^3 and e^3 are followed by falls to the lower octave, etc.

Thus, in the first section of the dance, the intonational line, over a bass D and beginning on d^2 (the melodic starting-point), reaches a^3—and having touched it, falls back to d^2. A new phrase rises to a^3 and $b\flat^3$, then falls back to a^2 and terminates abruptly. In the third section, over a bass C$\#$ (the leading-tone of the opening bass note of the first section), the intonational line moves from $c\#^2$ to $g\#^3$, lightly touches a^3, and settles back to $g\#^2$, the leading-tone of the final section. There, with a bass on contra-A and the upper line opening on a, the upper lines reaches a^3 without rising to the half-step above—that is, it spans three complete octaves out of the full range of five octaves. Here are the climaxes of the intonational line in order:

Section I: d^2 to a^2, $b\flat^3$, and back to a^2
Section II: $c\#^2$ to $g\#^3$, a^3, and back to $g\#^2$
Section III: a, a^1, e^2, a^2, to e^3, f^3, g^3, $g\#^3$, a^3

It is clear that in both sections I and III, the important factor in the climaxes is the pitch a^3 to which both b^3 and g$\#$ ^{3} have very strong attraction as leading-tones above and below.

The fleeting appearance of the opening material in the middle of the fourth section has no role in the gradual intonational ascent, because the material is held to a single level (d^2, e^2, c$\#$ ^{2}, c^2). But it has harmonic significance. The harmony of the first section is dominated by the tonic D in the bass. In the second section, the bass moves from G to D and thence to F and on through the F$\#$, G$\#$, B, and B$\#$ to c$\#$, which turns out to be the fundamental of the third section and is also the leading-tone of the previous tonic. The ostinato which forms the basis of the fourth section has A as its lowest voice. In the upper line the pitch d is predominant, and the fleeting appearance of the opening material uses D as a bass. The fifth section is firmly supported on A, which itself makes a natural transition at the end to D, the original tonic. Thus the use of the opening material in the fourth section is a necessary element in the broad harmonic plan.

Lest my analyses of the rise to the final climax have proven more difficult to understand than the course of the music itself, I have abstracted in the next example the pitches and rhythms of this intonational ascent [ex. 45].

I hope I have gone sufficiently into detail to show the inner logic and order of the conception of the dance. Only if one refuses to examine the new means of expression can one speak of them as chaotic and confused. As a finale, the dance brings the second part and indeed the whole action to its highest intensity. It is also the logical conclusion of the symphonic plan of the whole, and it conveys in sound the ultmiate overcoming of the "feeling of panic" through sacrifice, exaltation, ecstasy.

Each of the links in the chain of *Sacre* poses its own problems and finds its own unique solutions; in each, the artistic imagination of the composer is revealed in all its brilliance and originality. The originality is not whimsical—it proceeds from organic and natural premises. To understand this, one must be willing to enlarge the circle of one's ideas about what is permissible or not permissible in music and regard any technique as a temporary set of self-imposed limitations peculiar to a given epoch. Stravinsky finds it easy to exercise control over rhythms and intonations that are unusual but that have deep roots in European musical culture. One must first try to make out the inner logic: then Stravinsky's technical mastery becomes fully explicable. But even without such explanations, the music itself affirms its own rightness through its plasticity, its contemporary rhythm, and the great excitement of its sheer novelty. The colossal shock of the creative energy in *Sacre,* for example, cannot help overcoming inertia and must be enormously stimulating. Subsequent works may have a greater finesse or greater polish, but no matter what direction they may take, their seed was sown here, in this daring conception

Example 45

born at the end of Stravinsky's impulsive youth and at the beginning of his maturity. The impact of *Sacre* was so intense, its dynamic content, vitality, and the formal problems that it touched upon were so new and so daring that the composer himself could not work out all the unforeseen implications of his new music at one time. He had of necessity to deal with them gradually. *Noces* is the natural child of the techniques of *Petrushka* and *Sacre* and of course a completely integrated and finished work—though it could not have been what it is without *Sacre*. One is bound to suspect, further, that whatever the sphere—theatrical or non-theatrical—or the future direction of his work, Stravinsky will not fail to utilize the symphonic conception that he projected in those pages of *Sacre* (the introduction and elsewhere) where the principles of the dance suite proved no obstacle to developments of a symphonic nature.

After *Sacre*, Stravinsky turned to the lyric tale *Nightingale*, whose first act was written in 1909 in an atmosphere of impressionism, exoticism, and a fashionable Chinoiserie. At least that is the way the work was understood when it was first presented to the public in Paris in pre-war 1914. We can now see, however, that the work goes deeper, and that as the music moves toward the third act the work gradually frees itself—and in the third act is completely free—of the Chinese stylization. But *Nightingale* was and remains a work of a transitional time, and because of this it lacks coherence. Unevenness and inequalities in the works of the reckless, the daring, and the young are not exactly bad qualities. But in works that lack courage—in works portraying only beauteous refinements and contemplative moods—lack of coherence is a fault. The three acts of *Nightingale* represent three stages of the creative process, and of these, the third is the cleverest, the most extraordinary, and at the same time the most Russian, even if the most romantic. After this necessary transition, I proceed to an analysis of *Nightingale* with the hope that I may be able to point out, amid all that is nice and agreeable, that which has permanence and value.

Notes

1. The background in this case is actually the repetition of a single chord, but with accents on different beats of the measure [see ex. 13].

Example 13

2. In my opinion, the beauties of Debussy derive from the creativeness of his particular animism, his expression of the spiritual essence that flows through everything around him—a creative idea that dominates, for example, Jules Romains's *Mort de quelqu'un*.
3. How many rigidly regular eight- and sixteen-measure periods there are, whose rhythmic organization can never approach Stravinsky's. Stravinsky, furthermore, does it all without separating rhythm from intonations, without making rhythm abstract.
4. Here I am reminded of the "carillon" of *Firebird* (the awakening of the realm of Kashchey).

3

The Nightingale

Lyric Tale in Three Acts by Igor Stravinsky and S. S. Mitusov, after Andersen

Introduction: Larghetto (eighth note - 92). The opening recalls both Debussy and Musorgsky. It has a kind of idyllic intimacy and elegiac tenderness. Clouds—light, limpid—float by, quietly, peacefully. Soon an exquisite pensive melody is traced against this beautiful background. The melody becomes more animated, it takes the form of a langorous lament that dissolves in a series of descending sequences, and, without protest, melts away, leaving one final sustained noted. Over this note the opening harmonies, slightly transformed, emerge again.

Curtain. Darkness. The edge of the forest, by the sea. A fisherman in his boat can be barely seen . A few measures of transitional music: the rhythms of the undulating waves join the movements of the clouds (fragments of the opening motives). A second larghetto (eighth note - 60): the charming song of the fisherman amid the sound of splashing waters. Then, in a recitative, the fisherman muses—like a sort of Chinese Rousseau of the twentieth century (or Japanese, because Stravinsky's delightful musical paysage invites comparison with Japanese painting)—as he waits for the nightingale, expressing his rapture in the most touching fioriture. Again the naive and idyllic C major; the song is repeated. The voice of the nightingale enters—first instrumentally (an ornate improvisation), then in a langorous lyric arioso in G♭ major for high soprano, of exquisite grace and delicacy. This nightingale belongs not to the fields but to the porcelain of the salon, but the porcelain is nevertheless of Russian manufacture. The character of the melody and accompaniment (the undulations and rustlings of triplets, and chords descending by major thirds) suggests the style of certain songs and of the Russian operatic arioso that was created under French influence. Kuzmin and Verlaine, Rimsky-Korsakov and Debussy. The style is not literally derivative, but it has a mentality remarkable less for sheer invention than for the judicious selection and tasteful use of old materials.

The nightingale's song is interrupted by the arrival of the chamberlain, priest, courtiers, and cook (the symbol of the simple, trusting "nature" in the conventions of the court). Their grotesque entrance shows us another side of Stravinsky. The clumsy phrase characterizing the chamberlain is very amusing, as is indeed his whole musical speech, which is built almost entirely on leaps of diminished fifths and tritones. The priest's speech is similar, and equally amusing. The music of the cook, by contrast, is idyllic and tender throughout, suggesting the meditative "Maikov" style of Rimsky-Korsakov [Apollon Nikolaevich Maikov (1821-97), whose poems were set by Rimsky-Korsakov in opp. 40, 41, 45, 47, 50, 52, 56—Trans.]. The dialogue of the three, punctuated with choral endorsements, is amusing in its grotesque moments, but weaker in the lyric "intermezzi" of the cook. Because of a certain rhythmic monotony in the accompaniment (too many of those by now too familiar triplets) and a certain flabbiness of design and pace, the music begins to be tedious. The instrumental improvisation of the nightingale, a variation of familiar material, interrupts the "mistakes" of the noblemen, who have taken mooing of cows and croakings of frogs for the nightingale's song. I object to the fact that on both occasions the song of the nightingale is prepared by introductory passages of instrumental motifs (naigryshi), because these passages assume the character of prefatory "illuminations" whose color is so striking as to destroy the coherence of the form. It is very annoying.

To the polite and ceremonious entreaties of the noblemen, the nightingale replies in a marvelously refined arioso (the rococo style of the end of the Russian empire!) that although his song may sound best of all deep in the forest in the quiet just preceding dawn, nevertheless, should the emperor wish, the nightingale is ready to leave for the court. The courtiers depart (music of the first dialogue), gratified that their mission has been fulfilled. The music reverts to the opening—the fisherman's song—and ends. This song and the music of the introduction are without question the best moments of the first act.

The second act is a curious mixture of the descriptive (genre) and the expressive. But genre comes to dominate in the end—genre in its rich, impressionistic refraction. The act is preceded by an entre'acte—a marvel of little puffs of sound, now golden, now iridescent, that rise in front of the now veiled stage. One might call it a "Fantastic Scherzo," to borrow the title of one of Stravinsky's early works. The music, like delicate porcelain or exquisite illumination, traces a charming illustration of the words of the chorus:

> Et si l'on accrochait une clochette à chacune des fleurs
> Les fleurs au gré du vent doucement tintent.

Elements (popevki) of the pentatonic scale give the choral parts an archaic cast [see ex. 46].

Example 46

Ог – ни,   ог – ни   го – рят,   зо – ло – ты – е бле – стят

The movement of the music is light and fast (quarter - 144), the sounds flicker on and off like colored lanterns tossed by the winds, like fireflies flitting to and fro in the grass and among the branches. The glissando of harp, piano, horns, and trombones at the very beginning of the entre'acte has the blinding effect of a rocket whose sudden take-off signals the beginning of illuminations and festivities.

To questions about the nightingale, the cook gives simple, artless replies: he is a little bird, you would hardly notice him in the shrubbery—in a little half-aria, half-recitative, one of the most charming moments (with just a touch of Musorgsky) in this section. The exclamations of the chorus interrupt the cook. The combination of archaic materials and subtle harmonies, the delicacy of the patterns of color, the fragility of the design joined to the temperatment and crispness of the music—all these together convey the magic of a fairyland to an extraordinary degree.

The Chinese march that follows, still more refined and more gaily colored without being massive or heavy, adds to the novel excitement. It is magnificent as impressionistic genre-painting. At the very beginning the rhythms of three lines are combined: the "pinwheel" triplets of the celli, the downward leaps of flutes, harp, and violins, and the disjunct "Chinese" theme of the bassoons in fourths [see ex. 47].

Example 47

The use of pizzicato produces the effect of a muffled carillon of clicks and plucks. This is especially noticeable when the theme passes to trombones and trumpets and is heard in a pentatonic scale on D. Three measures of transition (harps, celesta, and violins) lead to a new thematic variation of the Chinese scale (trumpet over piano figuration, and flutes and clarinets in parallel fifths) [see ex. 48].

The celesta has a further variation over harps (the leaps of sevenths and groupings of threes again suggest pinwheels). Then the piano and violins

Example 48

pizzicato carry on the development of this motive over harps and celli, with the basses adopting the "turning circles" that the harp had previously suggested [see ex. 49].

Example 49

A new and sharply different texture commences when the pinwheel material is passed on to trombone and tuba, and the steadiness of the revolutions is interrupted. The pace of the march quickens; the bassoons, followed by trumpets, have a new variation of the theme [see ex. 50].

Example 50

The D-clarinet and the flutes join the "clumsy" tuba and bassoons in a grotesque variation of the pentatonic material and return the march to a variation of the opening material, the theme in fourths in the trumpets, the revolving sevenths in violas and violins. Over the revolving motion, the second Chinese motive of the march [ex. 48] returns, at first in the trumpets but an octave higher than before, then in the flutes surrounded by a little carillon of celesta and piano. The revolving motion continues all the while and even comes to predominate for a few moments, until it is replaced by the splendid solemnity of the third motive of the march [ex. 50], this time played by trumpets and tuba amid astringent harmonies and over the heavy ploddings of piano, harps, celli, and basses moving up and down by fifths and ninths [see ex. 51].

Example 51

This ceremonial passage is followed by the concluding section of the march—a musical fireworks in the fullest sense of the word. Over bassoons, horns, and celli in fifths, the second motive of the march, sounded simultaneously in the scales of g and d, whirls like a spinning wheel amid the ringing chords of piano and strings pizzicato, the flying sparks of the harps, and the rocket-like flights of flutes and clarinets. Festive, brilliant, colorful music.

Thus the whole march consists of a two-fold presentation of the three basic motives plus the concluding fireworks of the coda. It is interesting to note that one of the primary rhythmic premises (the "revolving motion" of the triplets) becomes a sort of leitmotif—a revolving wheel that gives unity and coherence to the march and that in the coda entwines itself into a principal melodic line [see ex. 52].

Example 52

Up to this point there has been no dramatic action. The paysage and idyllic intimacy of the first act and the magnificent genre-painting of the beginning of the second act have not exceeded the limits of pure sound painting and lyric romance. It is only in the center of the second act that one meets the rudiments of a drama whose substance is a quite novel application of the idea of the singing contest, an idea out of poetry and legend that has provided the motivation for a number of operatic actions. Stravinsky also used the idea later on in *Soldat,* where it takes instrumental form and is joined with the idea of the concerto. In *Nightingale,* the device is used to develop the opposition between two basic musical principles: on the one hand, the emotional, lyrical, improvisatory principle as the agent of compositonal freedom (and breathing as the agent of vital tension); and on the other, the mechanical principle as the instrument of a cold compositional style lacking freedom and dynamic vitality, where strong and weak, loud and soft succeed one another without nuance or ebb-and-flow, and produce a music that is flat and uniform. The contest here is between two singers: the live Nightingale and the mechanical (Japanese) nightingale, only of course without the full emotional context of a *Tannhäuser* or a *Meistersinger.* The "Nightingale of the Chinese Emperor" appears first— again, alas, only after the preparatory instrumental cadenza of the flute, as in the first act. The Nightingale's delightfully langorous arioso (which, without reproach, is a nice balance of the spicy and the bland) enraptures the emperor. The arioso's line is fragile and delicate, half-declamatory, with pauses after every phrase and with a gradual widening of the range after each rise and fall or after each return to the starting point. This is one of Stravinsky's favorite techniques of melodic development.

The "terraced" arrangement of ascending phrases, and the breaking of fragile and delicate lines are also characteristic of the melodic style of the *Three Poems on Japanese Lyrics* for voice and instrumental ensemble (2 flutes, clarinet and bass clarinet, piano, 2 violins, viola, and cello) written during 1912-13. Delicacy and transparency of figuration, tasteful selection of a few colors and shapes, a langoruous, hot-house quality—these are characteristics of Stravinsky's rococo exoticism—a passing style in his development, but one that had great significance for his taste and technique. In *Nightingale* the influence of this style is strong and, unfortunately, especially so on the Nightingale's melody itself, which is something quite different from the essence of Andersen's sweet and simple tale. There are no traces in the song of rural romanticism or the freshness and coolness of spring; the song is neither naive nor spontaneous. Here is one of the "lines" of the Japanese lyric (without accompaniment) [see ex. 53].

Here are the first measures of the Nightingale's song (again I call attention to the alternation of major and minor thirds) [see ex. 54].

The voice throbs amid the glassy harmonics of the harp, the porcelain

Example 53

Example 54

tinklings of the celesta, the twitterings and rustlings of muted violins and the dry chimes of piano and harp. Without doubt, a lyricism of such intimacy has its fascination, wholly apart from decor or subject. But nevertheless it is fortunate that Stravinsky quickly and easily freed himself from this fragrant and bewildering atmosphere. Little wonder that just those short-sighted individuals who detest and abuse Stravinsky's work chose to praise this kind of rococo lyricism, and with it the whole first act of *Nightingale,* for its "purity," taste, and obedience to the rules.

The poetic mood that has been created is somewhat disrupted by a grotesque interlude, during which the Nightingale's song is imitated by the ladies of the court, who fill their throats with water and emit gurgling sounds.

The Japanese ambassadors then arrive, bearing a mechanical nightingale as a gift for the Chinse emperor. The ceremony of their arrival is very wittily conveyed in musical terms: the two ambassadors sing together in a kind of organum (predominantly parallel fifths, but with exquisite deviations). The scene of the mechanical nightingale provides the occasion for ingenious orchestral tricks that are in the tradition of the carillons of Musorgsky and which sound very amusing. Background: piano, clarinets, and harps tremolo pp with one cello and one bass, plus the tweaking of pizzicato violins, the bubblings of flutes and the gentle bells of the celesta. Across this texture move the lifeless mechanical roulades of the solo oboe [see ex. 55].

Example 55

Meanwhile, having refused to await the results of this unforeseen competition, the real nightingale has flown away. The emperor, enraged, declares the live nightingale banished from the empire and designates the mechanical nightingale as court singer. The emperor and the chamberlain both speak in a dry patter full of awkward leaps over wide intervals, a style designed to convey the coarseness and magisterial stupidity of the two characters. The decree is received in silence.

There begins another procession back to the inner chambers of the court, a new variation of the "Chinese march," shorter, but just as elegant. The song of the fisherman—the voice of nature—follows on the march and terminates the "action-less" act. "Action-less" in the theatrical sense, but musically, the elements of drama are very much present. In the music, two worlds are contrasted: the cold lifelessness of the court with its elegant but ceremonial play, on the one hand, and on the other the naive idyll of the fisherman and the song of the nightingale, for all its delicate refinement of sublime and unaffected melody. Nothing emerges from this confrontation on the theatrical level, of course, but on the musical, a drama has been projected which may be developed.

The deadly rigidity of the court atmosphere is now intensified by the appearance of a new "factor": death itself. Opposed to death is nature, as the source of life: the nightingale flies back out of the forest and by its song restores the health and strength of the emperor. This little detail of the plot marks a significant moment in Stravinsky's work, because at this point he leaves the stuffy atmosphere of exoticism and apathetic impressionism behind: instead of trying merely to fix his impressions of phenomena, he now strives to express their vitality. The presence of Russian folk materials, vocal and instrumental, in Stravinsky's music has always implied its extra dimension of rich allusion; it is the character of this extra dimension that is now further defined by the introduction of mockery, buffoonery, and the sheer fun of irony and the grotesque. From the sunny pages of *Petrushka* and the elemental forces of *Sacre,* the way is now open directly to *Noces.*

Either because it suddenly takes on an added human dimension of its own, or because the development of the action has posed a genuine and forceful inner conflict, at any rate the third act of *Nightingale* has singular depth and significance. Contact with the subject of death has always stimulated Russian composers to write a deep and deeply felt music, regardless of their personal beliefs or attitudes. Of course, between the extremes of religious conviction and belief in immortality on the one hand, and on the other the fact (unassailable from the materialistic point of view) of the complete erasure of human consciousness—between these two extremes human beings occupy a great number of intermediate positions, all of which are characterized by a life instinct that is felt as incompatible with death and by the attendant emotion of fear. Skepticism defines one of these positions, and its strength is directly proportionate to the strength with which the creative imagination of the artist stubbornly proclaims the power of life—and yet finds that power not easily reconciled with the black hole "on the other side." The sense of irreconcilability, the instinctive horror in the face of utter finality have taken, as I have said, a host of forms, terrible, fantastic, grotesque, good and evil, benevolent and malevolent. They may be irrational and illusory, but their undeniable strength and power derive from the fact that they are the concrete expressions of vital sensations and emotions. In the world beyond there can be no fable, because fable is something that changes with the age of man and the state of knowledge, but the very concept of another world nourishes the fabulist in this one by evoking his insuperable horror of death—a horror springing in part from superstition, but in the main from the force of his vital instincts. Certainly, if it had not been for the idea of resistance to death, the art of humanity would have been without its most highly artistic and expressive creations, in which grief and suffering, sorrow and hope are found in an infinite variety of nuances and shades.

Russian life has always been difficult. Some people have even got to the point of regarding the gift of life not only as an accident but as an unjust accident. And when skepticism began to shake the customary and traditional beliefs, there came into being the Gogolesque grotesque—an attitude so affecting that its author himself took flight and refuge in a humble cassock. Among musicians of the nineteenth century the most grotesque was Tchaikovsky—and this was his strength. I know my statement will sound odd to all those who still look at him with the eyes of his time, who still hear his music as nice, sentimental melody. If such were really the case, we could think of him as we think of Arensky or Napravnik—passive illustrators of their era. But we know that we can love or hate Tchaikovsky, and his strength is in that, too. Indeed, it is just the keenness of his subjective awareness of life that makes us adore or detest his music. Tchaikovsky's grotesque has certain affinities with that of Tolstoy or Dostoevsky. For all that he loved to ruminate on life and death, Tolstoy of course loved the former and feared the latter, despite his faith. *The Death of Ivan Il'ich,* of which Tchaikovsky was so fond, is very instructive in this respect. Dostoevsky also feared death, and for just that reason he, like Gogol and Dickens, was acutely sensitive to life at the same time that his view of it was grotesque. Tchaikovsky moved nervously from one extreme to the other: though he could not believe in immortality, though he was madly in love with the artless simplicity of life, he nevertheless was frightened of death, and this fear expressed itself in an enormous expenditure of artistic strength aimed at maintaining a hold on life. I have already touched upon this matter elsewhere [cf. e.g., comments on Tchaikovsky's Sixth Symphony in *Russkaya muzyka ot nachala XIX stoletiya (Collected Works)* II, 186f.—Trans.]. I want here only to emphasize the powerful presence of the grotesque in his music, and the degree to which this presence stimulated his imagination to conceive brilliantly new instrumental designs and colors. This notion of the importance of the grotesque to any understanding of Tchaikovsky's work is not original with me. Tchaikovsky's sensitive contemporary and friend Larosh was keenly aware of it. I find the notion useful here to indicate a possible instinctive parallel between Tchaikovsky and Stravinsky and to designate an aspect of their work, otherwise so different in materials, character, and quality, which they have in common. If we reject emotionalism as the unique motivation of Tchaikovsky's work, then it is not difficult to find many similarities in the musical ideologies of Tchaikovsky and Stravinsky. For both, irony and the grotesque define the *direction* of their attitude toward life: on the one hand, it may not be so annoying to die if the human refraction of life is just a caricature of something better; but, on the other, death is still frightening, and its images are terrifying because life is still so full of sun and happiness.

The grotesque that is really funny marks a full reconciliation with life. The nightmarish and unreal, on the other hand, is engulfed in the horror of death and is not easily overcome. Compare *The Queen of Spades* with *Nutcracker, Histoire du Soldat* with *Pulcinella, Nightingale* with *Pribautki* or *Renard, Firebird* with *Petrushka:* in each case, the skepticism of the earlier fantasy finds release in the later one. Furthermore, Tchaikovsky and Stravinsky have identical attitudes toward native art: for both, it is organic material; for both, it is living language, and not an archaic tongue to be used as a basis for arrangements and stylizations. Neither arrived at this point directly, both began by borrowing and ornamenting tunes. But when they began to use folk materials, they avoided the application of formal rules for those general principles of formulation that are appropriate to any material, archaic or contemporary. Tchaikovsky was very close to the life of his times and the sounds of the city streets (whence the roughness and "vulgarity" that are so frightening to the aesthetes). Stravinsky was also intimately familiar with the urban and country street sounds of his times and with the many and diverse intonations of city and country, including those of the accordion and chastushka [popular Russian lyric, reflecting current events—Trans.]. A further characteristic that unites them (to which I have already referred) is their aspiration to be among the people, in the middle of the noise and hurly-burly, to merge with the collective vitality, to lose personal identity and rediscover the sensations of feelings en masse. They also share affinities for Italian melody, for French clarity, and for the dance, both in its native and in its general European refractions.

It was the third act of *Nightingale* that first made me instinctively aware of the relationship of Stravinsky and Tchaikovsky. I had completely missed the evidence of *Sacre*. Even during the first rehearsals of *Nightingale* I had observed that though the happy denouement was beautiful, it was not as convincing as the expressiveness of those moments when the power of death made itself felt. The salutation of the recovered emperor has almost the quality of a puzzled interrogation. The concluding song of the fisherman, which has repeated itself again and again throughout the opera, becomes something like a book illustration: illumination, vignette, and colophon—like the trumpet fanfares before the scenes of the *Tsar Saltan* of Rimsky-Korsakov. It seemed to me that Stravinsky was at a turning point, a fact that was confirmed by later events. Stravinsky's vital instincts were deepening at the same time that his skepticism itself was growing: the resulting sense of the grotesque provided a new impetus in a new direction.

The opening pages of the third act of *Nightingale* (the entr'acte and the chorus of ghosts) are remarkable for their seriousness, severity, and the concreteness of their expression. Here there is no decoration, illumination, or even description. The austere, commanding phrase of the trombone (continued by the trumpet) "opens" the music of the entr'acte [see ex. 56].

Example 56

The other important "factor" is the motive of the somber procession of ghosts, with tam-tam strokes like funeral bells (the court is prepared for the death of its sovereign) [see ex. 57].

Example 57

The alternation and variation of these elements over a cold and lifeless background reminiscent of the music of the mechanical nightingale (whose motive is heard in the trumpets) form the "content" of the first section. In the second section, the trumpet sounds the commanding phrase one tone higher, and it is carried on by the horns. Like a distant echo, the oboe repeats the theme (popevka) of the mechanical nightingale. There begin the chimes of harp and celesta. The color darkens. Over the low E of celli and basses, the horns intone a cold and horrible transformation of the ghostly procession. The idea is developed by the woodwinds with even more grotesque and somber harmonies. The horns repeat their terrifying command fff. This time, the strings take it up, in a whispering and rustling movement. Finally, all the strings join in a texture that becomes gradually thicker and more concentrated, as if the ghosts were closing ranks. More chimes (harp, piano, tam-tam). The chorus of ghosts (the dying emperor is terrified by his deeds) [see ex. 58].

Example 58

This simple, almost archaic lament (a three-note theme in a rocking, bell-like rhythm and an austere color) sounds like a nightmare that will not go away. Against this background, the cries of the emperor's delirious fright are terrifying. Only with the arrival of the nightingale is the nightmare dispersed. The nightingale's melancholy improvisation is the best lyric moment of the whole opera. Certainly it still has a lingering odor of the musical orangerie, but this is not dominated by the more highly developed and flexible design.

The ancestors of this melody were the reveries of the Tsaritsa Shemakha in *The Golden Cockerel* and other similarly voluptuous inventions. And how strange that a romantic élan vital should have been conveyed in a vocal symbolization of such fragility and tenderness: remember that it is with this song that the nightingale banishes death! But in a "porcelain" opera anything is possible, especially when fantasy takes such a beautiful and seductive form. And if, instead of solving the problem by the dynamic of events, or by adopting a romantic attitude toward nature and using some symbol of its mighty power—if Stravinsky is able to banish death only by the authority of beautiful sounds and the poetry of melody, who knows, perhaps he was right. Let us examine the conception more closely. The nightingale has always been a messenger of Eros, a singer of the songs of love, and always melancholy, sad, langorous songs. Why people who are longing for love and in the grip of their passions should be diverted by a meditative and even wistful music, is hard to understand. However, love songs of various kinds seem to confirm this, and even our traditional wedding melodies and the whole wedding rite itself are somehow related to funeral laments and have an air of sad presentiment.

The dialogue that follows the nightingale's song deals with the struggle between life and death. Death will return his victim if only he may hear the song of the nightingale before dawn. The nightingale in turn sings an even sadder and more wistful song about the gardens of the dead, about the moss on the graves of the forgotten. Stravinsky's fantasy is a texture of fascinatingly mobile figures, each more poetic than the last. Filaments—no, more exactly, gossamers of sound. The music itself becomes the mood of pre-dawn darkness, just before the sunrise, just before all life begins to stir anew. One senses that as the composer weaves the web of his dream and then breaks free of it, he is himself going toward life, he is anticipating life. Just so, strength returns to the emperor—he must live and, consequently, act, because his dream deserts him—the nightingale flies away. From this point of view, the whole conception of the opera becomes admissible. The dream that is finally brought on by the song of the nightingale engenders the passionate impulse that resists the specter of death.

The courtiers, believing the emperor dead, enter the anteroom to the accompaniment of a cermonial funeral march of measured and sombre tread (harp, piano, pizzicato strings, tam-tam). One of the motives of the Chinese march, in a suitably funereal transformation, is given to bassoons and oboes, and then to horns. All is somber, crepuscular, choking, oppressive: Stravinsky creates a mood of deep depression and anguish. The march itself is no less expressive than other more famous funeral processionals, but it achieves its results modestly and succinctly. When the horror has reached a sufficient intensity, Stravinsky dispels the gloom at a stroke: a harp glissando and a bright woodwind chord give the music an unexpected turn. There follows the emperor's salutation, and after the curtain has fallen, the fisherman sings for the last time his idyllic melody, a bright, sunny coda that brings the opera to a close.

In 1917, Stravinsky reworked the music of this opera into a new, exclusively instrumental version, the symphonic poem *Song of the Nightingale,* a beautiful orchestral work woven of wonderfully rich instrumental colors. But in the symphonic poem, the nightingale's music lacks some of the charm that derives from the fascination and intimacy of the sound of the human voice. To be sure, the unpleasant double aspect of the nightingale's melody has disappeared: the melody is wholly instrumental, and its line now has definition and personality. But the price of stylistic consistency and the banishment of the voice is loss of warmth. Furthermore, in the opera (and especially in the third act), the nightingale's song acted as the focal element that provided technical and emotional unity and coherence. In the symphonic poem, on the other hand, despite its relative brevity, one has the impression of a tedious succession of static episodes. Perhaps these inadequacies are imperceptible if one does not know the opera. But I think not. They are too obvious. One might have said that the operatic version of *Nightingale* was too instrumental; but when the vocal element is removed, as in the symphonic poem, artistic validity is also removed. For example, since there is no "competition" between the nightingales, the whole conception of the music of the mechanical nightingale loses point and is unremarkable. Also missing— because the warmth of the human voice is absent—is the contrast between the nightingale's singing and the horror of the death music (entr'acte before Act 3 of the opera). Comparisons with the opera wholly aside, the symphonic poem is still a motley and ineffective work. To be sure, its orchestral design is marvelously skillful, its instrumental colors quite wonderful, the imaginativeness of its ideas and its detail completely fascinating, and all these together help to hide the inadequacies. But when all is said and done, the music of the symphonic poem is wearisome, whereas that of the opera seems so good that one is inclined to wish there were more.

The symphonic poem is constructed as follows: the first act is out, the music beginning with the "Fantastic Scherzo" (entr'acte to the second scene). The whole middle section of the entr'acte is foreshortened and made over into a charming new episode (andantino, eighth note - 76), an improvisation of flute harmonies and string trills. Can this festive Chinese atmosphere induce the nightingale to appear? The music of the Scherzo then takes up again, as it did in the opera after the cook had reached the palace with the nightingale. The Chinese march is then heard in its entirety, and then (without the Chamberlain's recitative) the nightingale's song. First there is the flute improvisation, and then the whole song (the flute and the E♭ clarinet have the melody). The song is abbreviated and altered. There is another brilliant use of the Scherzo material, and the exclamation of the third Japanese ambassador (melody now given to trumpet, and the whole episode up a major third) serves as a transition to the music of the mechanical nightingale. This amusing passage is wholly preserved, but it serves less effectively as a contrast to the live nightingale's song than it did in the opera. Also preserved is the decree of banishment, that now serves as a transition to the recessional march and the song of the fisherman, which appears here for the first time and connects the festive recessional with the music of death (entr'acte before Act 3). The death music is now without the chorus of ghosts. The nightingale's reveries then commence, but in a treatment quite different from the operatic version. The introductory cadenzas of the first song are partially preserved but serve as codettas to the melody, which is itself taken from the second song (about the garden of the dead). This is repeated several times with occasional interruptions of motives from the first song (about the emperor's garden). If one did not know the opera, the interchange would not be noticeable, because the several motives are joined together with great taste and charm. Here is the basic theme (violin solo and clarinet) [see ex. 59].

Example 59

After the third statement of this refrain and its concluding "echo" (ppp), the orchestra is for a moment silent, and there begin the funeral bells—the ceremonial procession of the courtiers, as in the opera but up a half-tone. This episode is very effective. Despite the absence of the human voice and the use of a luxuriant instrumentation, the orchestral version of this symphonic procession loses nothing of its original sharpness and intensity. The harp glissando—a tried and true effect—signifies the return to life. The song of the fisherman in the beautiful key of $D\flat$ major concludes the symphonic poem (or suite?), a work rich in instrumental invention but lacking formal coherence.

The two halves of the symphonic poem differ greatly in tone. The atmosphere of the first is aglow with a variety of musical fireworks and illuminations, whereas that of the second is a chilling succession of two magnificently gloomy episodes.

Beneath all these reservations, however, both the opera and the symphonic poem have a quality that links them with Stravinsky's earlier and later works: the quality of festival, of celebration, with lights, fireworks, illuminations, and bells. The occasions may be gay, or funereally solemn. The bells may be happy, or sad. The place occupied by the sounds of bells and chimes in Stravinsky's musical texture is important in may respects. The rhythms of bells have a great influence on the design of his works. The intonations of bells (the dry pizzicato, the porcelain timbre of the celesta, the glassy harmonics of harps and strings) condition the character of the music and are intimately related to the general quality and specific nuance of the instrumental color. The previous history of Russian music shows many examples of the artistic use of the rhythms and intonations of bell-like sounds, but it is Stravinsky who carries this development to its furthest point by incorporating bell-like elements into the very material itself not as extraneous but as an intrinsic musical factor. The *Song of the Nightingale* is the first brilliant step, *Noces* the second and far more significant, because in *Noces* the entire orchestra (4 pianos and percussion) is treated from the percussive point of view, as strokes, thuds, bells, and chimes of every description: dry, wooden, muffled, unmuffled, bright, dark, brilliant, somber. It was Stravinsky who opened before contemporary art music this completely new conception of sound and new world of rhythms and intonations. (They had always been part of folk and ritualistic materials.) Note that this new intonational world is capable of the almost subtle nuances of every description. The performance of the four piano parts in *Noces* demands long and exhaustive study. For pianists, these parts are a veritable school of rhythm. They demand absolute exactness in performance, as do the percussion parts themselves. It is paradoxical that the performance of a work that is considered by many to be a musical chaos, cannot deviate by the slightest degree from standards of absolute exactitude without destroying the texture and the whole conception. The development of the intonations of bells and percussion instruments as a basis for Russian symphonic instrumentalism clearly points to the coming downfall of the old principles of compositon and their related textural and rhetorical conventions. The stroke (the accent) is a basic phenomenon of all music and a fundamental principle of ensemble; it is also the basic coordinator of collective work and life. The bell has an equally long history as a social phenomenon. Both reached a high degree of development in ancient cultures and were a part of European culture from the dawn of the rise of cities. Both have been intimately connected with war, with festivities (play, dance, procession), and with all the brilliant manifestations of social life. Having created a new festive music in *Petrushka, Nightingale,* and *Noces,* Stravinsky can surely find the way to the great festive symphonism of our times.

There is a further point. These two elements (accent and the bell) are also very firmly embedded in our folk instrumental culture, at least in the form in which it has come down to us. Even in the rhythms and intonations of purely lyrical melodies—not only dance songs—it is easy to discover traces of the rhythms and melos of bells. The sound of ringing bells has also formed a part of the tradition of our art music. The tocsin, gay bells, funeral bells—all these belong to Russian music, not just as bells introduced into an orchestra, but as part of the very pattern, character, and style of the music itself. It was in *Noces* that Stravinsky first utilized the sonority of bells not as an element of pictorialism or as something added for theatrical effect, but as an intonational principle basic to the work, a principle whose rich possibilties inhered in the very materials themselves. No one—not even Musorgsky—had succeeded in doing this. In no collection of Russian songs, or in their accompaniments, can one find a trace of the conception of instrumental writing on a plane with that found in *Noces*. I do not dispute the fact that Russian composers have shown a great fondness for folk musical art, but they never had real confidence in its strength and originality as a system of organized sound. They considered that the formal principles worked out in this peasant art over the centuries were casual in comparison with the rigorous principles of art music that are expressd in the canons of harmony, voice-leading, etc. Since they laboured under distrust and delusion, they preferred to raid the treasures of folk music for materials for variations, symphonies, and the like and palm off on the listener arrangements that were often out of character with the material, rather than work out ways of developing the material that would inevitably have more energy and more logic and be more consonant with tradition than any methods derived from "elementary theories" and harmony courses.

I do not mean to imply that the "advance" from *Nightingale* to *Noces* consists solely in the fact that the use of accent and the sound of bells which was a special particularity of certain passages in *Nightingale,* grew in *Noces* into one of the important factors of the musical movements. This is a severely limited view of the matter. The fact is that such "advance" had its roots in the whole trend of Stravinsky's creative work during the first years of the war (1914-15). At this time, after *Nightingale,* a long anticipated crisis in the composer's style led him to undertake serious work on Russian rhythms and melodic design with a view to uncovering certain principles of musical formulation. These principles should be simple, indigenous to the art, and yet of such scope and strength that they could have relevance not only to the European music of the eighteenth and nineteenth centuries but to the musical culture of the whole of humanity. Stravinsky was not looking so much for the new as for the primordial, the basic techniques and forms that unite and clarify the whole world of musical phenomena and not just the narrow confines of so-called art music. He began—whether instinctively or unconsciously, it matters not—he began by trying to understand the suppleness and distinctiveness of the rhythms and intonations of Russian song and dance—Russian not in the ethnographic or aesthetic sense, but Russian as qualifying the fundamental principles of a musical language peculiarly well preserved in the "music of the oral tradition" of our peasantry and our Eastern peoples.

We must understand an important distinction with respect to the use of folk materials then and now. It is one thing (as has often been done in the past) to *imitate* archaic intonations and rhythms. It is quite another to forge one's musical language and deepen one's artistic and creative point of view through a broad study of a basic socio-musical tradition which leads to a mastery of the riches of melodic phraseology and rhythmic formulas, elements that have almost no part in the rationalized music of Europe. After our analysis of *Nightingale,* we must now pass on to this period of Stravinsky's development in order to understand *Renard* and *Noces,* and not just these alone.

4

Toward the New

The early years of the war coincided with a temporary lull in Stravinsky's creative work, but this comparatively quiet period was filled with a whole series of smaller works in which the new direction of the composer's thought can be perceived. Signs of the new appear in both the vocal and the instrumental works. The vocal works of this "borderline" period are especially interesting with ultimate reference to *Renard* (1916-17) and *Noces* (1917), because they reveal with unusual clarity the gradual development of the supple rhythms and intonations that distinguish these two major works. The instrumental pieces likewise anticipate the contemporaneous trend in Stravinsky's work that can be called the "new instrumental style" (no, I did not say "new symphonic style"). Any division, of course, of the continuous line of creative development is arbitrary, and the road to *Renard, Noces, Histoire du soldat* and *Mavra* begins long before 1914-16. But the sounds of this period have a common and a special interest with respect to the delineation of the new principles of writing which rose out of Stravinsky's mastery of the rhetoric of folk music and ultimately produced the wonderful perfections of the major works.

In 1913 Stravinsky had already completed the *Three Little Songs (Memories of Childhood)* for voice and piano: *The Magpie, The Crow, and Chicher-Yacher.*[1] These are pribautki of a rather hybrid type. There is a little of Musorgsky and a little of Liadov mixed with the traditional treatment of Russian songs for voice and accompaniment. Despite harmonic audacity, despite the movement of the inner voices in chromatic fourths, the vocal line has still not emerged from its status as a dutiful daughter of metrical regularity. Above all, there is still no mastery of the material: these are songs with accompaniment, and not an artistic refraction of original folk intonations in terms of voice and piano. Indeed, although the piano figurations are comparatively audacious, there are still no new intonational formations derived from the nature of the instrument or the vocal line. The piano part is just accompaniment, no more. In *Chicher-Yacher,* the density of the piano writing even suggests orchestral sonorities.

The concluding chorus from *Khovanshchina* (on an authentic folk theme given by Musorgsky) is unexciting and of no great importance. The work lacks a certain asceticism, and the musical imagination is not sufficiently disciplined. Indeed, the desire to be impudent at all costs leads Stravinsky to give the archaic material an incongruously ornate setting, and the result, though fresh, bold, and often inventive and tasteful, is not effective. Stravinsky seems to have done this not because it was necessary but because it was a way of being different. The chorus does make a magnificent, baroque impression. But in no sense is it a new language, a new principle of the expression of ideas, or a new world of sounds, but just one more item for discussion. If only the item were not so old-fashioned! (That is, so much in the style of Rimsky-Korsakov.) At the time of its first performance, the chorus was something of a disappointment.[2] It is constructed on the responsorial principle: the leader intones a basic motive, and the chorus repeats and develops it.

In the Pribautki (1914) for voice and 8 instruments (flute, oboe [English horn], clarinet, bassoon, violin, viola, cello, bass), *Berceuses du chat* (1915-16) for female voice and 3 clarinets, *Renard* (1916-17), of which we shall speak separately, and the *Three Stories for Children* (1917) for voice and piano, Stravinsky begins to reveal the new style that finally reaches maturity in *Noces*. The *Four Russian Songs* (1918-19), which follow *Noces,* form a sort of little suite in which Stravinsky makes a synthesis, a codification of what he has accomplished. He had by then acquired such mastery of his own experience that he could make a brief summary of its basic tenets and be fully cognizant of their value and immutability. They are in essence quite simple: (1) rejection of a large and complex orchestral apparatus; (2) the treatment of each instrument as a character with innate qualities and properties that conditions the material and the whole texture, and not vice versa; (3) the conception of instrumental counterpoints [*podgoloski*] as outgrowths and extensions of vocal lines; (4) the design of instrumental counterpoints that envelops the vocal lines in timbres of tinkling bells and in rhythmic patterns characterized by prominence of accent and pizzicato; (5) rejection of metrical regularity in favor of lines with individual patterns of accentuation.

In addition: (6) the measure reassumes its originally modest role, as a guidepost, a landmark, a counter, an indicator of a unit in the passage of time that does not impose rhythmic uniformity; (7) the tonic-dominant formulas are superseded; (8) it is no longer obligatory to make a design composed of measures filled with a monotonous and formal figuration; (9) it is no longer compulsory to resolve intervals according to the formulas that the ear has learned by rote in school and that have no necessary relation to the basic properties of sound. One result of this liberating attitude is an awareness of the functional relationship and interdependence of the various elements composing the texture of sounds, and a wonderful sensitivity to intervallic distance and to the varying tensions of the degrees of the scale and melodic groupings.

There are four Pribautki: *L'Oncle Armand, Natashka, The Colonel,* and *The Old Man and the Hare.* These already reveal the essential elements of the new trend. Though the vocal lines are terse and, of course, idiomatic, they combine clarity and austerity with a surprising degree of variety. It is easier to describe some lengthy aria in which the melody is disposed in broad periods than to speak about the melodic designs of these amusing little works. The simplest material is in *The Old Man and the Hare* (No. 4). The first half is a series of ornamental variations on a Phrygian theme of four notes [see ex. 60].

Example 60

In the second half (con moto, quarter note-66), the melody has the range of a seventh and forms two conjoined Phrygian tetrachords [see ex. 61]. Its last appearance is shortened [see ex. 62]. Thus, the Phrygian tetrachord is presented over the range of an octave at three levels, the upper and lower being joined by and to the middle. The accompaniment is in sustained notes with a clarinet theme in its upper register and with Stravinsky's characteristic semitone clashes (for example, g♯ heard against the melodic tonic A and the F below). In the second half, the instrumental melody is given to the bassoon, while pizzicato strings form a background of an amusing dance-like character with interruptions and leaps: essentially, this is a grotesque reflection of the vocal element.

Example 61

Example 62

In the third Pribautka, *The Colonel,* we again find development of the vocal theme (a three-note element) by means of transposition, extension, and the introduction of a burlesque psalmody [see ex. 63].

Example 63

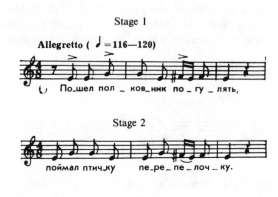

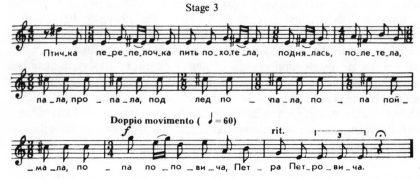

In contrast to No. 4, the melodic material of this Pribautka is made to grow away from its starting point. In addition, it is interesting to note that the third statement takes off from the leading-tone $d\sharp^2$, which receives its resolution only after the recitation on the $c\sharp$ and the leap to the highest point g^2. The accompaniment moves in ostinato, with the material given to clarinet, bassoon, oboe, and flute. The imitations of birds that do occur are done expertly but with great reserve [see ex. 63].

In the first half of the second Pribautka, *Natashka,* there is a two-measure melodic element, the Phrygian tetrachord $e\flat^2$-$b\flat^1$, which is repeated four times with minor variations of an ornamental character. To the $e\flat$ in the voice, the accompaniment simultaneously presents $f\flat$ (e) and d, the leading-tones that produce the characteristic semitone clashes. The second part, a development of the melodic element, is more complicated. The opening $e\flat^2$, $d\flat^2$, c^2, $b\flat^1$ becomes the following [see ex. 64] and resolves in the coda quite logically [see ex. 65].

At the same time, over the D-c♯ in the accompaniment is a figuration that gives unity to the two distinctive intonational elements of the two movements by the clashes d-c♯ and f-f♯.

The first Pribautka, *L'Oncle Armand,* is still more complicated. The original melodic element, suggesting E♭ major [see ex. 66], reaches a climax with the pitches g, a♭, b♭, and the undulating motion proceeds to the meno mosso [see ex. 67].

Example 64

Example 65

Example 66

Example 67

Сто _ ит браж.ка   в ту _ яс _ ку

The cadence begins in the following way [see ex. 68] with its characteristic snap and fall. (There is a similar passage in *Noces,* beginning on the pitches f♯^{2} and e♯^{2} and then leaping to e^1.) Against the F♯ in the bass of the accompaniment are opposed the clashes of f and g. The instrumental postlude has a tremolo d♭-g in the clarinet, over which the oboe plays the cadenza. How is the sequence of the melody throughout the piece to be understood? It seems to proceed from E♭ major through C major to conlcude in c minor, but with a final melodic d♭ just before the tremolo d♭-g. If we take the single note g as the intonational base, what about the f♯, with which it oscillates? If we take the c at the end, then the final d♭ seems to destroy it, as the e ultimately destroys the e♭. The pitches g and e, however, are displaced by oscillating half-steps only in the accompaniment—in the melodic lines they are constant. These three constants seem to be the intonational elements that articulate the construction: from e♭, the movement goes up (e♭-g-b♭), from g, down: first g-e-c, and then the fully symmetrical g-e♭-c. In other words, g is the unifying pitch. The scheme is as follows [see ex. 69].

Example 68

браж _ ку пор.няй   вы _ пи _ вай

Example 69

All this takes place in a vocal line with a span of only twenty-one measures. I have dwelt purposely on the "content" of all these vocal elements in order to point out their nature and construction, their mobility, flexibility, and sharply shifting balances.[3] The score of the Pribautki also shows a special use of the pizzicato, both as an accentual and as a bell-like intonation. The frictional clashes of a leading tone—or, more accurately, a *note sensible*—with the fundamental, occur most often either as pizzicato, or as arco with an added sharp staccato or sforzando. Therefore, they produce an effect suggestive of bells. When a bell is struck, the fundamental tone or timbre does not reach the ear immediately: after the stroke, there is a brief moment of flutter and blur—of vibrational confusion, and precisely this effect is created by the semitonal clashes. (See the first two measures of the first Pribautka [ex. 66], voice and strings alone without flute and bassoon.).

I stress this technical point because it has great significance for *Noces*.

My explanation of the semitonal "clash" makes sense, of course, with reference to the intonational impression—it derives from perception, and not from harmonic theory, according to whose rules the f♯ in this case is auxiliary to the third of the E♭ triad and resolves to g. The trouble is that such explanations are formal and static; they do not relate to the dynamics of the intonations, and if one is readily to approach *Noces* and the other works of Stravinsky's latest period, then one must understand a simple truth: one cannot learn, from rules about the resolution of intervals, how, where, and when voices should move; one cannot hear and evaluate the movement of musical compositions in terms of principles derived from static premises. If one does, the most important factors pass by unapprehended: the sensations of intonational tension, of functional relationships, and of the dynamics of the melos. The unfolding of musical motion has nothing to do with the mechanical resolutions of intervals, but only with the functional interdependencies of tones, given the specific conditions and the specific relationships between the elements. Abstract rules play no part in defining those relationships; they are determined by the positions of the tones in the scale system and the character of their function. In the example to which I have referred [ex. 66], the low F♯ and the g above might have quite another significance if the basic materials had a different melodic structure.

The four pieces of the *Berceuses du chat* date from 1916-17, according to the piano score. The ensemble consists of alto voice and three clarinets: E♭, A-B♭, and bass in B♭. Obviously, Stravinsky loves the clarinet. For it, both as a solo and as an ensemble instrument, he has uncovered hitherto unsuspected intonations of the greatest interest and has utilized the richly expressive properties of the instrument in a new way. In *Histoire du soldat* the role of the clarinet has extraordinary and perhaps even primary importance, yielding nothing in this respect to the violin. In the Three Pieces for Clarinet Solo (1919), Stravinsky's treatment of the unaccompanied instrumental line is a model on a par with the Bach sonatas and suites. We shall return to these pieces later.

In the *Berceuses du chat,* Stravinsky achieved a wonderfully simple, and at the same time highly refined, ensemble. The network of lines surrounding the archaic intonations of the voice is always organically related to the compositional idea and reveals the remarkable ingenuity of the composer by the degree to which, despite the basic uniformity of timbre, Stravinsky achieves variety of nuance and plasticity of line. The characteristics of the "clarinet family" are such that a composer may divert a melody, pass it from register to register, and make separate lines of it without risk of losing melodic coherence or fear of falling into monotony. The qualities of clarinet timbres—gentleness, suppleness, capacity for blending, and a certain feminine passivity—these qualities make the instrument remarkably well-suited to convey movements and moods that are voluptuous and langorous or that in certain cases could be described by the nuances: lazy, stretching, arching, purring. All this, of course, must be taken not in the sense of literal description but only as characterizing the general aspect, the dynamic "content" of the "cat" melos, a description of muscular exhaustion in musical terms.

It is difficult to say which of the songs is wittiest or most expressive. In the first *(On the Stove)*, the voice ranges over the seventh a-g^1 (two conjoined tetrachords, the lower one of which is not complete, while the upper d^1-g^1 has a "limp" where the e and the e♭ alternate). The tremolo of the "middle clarinet" (c♯-g♯) forms a background, and around this Stravinsky coils, like water plants, the whimsical intonations of the E♭ and bass clarinets.

The second song is an idyll *(Interieur)*. The range of the voice is the same, but the line is now adorned with chromaticism and glissandi. A sensation of shimmering color derives especially from the way in which the melodic fifth a-e^1 is playfully filled in—either by glissandi or by the cross-related major and minor thirds. The clarinet writing is very ascetic here: the high clarinet is a beautiful counterpoint [*podgolosok*] to the voice, now joining it, now branching out, now completing an unfinished thought. The bass clarinet does amusing musical bends through wide intervals. The middle clarinet enters only toward the end and concludes the song on a capricious gesture.

The melody of the third lullaby utilizes the fifth d^1-a^1, even though a^1 is sometimes reached via detour to the b^1 above, and d^1 via c^1. The accompaniment consists of a counterpoint [*podgolosok*] like that of the second song but still more "modest," and of two additional accompanying voices below. The pitches of these two lower voices are chromas of the vocal line and for the most part move in parallel fourths. The combination of the archaic melody with the bare chromas of the fourths, whose course is so calculated that they always seem to be trying to raise the vocal line to a more intensive "tone"—that is, the chromas often sound a semitone above the vocal line—this combination also creates a sensation of shimmer by the colorful oscillations of the vocal and instrumental pitches and timbres. I should even risk likening the combination of the austerely designed vocal line with the eccentric chromas of the accompaniment to painting on glass, where a similar contrast might arise from the irrational combination of an austere, objective outline with a chromatic background that "irrealizes" the design.

The fourth lullaby is the smallest: only seven measures (I, 16 measures; II, 19 measures; III, 16 measures). It is wholly diatonic. In the first half, the melodic line utilizes the fifth g-d^1 and terminates on a^1; in the second, the line utilizes the third a-c^1 and terminates on g^1. Thus even in the course of so short a piece, there is set up a tension between the two poles of attraction a^1 and g^1, giving the melos a vital freshness.[4] The clarinet accompaniment is in three contrapuntal lines [*podgoloski*]. The archaic quality of the song is emphasized by the use of parallel sevenths (measures 5 and 6) instead of the more commonplace thirds and sixths.[5]

The *Three Stories for Children* (for voices and piano) are in essence also pribautki. The last, *The Bear,* a tale with music after Afanas'yev, was written in 1915; the other two, in 1917. Like the other vocal works of the period, these have no extensively developed melodic form. It is as if, after the big dimensions and elaborate decorativeness of the ballets, Stravinsky had set himself the task of working out a terse language and a style of exposition that would be as ascetic as possible. This is just the road that leads to *Noces* and *Histoire du soldat,* which are themselves the results of the labors he had undertaken on language and style. The problem was how to create colorful works of large dimensions and full sound, whose textures would have a new intensity and whose lines a new muscular strength and resiliency resulting from experiment with the minute details of linear and rhythmic differentiation and dynamics. Stravinsky had of necessity to acquire training and skill by writing small ensemble pieces of limited dimensions before passing on to the larger works which, despite their size, display the new leanness of texture and economy of expression.

The first of the *Three Stories for Children* is called *Tilim-bom.* The bass is a one-measure ostinato that sounds unchanged throughout the piece. Over it, the voice chimes a short melodic peal that has somewhat the character of a call of alarm and that periodically disappears and reappears. In its absence, the voice has other melodic materials that share the character of chimes. Above all this are the little chimes of the accompaniment's upper voice, also an ostinato, one-measure pattern. The charm of the work lies in the way the basically one-measure ideas combine, alternate with, and displace one another, to produce an effect of anxiety and uneasiness [see ex. 70].

Particularly amusing is the way the figuration of the two outer voices surrounds the melodic material but just manages to avoid being consonant with it.

The second Story is entitled *The Geese and the Swans.* The background, which remains constant throughout, consists of the "clash" of the nineth c♯-d in the middle register of the piano, forming a rustling movement of sixteenth

Example 70

notes that is nudged forward from time to time by little darts into the lower register (E♭, B♭). Over this there is a scurry of little vocal elements, sometimes little cries, sometimes a sort of comic patter. After the first-three pairs of measures (each measure of three units), there is a rhythmic change: the meter remains triple, but the melodic segments are now four units long, while the accompaniment is an irregularly foreshortened variation of the original figure [see ex. 71].

Example 71

The triple meter remains constant throughout. But the apparent elongation of the measure by the introduction of a four-unit melodic element in a texture of three-unit measures is one of the ways of avoiding monotony. Another is the insertion (into the accompaniment) of what amounts to a new figuration with a numerator *shorter* than that of the basic one.[6] How often Beethoven inserts duple patterns into measures of three units!

A third method of destroying metrical uniformity is to combine rhythms and melodic lines of varying lengths, so that there is almost continuous metrical alternation. Examples of this appear frequently in *Renard, Noces,* and *Histoire du soldat.* Sometimes the line itself is lengthened or shortened. Sometimes the addition or subtraction of a word or syllable (usually in the form of an exclamation, as happens so often in folksongs) will increase or decrease metrical length. From this results a frequent juxtaposition of 6/8 and 5/8, or 5/8 and 4/8, or other similarly related meters. Sometimes an extra measure may be inserted as a rhythmic anticipation and produce an effect of elongation in this way. Sometimes, also, moments of silence appear on strong beats in place of sounds. By this rhythmic idiosyncrasy, Stravinsky may be trying to convey the image of a physical gesture that is trying to reassert control over the impetuosity of the motion, or he may be prescribing a moment for the intake of air—that is a moment of interruption or caesura, designed for the taking of breath but written into the texture itself. Breathing is organically related to rhythmic pulsation, and in the presence of such pulsation breathing ceases to be a voluntary act independent of the musical context. Thus a pause on a strong beat inevitably awakens a sensation of the delayed arrival of something important and thereby reinforces the tension of the sound. It is a pause of a dynamic order. Here are examples [see ex. 72]. The third of these examples illustrates Stravinsky's use of polyrhythms. Here is an instance of rhythmic interruptions [see ex. 73].

Example 72

a) С-под ка_мушка,   с-под бе _ ло _ го

b) Баслави божа   до двух по.ра_жден,   баслави божа   до двух...

Example 73

In *Renard,* there is an excellent illustration of dialogue with constant changes of measures and interruptions—the dialogue of the Fox and the Cock, particularly that of their second meeting. The following is an exchange of compliments [see ex. 74]. And next, the length of the measure is gradually extended [see ex. 75]. Any of the pieces making up *Histoire du soldat* contains marvelous examples of "metrical variation" and rhythmic play, with the greatest variety in the permutations of the elements. Especially remarkable are the Soldier's Violin, the Royal March (containing masterly treatment of pauses), and the Little Concerto.

Example 74

Example 75

Тюк, тюк, да за_гу_ла, а дру _ га _ я при го_ва_ри_ва _ ла

I have dwelt at some length on this small area of Stravinsky's craftsman-ship because, beside the community of sound qualities that unites the vocal miniatures and the later, larger works, I wanted to stress another, linear, connection: the gradually increasing use of variable metrical durations and a growing rhythmic elasticity. The *Four Russian Songs* for voice and piano (1918-19), written after *Noces* (but, it appears, before its "orchestration"), are especially interesting in this respect. They prolong the lineage of the miniatures and at the same time bear traces of Stravinsky's new manner, the broader and richer fresco style that made its full appearance with *Noces*. Of all the miniatures, these songs are the richest in content and the most remarkable in technique. They form a complete vocal suite. The first song (quarter note-116) is entitled *The Drake*. After the piano introduction (a B♭ major motive over a C major ninth c^1-d^2 in ostinato), the voice leads off with an undulating line that again suggests the rocking movements of bells [see ex. 76].

Example 76

Се_ле_зень, се_ле_зень, сиз го_луб_чик се_ле_зень, хох_ла_тый се _ ле _ зень,

The next melodic element starts within the range of the fifth as $a♭^1$-$e♭^2$, then widens that range to the sixth $a♭^1$-f^2, and finally rises to $a♭^2$. This is the first section. After two measures of silence, the voice begins again with a variation of the opening material, but the melodic line that grows out of this has much greater intensity than before and moves past the A♭ Mixolydian to B♭ major and rises up to $a♯^2$.

The logic of the melodic design is startling. The direction of the first section is toward the cadential enharmonic change $e♭$-$d♯^2$; the second section begins on d^2 but comes to center around $d♯^2$ and concludes with an enharmonic transposition of the first cadence ($d♯$-$e♭^2$). The third and concluding section begins with a sudden shift of the melody away from $d♯^2$ ($e♭^2$) to d^2 and then moves into the tonality of B♭ major (suggested by the melodic sixth $b♭$-g), from which it breaks away at the very end to cadence in the tonality of B major (established by the melodic sixth b-$g♯$), thereby completing the pattern of the first two sections. The following example quotes the three sectional cadences [see ex. 77].

Example 77

Of course, only a view of the linear development as a whole can show how Stravinsky has created a melodic style of genuinely contemporary cast which at the same time perpetuates the essence of the archaic folk intonations.[7]

The second song is called *Counting Song* (quarter note-168). It is a pert and lively pribautka with, in the first half, a certain overtone of lamentation arising from the alternations of the melodic progressions b^1, c^2, d^2, e^2 and $e\flat^2$, d^2, $c\#^2$, b^2, thanks to which the implications of the minor third b—d^1 are alternately varied. The melody of the second half is purely diatonic, remaining within the framework of the antique Dorian tetrachord on $c\#^2$ [see ex. 78].

Example 78

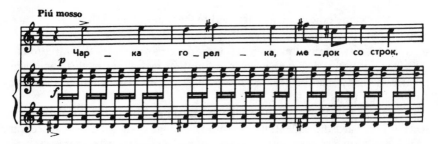

The vibrating accompaniment of the first half (tremolo on d^1 and glissandi) gives way in the second half to a reiteration of the oft-mentioned "clashing" seconds and ninths, again suggesting bells. [See ex. 78 above.]

At the end there is a bell-like instrumental passage in the high register of the piano.

The third song is entitled *Table-mat Song* (quarter note-112). The song has the form of six statements of verse and refrain, and this solo piece is thus composed after a "choral" principle. The four inner verses sound like repetitions or variations of the first, which is built on the Phrygian-Lydian tetrachords a^1, b^1, c^2, d^2 and d^2, $c\#^2$, b^1, a^1. Each verse except the last terminates on a sustained vowel (e, u, a, a, u) and thus acquires a final intonational color and a point of climax. The cadence, like a question, evokes the refrain as reply, and thus each refrain is dynamically induced, and each repetition of the whole cycle (complete statement of verse and refrain) seems like a variation of the original impulse. I shall quote the first and all variations of the refrain because they so clearly show Stravinsky's art of melodic development. The last variation I give with the preceding verse, which is of all the most sonorous and strident and which sounds less like a variation than like a wholly new version of the basic rhythms [see ex. 79].

Example 79

The two patterns of figuration in the accompaniment, one for verse and one for refrain, are separated each time by a tinkling sforzando chord.[8] The accompaniment to the verse, a chirring staccato figure, is composed of two tetrachords a^1-d^2, one with a major and the other with a minor third, both being heard simultaneously but moving in opposite directions. The accompaniment to the refrain has bell-like rhythms and timbres.

With respect to the "tinkling" sforzando chords, note that they are only one of a number of methods of accentuation by means of percussive intonations which may evoke sensations such as "tinkling," "beating," "clanking," "knocking," "popping," etc. From the dry, non-resonant pizzicato of a single sound to the heavy strokes of bells, there are innumerable gradations in the scale of percussive intonations which have recently been revived for use as musical materials. I repeat that in *Noces, Histoire du soldat, Pulcinella,* and other works, such intonations are not surplus or subordinate factors but are assigned unique functions and participate directly in intricate relationships with the rest of the elements composing the musical texture. Though their primary function may be to give the intonational heterophony a rhythmic unity, they can nevertheless be combined into intricate vertical relationships with an almost infinite number of nuances in timbre. The scores to which I have just referred contain wonderful examples of the use of "percussive color," and a detailed study of this whole area and the diversity of its materials and their uses would be very instructive. I have often referred to this subject and have stressed the expressive significance of percussive intonations and the extensiveness of their use. But beyond pointing out Stravinsky's technical virtuosity in this field, I have not analyzed his accomplishments in detail because this book would thereby have to be much larger and much more heavily sprinkled with musical examples. The remarks I have already made on this subject will be presented in greater detail and depth in a short essay in connection with my analysis of *Pulcinella.*

The fourth song of the cycle bears the title *Dissident Song* (1919) and is unconditionally the best—the deepest, the most expressive. This is not the first time Stravinsky has made use of melodic elements from the musical legacy of the old Russian religious culture. But he does not borrow melodies whole— rather do his original melodic formations reflect and refract the general aesthetic character of the old. From Stravinsky's early period there are two examples, both wonderfully fresh and strong: the songs *Spring* (1907) and *A Song of the Dew* (1908), both on texts of Gorodetsky.[9] To them we may also add the cantata *The King of the Stars* (1911-12), on a text of Bal'mont, for male chorus and orchestra, because it is aesthetically similar even if its material is much more highly refined, and the concluding chorus from *Khovanshchina* which I have already mentioned. *The King of the Stars* is written in the amphibrachic declamation of the old ballads, with a preponderance of undulating lines in triplets. In its instrumentation one can already sense the dynamics and timbres of *Firebird.* The airy effects of musical impressions predominate (tremolo sul tasto and sul ponticello, glissandi of harmonics, flutter-tonguing in the woodwinds, etc.), the sound trembles, and one has the impression of limitless distance (instrumentation without perspective), and an atmosphere filled with magnificent visions and swept by mighty sounds. The harmonics already show some resemblance to the style of *Sacre*—as, for example, in the opening motto [see ex. 80].

Example 80

Tenori

Зве _ здо _ ли _ кий

Bassi

I believe that all the small works that I have mentioned, which were written before *Sacre* (excluding the chorus from *Khovanshchina* which dates from the period of *Sacre* itself), form a very important link between the other works contemporaneous with them and the later experiments of Stravinsky. But the *Dissident Song*, which was written eleven years after *A Song of the Dew* and eight years after *The King of the Stars,* is very far from them in style. Here there is no groping, no mixture of styles, no inclination to use melodic elements whose style is alien to the context, no deliberate impudence. In rhythms and intonations, this song does closely resemble the three that precede it: it has dry, "tinkling" chords in the accompaniment, free meters, and a dualism in the basic melody whereby the major second a^1-b^1 is heard in the "sharp" intonations, and the minor second a^1-$b\flat^1$ in the "flat." The music also has something in common with *Noces,* but it is more severe, more ascetic, I might even say more subtle and more direct. The line of the melody is a unit, a whole. It gradually flows out of a melodic cell that oscillates between a^1-b^1 and a^1-$b\flat^1$, with a wavy figuration. This figuration gradually falls by whole and half steps from a^1-b^1 to $b\flat^1$, a^1, $a\flat^1$, g^1, $f\sharp^1$. A variation of the original rises to c^2 and alternates between the Phrygian ($g^1a^1b\flat^1c^2$) and the Lydian ($g^1a^1b^1c^2$) tetrachords. Then a sudden leap to $f\flat^2$ and a new descent to b^1, followed by a similar pattern descending this time from f^2 to $b\flat^1$. The end of the pattern converts itself into a new melody with a sharper profile, that alternates between the tetrachord $b\flat^1d\flat^2e\flat^2$ and $b^1c\sharp^2d^2$. Victory goes to b^1 as the stronger foundation, and the line undulates for some time, locked within the confines $b^1c\sharp^2d^2$. But since a^1 was the starting point, a return to it seems natural. This whole episode turns out to have been preparation for the magnificent blossoming of melodic jubilation in the concluding section of the piece. From a^1 again, and in the same wave-like style, there is a tense rise to $e\sharp^2$, whence the voice returns to the starting point. But, as often occurs in folksongs, it does not come to rest there but slides down through a^1 to $g\sharp^1$. From this point there is a new ascent and a new "jubilation," after the model of the old lyrical improvisations on cadential fragments. This time the line breaks the fetters of the measure and assumes the rhythmic freedom of respiration and the ebb and flow of a melodic wave. It stays within the limits of the fifth $f\sharp^1$-$c\sharp^2$ with interior chromaticisms [see ex. 81]. Since the reproduction of the entire musical "text" is impossible, I confine my examples to the important moments of the development with the additional reminder that the development is continuous and that sectional illustration of it interrupts its flow. The example [ex. 81] shows: (a) the original material and its downward curve; (b) immediately after the first leap to $f\sharp^2$; (c) the transition to the final section; (d) the last section of the "jubiliation."

Example 81

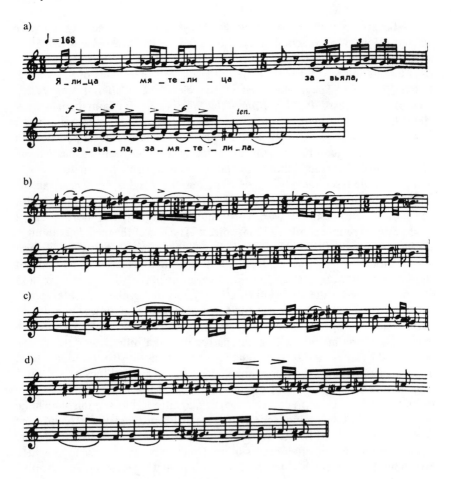

I call attention to the fact that Stravinsky establishes no final cadential point, and that the end of the piece consists only of a concluding melodic line: this is an example of a purely linear melodic cadence which usually contains all the basic elements of the scale or of the original melodic idea, just as the harmonic cadence contains all the essential elements of the tonality.

I now pass to a consideration of Stravinsky's style during the transitional years 1916-18 as that style expressed itself in instrumental works. In 1914, Stravinsky wrote the Three Pieces for String Quartet, works modest in size but remarkable for their novel treatment of material and form. They are principally significant, however, for the dynamics of their organization. One of the most difficult problems in contemporary music is the dynamics of the chamber ensemble.

For the very concept of chamber music has been altered. The chamber ensemble as an ingenious salon dialogue or an exquisitely refined conversation, the chamber ensemble as a self-contained area of personal experience and ratiocination—a monologue of the deep sentiments of the soul (the last quartets of Beethoven)—these concepts cannot contain the contemporary chamber style. Its content is much wider, and its quality is different. Contemporary life, with its concentration of experience, its capricious rhythms, its cinematographic quality, its madly fast pace—the quality of this life has weaned us away from slow and leisurely contemplation. I said earlier in one of the issues of *New Music*[10] [*Novaya Muzyka,* Leningrad, 1927 (4 issues)-1928 (1 issue). Cf. no. 1: "From 'New Music' to a New Musical Perspective" (pp. 20-28); no. 3 "Contemporary Instrumentation and the Treatment of the Ensemble" (pp. 5-9).—Trans.] that contemporary life demands discipline of the will and a steady concentration of all the faculties from those who wish to be in the mainstream of work and affairs and not be left standing on the bank observing the swift current of events with a growing sense of panic. The field of music makes the same demands, and the responses can be seen in the striving for severity of construction, for clarity of writing, for concentration of the greatest tension within the shortest possible time, for the attainment of the greatest expression with the most economical expenditure of performing forces. As a result, there is a growing contrast in contemporary music between works built on the principle of maximum concentration, economy, and conciseness, and those which dispose their materials in breadth and employ the largest possible number of performers. The former are notable for emotional and formal conciseness, for intensity of expression: if there are only a few players, then there must be an increase in the number of ways the separate units can be combined, based on a careful calculation of the properties of each. Emotional outpourings and formal breadth characterize the latter: there are broad periods of accumulation and release of tension, long lyrical digressions, a tendency to write the sounds of music *an und für sich* and a love of sound combinations wholly out of style with salon lyricism, even if their quality is beyond reproach.

In the first case, the music asserts the dynamics of life; in the second, it is hypnotic, sterile, hedonistic. It is natural, therefore, that the new chamber music should have chosen the first style. Its literature—in its best and most serious manifestations, no matter how deeply contemplative or severely intellectualized—its literature has always been unavoidably influenced by the impetuous current of our lives with its elastic rhythms, its fast tempi, and its obedience to the pulsations of work. Moreover, it has not been able to escape the influences of contemporary city streets and their intonations.

One can observe, together with the striving for conciseness and concentration of expression, the attempt to utilize musical materials and the expressive possibilities of the instruments to the greatest advantage. Each instrument is made to find its characteristic sound, the sound peculiar to it and producible only by it in the given context. This, together with the factor of wartime economic conditions, leads to a decrease in the size of orchestras, and to the use of small performing ensembles in all kinds of formal musical situations. The trend was also doubtless influenced by the increasing number of indoor and outdoor orchestras (restaurants, street bands, and the like). The jazz band helped the trend through the evidence it gave of its wonderful rhythmic discipline and its ability to make a lot out of a little. As the nervous mobility of life gradually became more intense, a new technique was needed to observe the rapidly changing phenomena, a technique that permitted greater and greater concentration, that attended only to what was characteristic, important, essential (the poster!). It was just demands of this sort that found their answer in the field of music in a technique combining formal conciseness with economy of performing means and that led, as I have already said, to the careful exploration of the expressive possibilities of each instrument. One result was the appearance of a multiformity of versatile and mobile performing ensembles which came to occupy a middle area between the large symphonic and operatic complexes and the ordinary ensembles that performed the usual kinds of chamber works, like string quartets and trios. In their turn, these new ensembles evoked new intonations from life. In a certain sense, also, they mark a return to the old practise of the town musicians of the sixteenth-seventeenth centuries, to the rich instrumental culture of the Renaissance city with its public openness and accessibility.

There is no doubt that the present attempt to widen the whole concept of chamber music points toward a definite goal: to bring the virtuosic but intellectually passive chamber ensembles out into the world of actuality, and to replace the neutrality of their instrumentation by a combination of instruments of diverse origins and thereby create individual ensembles with differing capabilities, mechanisms with particular intonations and coloristic qualities, a whole host of characters each with its particular group of unique conflicts. As a natural consequence there followed an extraordinary complication of the linear technique of composition and a polyphony unique in its use of polyrhythms and in its tendencies toward polytonality. Stravinsky took, and still holds, a position at the head of this movement, and his experiments in the new chamber style served as models for almost all the best French, Italian and even German composers. Of course, the new chamber style is nearer to the street than to the salon, nearer to the life of public actuality than to that of philosophical seclusion. It stands midway between the self-contained chamber style of the recent past and the operatic and symphonic-concert styles. But it is not a new phenomenon in European culture but rather a rebirth—deeper and more complex—of the profession, techniques, and renowned traditions of the town musicians. Its style is essentially dynamic, for it is rooted in the sensations of contemporary life and culture and not merely in personal sentiments and emotions. Its style is energetic, active, and actual, and not reflectively romantic.

Stravinsky experimented with resolving the problems of chamber dynamics in the Three Pieces for String Quartet (1914), in which he confined himself to the standard instrumentation: two violins, viola, and violoncello. Of course, the ear is immediately struck by devices now familiar to us: percussive intonations (the "pizzicato" qualities of the sounds), the "play of melodic elements" (variations and rhythmic alterations), the avoidance of metrical uniformity and monotony, the use of timbres for expressive purposes, the careful calculation of dynamic accent and nuance and the designation of it in the most precise terms, leaving no room for arbitrary emotionalism. The "character" of the movement is not designated: there is only the neutral measurement of time that sets the pace. In the first piece, which has a static scheme (the organ point of the violoncello, viola, and second violin is a kind of passacaglia bass that gives the impression of being constantly diminished or augmented), the dynamics of the texture of sound are defined by the interrelationships of the lines in the opening measures, though strength and intensity remain constant throughout. But thanks to the diversity of accents, there seems to be a constantly undulating movement. The musical sense of the first piece (quarter note-120) lies in the rhythmic and metrical variations of the melodic opening set against an essentially motionless background (the elements of which only move by a shift of position). The procedure has something in common with the old epic tale in which adaptations of the opening theme reappear in each of the episodes throughout the whole length of the poem [see ex. 82]. This is the basic melodic element, the various particles of which come sometimes on strong beats, sometimes on weak, and sound sometimes in the foreground, sometimes not. In order to augment the number of possible combinations and to avoid reappearances of the same particles on the same beats of the measure, Stravinsky changes the lengths of the measures

Example 82

Sur le sol

and also, at unequal time intervals, breaks the basic diatonicism of the material by inserting a chromatic progression of eight notes (twice $f\sharp^1$-e^1-$d\sharp^1$-$e\sharp^1$). Thanks to this, parallel repetitions of sounds and identical combinations reappear infrequently: in other words, what is the same, seems really not so.[11]

The second piece, which uses thematic fragments melodically and rhythmically quite unalike, has a rather dappled quality. Its dynamic energy rises from the differentiation of sharp contrasts. A procession of little machinelike shocks or, rather, clicks (like moving train wheels) moves toward a terse melodic phrase (basically vocal in character) which, without undergoing development, is interrupted by a nervous and fussy motion (like a scherzo) that suddenly comes to rest on a single tone (ppp and a fermata). After another of these convulsive interruptions, the scherzo rhythm and a steady pace are for the moment reestablished, and then there is a brief reflective episode (two measures, tempo primo). The piece suddenly takes leave of this lyrical obsession and proceeds to a dance movement (like a rondo), but not for long. Again there is a sharp, impulsive shock (ff), an echo of the earlier airy fanfare in harmonics, a pause, and a return to the opening material: the first rhythmic formula is restated in a higher register. This is again followed by the terse melodic phrase which is again cut off by a short, sharp stroke—sforzando (pizzicato).

The melody makes another attempt to advance, but it yields to a terse restatement of the first rhythmic formula. The nervously convulsive passage, immediately cut short, closes the movement. As in much of contemporary music, the section gives evidence of a surprising concentration of material, however much the material is diffracted or broken up, and the movement returns ultimately to the initial element out of which it rose. Thus the old principle of tripartite construction is applied anew, and out of the very small and clearly delimited "field of sounds" there arises a sequence of melodic particles differing in pace, color, and character that forms a pattern of great intricacy. I should also like to call attention to the importance of the pause and fermata as factors of "respiration" which take an active part in the formulation of the movement. And whereas the first piece was built on the uninterrupted and almost mechanical displacements of a single element, in the second piece, by contrast, the flow of the musical ideas is nervous, capricious, intermittent.

The third piece is much simpler: here there is a slow succession of a number of heterogeneous metrical schemes (3/2,5/4 and 2/2,5/4,6/4 and

2/2,3/2). The dynamics of the movement are determined by the succession of vivid harmony-timbres of different degrees of intensity and by the interrelationships of "feet" of different lengths within a single metrical frame (units of three in a duple measure, a whole measure of triple units, etc.) The sonorities are strange, sinister, repressed, crepuscular. It is a sort of requiem, almost "without sunlight." The opening measures sound like a choral exclamation. They ultimately become a refrain, a responsorial cry, and assume a kind of cadential significance. Between their appearances are variations of a rather severe melodic element [see ex. 83]. This beautifully ascetic idea is wonderfully harmonized, with one voice doubling in fourths and the other two creeping chromatically below. The effect of its repetitions is a kind of soporific blur: sometimes the severe outlines of the melody stand boldly out, sometimes they are overshadowed. Further along a new idea enters (cello harmonics), a development of the original material but on quite a different intonational plane. A short development ends in mid-air (a tutti in harmonics). The refrain, as I have already said, concludes the movement, but not with a full cadence: the work ends with a question, ppp. I consider these three pieces highly significant in the whole body of Stravinsky's work, and considering the moment of their composition, I should characterize them as being "on the brink." In each, there is a highly concentrated, new idea; each of them has a special plan, and each is a kind of sound-model that leaves a deep impression on the consciousness. Stravinsky achieves a continuity of motion and a blend of elements through an extraordinary detailed working-out of all the dynamic relationships, nuances of timbre, methods of sound presentation, the intermarriageability of rhythms, and the careful calculation of pace. A close analysis of the eight pages of this score exposes Stravinsky's thoughtful concern with the tiniest details of writing to achieve the finest and most exact fixation of the sounding process as he heard it at the time of writing. The mechanical formation of the first piece, the tense dramaticism of the second, and the tragic repression and concentration of the third: the sum of these conceptions creates a new dynamic, a new resolution of the problem of the chamber ensemble for strings. A miniature of art becomes a microcosm.

Example 83

Tutti sul tasto

pp

The next experiment of Stravinsky in this direction (the dynamics of the chamber ensemble) is in a more open, brighter mood, and touches the sphere of "house music" with its charming rhythms and intonations. I speak of the Three

Easy Pieces for piano four hands (march, waltz, and polka) written in 1915, and the Five Easy Pieces, also for piano four hands: andante, espagnola, balalaika, napolitana, and galop.

In the first set, the lower part is the easier one, and in the second, the upper. The rhythms and dynamic plans of both are wonderfully precise. Never have pieces of this kind been equalled for exact registration of materials, for fullness and intensity of expression with economy of means, for ingenious use of self-restraint as a principle productive of the maximum of inventiveness within modest but extraordinarily precise limits. The study and performance of these pieces alone is a study in attention, rhythms, and self-discipline. At first hearing their light and playful exterior is deceptive—they give far greater pleasure on closer acquaintance. Their grotesque humor sometimes has the quality of "musical anecdote," their irony is light, pure Pushkin-esque, their choice of themes witty, their combinations of rhythms and melodies imaginative. One senses throughout the shrewd and incisive intellect of a great artist, and the great technical skill of a composer who playfully overcomes every difficulty. Since Stravinsky orchestrated a few of these pieces (two Little Suites), we shall have occasion to return to them again. These charming little works are saturated with the intonations and gesture of life, with factors of rhythm, dynamics and tempi that belong naturally to music to be played in the home. To a certain degree, they are also related to the sounds of the "old-time" streets, parks and boulevards, when the waltz, polka, tarantella, Spanish dance, and galop had not yet been affected by the rhythms of contemporary dance. Stravinsky regarded each of these aspects of musical movement as detached and self-contained. He did not try to write a new, original waltz, a new galop, etc. No, he sought only to give the quintessence of the waltz, of Spain, of the march, selecting from each of these movements only those dynamic features by which its nature is defined. His waltz, galop, polka are typical, distinctive formations, and in no sense stylization or affectation. All the pieces are very expressive, and deeply contemporary. They do not represent a transplantation of the past into our life, but a new interpretation of the rhythmic formulas and the intonations characteristic of another epoch in the context of our energetic twentieth century, with its dynamic perception of life and obedience to the discipline of work and the steady beat of the pulse of the machine. In my personal opinion, the best of the pieces are the espagnola, galop, and polka. But immediately one thinks again of the napolitana, waltz, balalaika, and the idyllic andante. All the melodies have a strictly diatonic outline. There is sometimes an exquisite chromaticism in the accompaniment: the "poly-chromas" in the Spanish dance, for example, to go with the "polyrhythms." The galop is marvelously contrived: the irresistibly impetuous "stretto" movement is hammered out with an iron rhythm. The piece is full of joy, nerve, brilliance, and has the amusing hustlebustle of the "sixth figure of the quadrille" [i.e., a frantic coda-Trans.] The balalaika marvelously conveys the mannered dynamics of the chastushka, with its "loud" cadences and abrupt interruptions and turns, for all the mechanical steadiness of the basic pace. In the tarantella, the rhythm (suggesting on orgiastic whirl) and the typical melody floating above, form together a genre-like episode but one without any descriptive inclinations. It is simply an expressive gesture which conveys a grotesque aspect of the dynamics of contemporary life in the most ordinary intonations and rhythms, the very possibility of whose use is evidence of the tenacity of life itself. I need not add that the construction and dynamic conception of the pieces in both series naturally bear the imprint of cinematography and the jazz band—even the idyllic andante, whose calm pace is suggestive of a landscape travelogue.

Notes

1. A theme also used in the finale of his youthful symphony.

2. The impudent imagination of youth, energy, archness, even the consciousness of being old-fashioned—all these impulses doubtless were present in the early work of Stravinsky (how much was instinctive and involuntary, and how much deliberate, we shall never know). Therefore, by using any such terms in making a judgment about this chorus, I mean no reproach—although no matter what role any of them may have played in this specific case, the result tends to be negative.

3. The effect of oscillation or undulation is produced by a heterophonic texture whose images may be presented simultaneously or consecutively.

4. The undulating line moves in a gradual descent (after ascent as the anacrusis) from e^2 to g^1. In general, the melodies of the lullabies move in gentle undulations. Glissandi and "curls" are used to fill out wide intervals.

5. There is no basis for regarding parallel sevenths as inadmissible due to an inherent "falseness." Thirds and sixths are no less "false" from an acoustical point of view; and yet they have long been heard as unisons and have played the role previously played by parallel fifths, whose proscription was in turn probably motivated by the "together-ness" or "unison-ness" of their sound, a texture of four voices being heard as three voices, one of five voices being heard as four, etc. The principle of parallelism demands of necessity some perception of the separateness of the voices: otherwise, how can parallelism be distinguished from unison writing?

6. Stravinsky compresses three units into two and one-half when he writes his accompaniment in 10/16.

7. I call attention to the fact that the whole piece pivots melodically and harmonically on the ninth c^1-d^2, which also underlies the chordal tinkle c, g,a^1, $d\#^2$, b^2 that provides occasional sforzandi and that closes the movement.

8.   Like the C major cadential complex in the second song.

9.   Even in a work as early as *Spring*, the accompaniment clearly suggests the sounds of bells.

10. Statements which I now paraphrase, with changes and additions.

11. In *Histoire du soldat*, Stravinsky often uses the same technique but in a more difficult context, for there are several melodic elements instead of just one. In addition, in *Histoire du soldat*, Stravinsky makes use of the principles of improvisation.

5

Renard

The Fox, The Rooster, and the Sheep.
A Diversion, with Singing and Music

Renard was composed by Stravinsky in 1917—that is, at the same time that he was composing *Noces*. The essence of these two works is the revival of buffoonery, of the art and profession of the buffoon, of the authentic "old" Russian theater with its jesting, sporting, tomfoolery, and mischievous satire— the quintessentially grotesque folk art. Neither *Renard* nor *Noces* was intended, or can be understood, as stylization or ethnographic spectacle. If the ritual nature of the subject of *Noces* does not result in the maintenance of sheer buffoonery throughout, in *Renard* we find it pure, controlling the character of the whole work and its materials—songs, dances, and vocal and instrumental themes. Buffoonery—or Russian grotesque art, which had been suppressed by hundreds of years of every kind of hypocrisy, had sooner or later to manifest itself in our lyric theater. Persistently and steadily, it had beaten its way through obstacles and impediments. There is one great Russian opera—the *Prince Igor* of Borodin—in which Russian folk epic and folk music are transmuted into contemporary form. (The chorus of peasants, as I have frequently said, is an organic synthesis—an art completely without artifice—of the essence of Great Russian lyricism.) In the parts of Skula and Eroshka, buffoonery finds a new musical language that is completely expressive and original. Glinka's Farlaf also represents a breakthrough, but Farlaf is, so to speak, the "universal" buffoon who has absorbed the traditions of the mimes, wandering minstrels, jesters of the commedia dell'arte, and the closely related Italian opera buffa (portions of which even appeared in opera seria).[1] Borodin, on the other hand, rid Skula and Eroshka of the layers of convention that had gradually attached themselves to "comic characters" during two centuries (seventeenth-eighteenth) of operatic practise. He thereby was able to reveal a direct relationship between these characters and the (traditional) buffoons of the past—those described by the saying: "God gave us the Pope; the Devil, the buffoon." The people venerated the Pope on principle; but they loved the buffoons, who were merrymakers as well as living newspapers with a strongly ironic and grotesque bias. No side of private or official life escaped their banter; and however meagre may be the first-hand evidence about them (it has come down to us in droplets), what there is, enables us to reach certain conclusions about the character, the strength and influence, the technical methods and substance of the profession. Often, to be sure, this evidence must come from its "opposite"—from evidence of attacks on buffoons, or measures of repression. The disappearance of buffoonery as a profession did not and could not mean the eradication of the elements that had created and nourished it. The profession vanished, but the "mask" has remained—the mask of the puppet booth and of the "high-class" theater. Buffoonery has always been an important element of Russian life.

In folk song, of course, buffoonery was fully preserved. The origin and spread of the chastushka was a surprise only to those who thought of the folk art of the peasants as something inert and long ago solidified into the "model" folksong in its "highest aesthetic" sense, and who denied to this area of art the possibility of a normal development. The cast of the chastushka incorporated many of the essential elements of buffoonery: its ironical character, the material of the instrumental themes, its generally "grotesque" aspect. It is impossible to explain the chastushka completely in terms of the "evil" influences of the city, its factory songs, sentimental romances, and other similar influences. Its comic strain runs far deeper. Think for a moment of how much the chastushka contains of the postures of theatrical eccentricity, of exaggeration, comic pathos, and the grimace of the clown. The energy of the quintessentially "comic" had never vanished from the songs of either city or country, just as it had never disappeared from life.

The example from Borodin's opera is clear and apposite (and the more so in that the music of Skula and Eroshka already shows traces of the chastushka), but it is not unique. I cite again Serov and his Eremka in *The Power of Evil,* and particularly the carnival scene. It now seems clear that Serov felt instinctively close to the new elements of society that were beginning to be active in public life (the new intellectuals, the merchants, the members of the petty bourgeoisie), and that he tried to write an opera based on the musical language of the merchants and the petty bourgeoisie, with an assist from the sentimental songs of the provinces. He became stuck between the style of Ostrovsky and Reshetnikov (I cite these names to make the analogy clear), and the opera is uneven. But Serov's instincts were not deceiving him, and the composer was right, and pointed to one of the real avenues open to Russian opera, which had no desire to leave behind the formal traditions of epic, tale, and history for a musical realism that was closer to the Russian city and to Russian society— even if on the plane of the grotesque. There are other isolated examples: *The Marriage* of Gogol-Musorgsky, and *The Gambler* of Dostoevsky-Prokofiev, but these are insignificant considering the great number of other works. Even such outstanding masters of the grotesque as Leskov, Gleb Uspensky (the grotesque of the petty bourgeoisie and factory workers), and Chekhov (the grotesque of the civil service and all such attitudes) have not touched Russian musicians, who have stayed on a higher level. However, to everything there is a season, and, as we shall see, the *Mavra* of Stravinsky, which returns to the grotesque of Pushkin and to the old opera-vaudeville—*Mavra* shows that it may not be too late to fill in the gap.

However, such elements of buffoonery as we have described are the surface manifestations of specifically Russian attitudes that lie beneath. Throughout their history, Russians have always expressed these attitudes in "masks" of song, dance, and music that portray the measure of mockery, insolence, cunning, and irony which they find in life. Besides using peculiarly Russian intonations and rhythms, the specifically grotesque in Russian life also finds expression in one aspect of the skeptical attitudes of the "philosophy" of buffoonery that is really frightening: in the destruction of any foundation just because it is foundation, in mockery for the sake of mockery. After all, life is just a game on the edge of the grave. The game may be military, domestic, religious—but in sum, life is either deception, or pure lust. Another, no less dominating, element of buffoonery (the "curved mirror" of Russian life) is merrymaking that finally makes contact with freedom, a freedom for which life itself is not too great a sacrifice. And then the wheel comes full circle: from the anticipation of this freedom, buffoonery passes over to the vicious taunting of everything that stands in its way, every chain, every fetter that keeps it from pure debauchery and violence. Whether this is healthy or unhealthy, it is difficult to say. But for the individual Russian, there was no other escape from oppression. Laughter comes to the rescue as a lifegiving, health-giving force; even ironical laughter and sarcastic laughter serve life. And especially in the theater, and in the theater with music. Deprive life of laughter, and you take away its real mirror, its self-criticism.

The structure of *Renard* is simple. The general observations that precede the action explain that *Renard* is played by clowns, ballet dancers, or acrobats, preferably on an empty stage, with the orchestra behind. The actors never leave the stage, staying in full view of the audience from the time the "procession" brings them in until it takes them out at the end. The music of the procession (bassoon, horn, and trumpet over percussion playing a motive evocative of clowns and mountebanks, with a very Russian manner in its second part) is thus a kind of illustration that both precedes and follows the action. The action itself has the typical plot of a folk tale.

The rooster is bustling on his perch. The fox, in the garb of a nun, sanctimoniously admonishes him to confess. When the chipper rooster jumps to the ground, the fox seizes him. The cat and the sheep answer the rooster's desperate cries and rescue him. The victory dance, which mocks the sanctimonious fox and humorously imitates his cunning advances, closes this scene.

The rooster regains his perch, and the whole "incident" repeats itself. But this time things go badly for the disgusted fox. The others pluck him by the tail out of his hole and kill him. Again an even more burlesque victory dance, a closing salutation to the audience (as in vaudeville), and finally the procession, to whose music the actors quit the stage.

The musical elements which form the intonational basis for the action are extremely concise. In rhythm and character of sound they are deeply folk art, without being limited by any requirements of ethnographical exactitude. They seem to come directly out of the everyday world of the wandering buffoons who, according to the account of Dal', carry bagpipes made of whole calfskin hung all over with little bird whistles, and do enough talking for three. The singers (two tenors and two basses) sing from behind the actors. Sometimes, to achieve an intensification of sound, two voices combine to characterize one actor, and sometimes the voices are arranged as chorus and leader (a "responsorial" style in couplets).

The buffoon, absolutely and always, is an imitator. Thus the material of *Renard* always implies the quality of imitation—plastic imitation, sound imitation. The action centers around the two very witty dialogues of the rooster and the fox. But here I must make an important amplificatory digression. The buffoon is an imitator, but even before that, he is a clown, and most of all, an acrobat. Thus the element of the circus enters into the work of Stravinsky. How is this important for the music? In two ways. First and foremost, in the area of musical construction. The circus and acrobatics demand an ideal musical discipline: exactness, terseness, and a complete absence of lyrico-emotional turbulence with its arsenal of mobile nuances that "gypsy-ize" the musical pace.[2] One can thus describe the musical action of Renard as one in which every rhythmic moment is plastically coordinated with every other, and every duration is controlled "at long distance," so to speak, by the brevity of the conversational instant. The art of Stravinsky is not an art of idle hours with thousand-page novels (and even such novels, in their turn, are only drops in the sea of literary time): his art lives and breathes contemporaneity with its "differentiation" of time and its intensive economizing of time. Therefore, this art maximizes the intensity of every "musical moment," every line, every measure, every kind of complex. All this is not disproved by the possible appearance of a second Schubert, who will say: to the devil with such an attitude, let us revel leisurely in life as it presents itself to our senses, let us sing and to our hearts' content. This is possible. But the Schuberts of our present are quite different. And history may really say something quite different about the historical Schubert: that he was *consumed* by life, and that the surface leisureliness and longueur of his work were really the result of the dynamic exhaustion of the tension of every moment.... However that may be, we have in *Renard* a muscular discipline of the whole organism. By its very nature, this kind of disciplined attention belongs not to the mere speaking actor, but to the universally gifted actor—ideally, to the complete acrobat. When the circus makes contact with another art, it brings with it its intense watchfulness, discipline of gesture, and accuracy and elasticity of movement. And if music has always received from the dance the very salutary influences of rhythmic exactitude, proportion, and general economy of movement, then the influences that may come from acrobatics and feats of equilibrium may turn out to be so much the stronger. I repeat, therefore, that in *Renard* we are not dealing with the stylization of buffoonery, but with a transmutation of the musico-theatrical elements of buffoonery under modern conditions.[3] A second element coming from the circus buffoons and making itself felt in the music and action of *Renard* is connected with the profession of clowning—of buffoonery in masks. The buffoon-imitator will not strive for an imitation of real sound; he is not a rooster or a fox, but a buffoon-rooster, buffoon-fox. His musical imitations are accomplished through a humanization of the song, the cry, or the language. The animals of *Renard* are therefore characterized by sounds which are not imitations of the sounds of nature, but imitations of sounds that human beings make when they imitate natural sounds.[4]

Imitation and acrobatics, in the senses in which I have used the terms, determine the construction and intonations of *Renard*. One could imagine that acrobatics would be incompatible with completely unstable, arhythmic alternations of sounds that give the impression of complete assymetry. In actuality, the dominant principle of the music of *Renard* is one of continuous motion and unstable equilibrium. This instability of equilibrium manifests itself not in regular shifts of two-measure, four-measure or other rounded musical periods, but in a constant modification of durations, clashes of accent, and crossing of motives and phrases from different rhythmic configurations. The principle behind all this is not the coordination of sound complexes connected in series, but the functional interdependence of sound moments that are sometimes remote from one another. One has the impression of a continuous and clearly organized musical motion in which the mutual interdependence of the elements is determined not by their proximity but by the character of the motion—its speed, degree of difficulty, etc. Therefore, what is assymetry to the eye may not be to the ear, and the motion of *Renard* fully meets the requirements of precision demanded by pantomime, dance, and acrobatics.[5] One need only move an accent or sound from one beat of the measure to another, to postpone or upset the moment of equilibrium. A new musical motion, by the very fact of its appearance, and without any formal cadences, severs the previously "established" musical motion, breaks it, stops it, and begins to beat out its own pace with the precision of a watch mechanism.

At the same time, the sinuous instrumental lines gaily go on weaving their designs. For example, let us take the first moments of the action: "the rooster is bustling on his perch." This is his cry [see ex. 84].

Example 84

There are no balanced periods in the vocal line, because it grows like a branch, containing within itself the implication of two sets of fifths—g^2-c^2-f^1 and f^2-$b\flat^1$-$e\flat^1$, the second of which branches off from the first. (The fifths occur in the sequence g^2-f^2-$b\flat^1$-c^2-$e\flat^1$-f^1, the g^2 and c^2 in the upper line acting like pedals.) As is usually the case in folksong, this opening passage with the tonal implications of its fifths is interrupted constantly, and alternations of these interrupted sections form the basis for almost the entire vocal configuration of sixty-two measures (the tempo of the section: quarter note-126), complicated, after the second statement of the cry, by another element that makes use of other degrees of the scale [see ex. 85].

Example 85

Beneath the rooster's cry, there is the following organ point [see ex. 86]. Within this section, the E♭ clarinet theme has the following aspect (in constrast to the rooster's cry, this theme has a very narrow range and is held to one level) [see ex. 87].

The flute and trumpet counterpoints form offshoots to this theme. The stronger the rooster crows, and the more fearsomely he frightens his supposed enemies, the more intricately branched becomes the texture of counterpoints.

Example 86

Example 87

    Let us see what results from our analysis of this section. The cry of the rooster moves with a steady pace. It is supported beneath by the persistent beat of the basic rhythmic motive. Above this motive are woven the instrumental counterpoints, now imitating the rooster's music, now ornamenting the intervals between periods of song. The vocal phrase is divided into two lines and tends to describe two different ranges, the ninths g^2-f^1 and f^2-$e\flat^1$, a fact that is also reflected in the parallelism of the cadential turns [see ex. 84, a, b, c]. The fact that the transposed version of the diatonic theme is a "twin" of the original [ex. 84, measures 5-6 of first variation, second voice] is a very important clue to understanding the structure of the whole work. A scale such as the following, composed of pentachords, is not infrequently met in folk art [see ex. 88].[6] Specifically, one can find similar ones with ranges from a^2 to g^1 and g^2 to f^1 in Rumanian folk music (*Volksmusik der Rumänen von Maramures* von Bela Bartok, München, 1923). Notice that when Stravinsky introduces a melody with f♯ into this section [ex. 85] he expands the series by introducing implications of the "dominant" in the upper part of the scale. But the introduction of a half-step in the upper register need not imply, in folk art, a corresponding step in the lower register. In Bartok's book, there is, among others, the following interesting illustration [see ex. 89].

Example 88

Example 89

As a result of the shift of the melody, the final cadence is approached from the whole step below. This also happens in Russian and Eastern folksongs. I point out all this only to give evidence of the shrewdness of Stravinsky's conception, to define the stylistic consistencies of the melodico-linear formations, and to point out the principles which underlie the process of formulation.

The opening of the next section is marked by the rooster's screams (English horn and cymbalum) that interrupt the established movement, after which the rooster's song expresses a more peaceful, quieter mood of watchfulness [see ex. 90].

Example 90

Сижу на ду _ бу, си_жу, дом сте_ре_гу.   Пе _ сню по_ю.

In the orchestra the music undulates drowsily (bassoon, French and English horns).

The fox arrives in the garb of a nun and begins his speech of hypocritical flattery. The speech is sweet, saccharine, ardently adulatory [see ex. 91]. Here Stravinsky is following the footsteps of Musorgsky. A type of hypocrisy that has taken many forms in Russian life and that has been immortalized in numerous literary works, receives a worthy musical characterization.

Example 91

Здравствуй,   красно _ е ча _ до,   пе _ тел!

The rooster becomes excited: his original motive ("O sister dear, o sister fox, I have not fasted, I have not prayed") reappears with slight changes over a bass, also somewhat altered. The fox continues his entreaties, and the rooster finally weakens and drops into his clutches. The character of the music changes and becomes agitated (resembling the beating of wings); the rooster wails desperately. The rhythm is a series of unequal durations:

$$\frac{3+4}{8} \qquad \frac{4+3}{8} \quad , \text{ then } 6/8, 7/8, 5/8, 3/8, \text{ etc.}$$

The strummed improvisation of the cymbalum, as is the custom in this piece, sharply and unexpectedly changes the direction and character of the musical motion: the cat and the sheep appear. The wailing of the rooster is followed by a wonderfully bold, song-like instrumental theme (con brio) [see ex. 92] around which a "polytonal" texture winds itself. The theme above is joined by a new vocal melody ("Ah you, my little woman, my little dove" in E♭ major with a lowered sixth degree), which is slightly altered in further repetitions. Notable among the pitch identities of the texture are the enharmonic equivalents b-c♭, g♯-a♭, and c♯-d♭. The splashes of the cymbalum make a kind of mottled accompaniment whose forceful little gestures cut through the texture of melodies. Finally, an energetic "whistle" (piccolo, clarinet, oboe) and a supporting trumpet call cut across the texture: the fox drops the rooster and flees. Then begins the buffoonery of the dance of the rooster, cat, and sheep, accompanied by the singing of pribautki (solo, with support and participation of the other voices). The imaginative dance is a caricature of the unsuccessful plot of the fox and his conversation with the rooster. Its principal vocal and instrumental materials are as follows [see ex. 93].

The dance has the function of a first finale. After it there comes a second "monologue" of the rooster and his conversation with the fox, which are much like the first, though with some variations.

Thus in the first section of *Renard* there come in sequence: the call of the rooster, provocative, apprehensive, full of a fake fearsomeness (quarter note-126), the drowsy song of the weary watchman (quarter note-63), the dialogue of the rooster and the fox (alternations of the two earlier tempi), the wailings of the rooster (dotted quarter-126, then 84), the "procession" of the cat and the sheep (quarter-126), and the final dance (the same).

The dance is based on the steady pulse of an ostinato rhythm in eighth notes, over which are woven and unwoven the distinctive instrumental and vocal elements that are based on the first melody [ex. 93], which is used as the material for ever new developments. Stravinsky's wit and keenness of observation are shown at their best in his musical caricatures of the dialogue of

Example 92

Example 93

the rooster and the fox with its contrasts of cries, prayers, exclamations of greed, moans, laments, and calls for help. Here, for example, is the grotesque imitation of the dialogue of the strong adversary and his victim [see ex. 94].

Example 94

The dance does not cadence in the obvious way. A deft stroke of the cymbalum signifies the end, and the situation changes: the cat and the sheep depart, the rooster reoccupies his perch. But here a show of bravado would be out of place: the rooster is weary as he intones his lullaby: "I sit on my perch, I watch the house, I sing my song" [ex. 90]. Again a cymbalum stroke, and the fox reappears without his disguise. He has the attitude of the hunter who knows for sure that the game is up and that all he has to do is to choose the proper moment. He is the sweet flatterer whose amiability reflects his anticipation of edible goodies. Just as folk art often deals with generalized formulations of deep human feelings within the traditional formalities of lamentations, tales, and pribautki, so does the dialogue of the rooster and the fox express human intonations that are as old as time. On the one hand there is the ingratiating voice of the predator sure of his prey; on the other hand, the weak, doomed victim who nevertheless tries to resist the strength and attraction of his opponent. The whole dialogue, therefore, has a somewhat different intonational plan than before: it has the character of children's pribautki and rhyming songs.[7] Here is some of the basic material: (a) the salutation of the fox; (b) the "argumentation" of the fox (falsetto) [see ex. 95].

Example 95

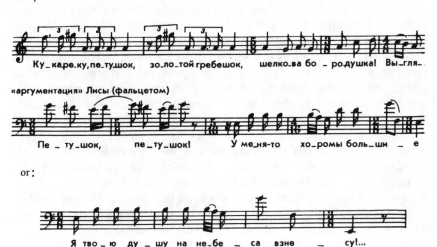

These two examples typify a practice followed by Stravinsky in his dialogues. The accentuation of the words is not always made to conform with the strong beats of the measure, but the most significant intonational accent is produced on a strong beat which in turn becomes the principal stress and the center of a group of other subordinate measures whose beats are neutral with respect to the pattern of word accentuation. The phrase in the example [see ex. 96] is not sung: *v kazhdom uglu pshénichki po mérochke* but naturally: *v kázhdom uglu psheníchki po mérochke* [i.e. the phrase is sung not with accents at the beginning of every measure, but on the second sixteenth of the 4/16 measure, corresponding to the spoken accent.—Trans.]

Example 96

В каж дом у _глу пше _ нич_ки по ме _ роч _ ке

The question arises: why does not Stravinsky pay attention to the accentual patterns of the words and place their accents on the first beats of measures? Obviously, it would be impossible to put the material of the example into measures of equal length (one would either have to *lengthen* the accented beats or make the metrical arrangement 4/16, 2/16, 3/16, 2/8, 2/8). Actually, the answer is very simple. Stravinsky wants to preserve the freedom and natural flow of the prose recitative become musical speech. He therefore prefers not to associate each accent of each word with a note of relatively greater length, but to free the song from the grip of poetic meter while at the same time confining the measure to its mechanically important function as a vertical indicator of simultaneity. By neutralizing the beats of the subordinate measures (in the way I have already described), he secures for one measure a real hegemony over the others. The measures retain their significance as such, and the intonation of the prose phrase retains its character—its tone, its elevation. For example, the phrase *Petúkh káshky kúshaet, lisú ne stúshaet* might be placed in a rhythmic setting like this [see ex. 97]. But Stravinsky does otherwise: emphasizing one word, *lisú,* by an amusing combination of bassoon timbre and rhythmic accentuation, he gives the measure the following durations [see ex. 98]. The fourth measure thereby becomes the "strong beat" of the whole series of measures. Pauses are punctuation marks in the full sense of the words, and the musical prose, which (like psalmody and recitative) ignores arbitrary metrical divisions by nature, receives a proper musical formulation.

Example 97

Example 98

Пе_тух каш _ ку ку _ша _ ет, ли _ су не слу _ ша _ ет,

When the rooster has hopped to the ground and the fox has seized him (as before, his salto mortale, preceded by a snare drum roll, is marked by a whack on the bass drum—a "march to the scaffold" all its own), the rooster's wails are repeated ("the fox has got me"). But this time the moment of freedom seems to be somewhat further away: the fox carries his victim to one side and begins to pluck out his feathers. The victim begins to whimper and pray. As he prays, the frightening "dactylic" chords of the strings sound like tolling bells [see ex. 99].

Example 99

The rooster's prayer, interposed to delay the course of events and to heighten the emotional tone of this point in the action, is an important passage, musically and formally. After all, it is the traditional comic situation: the fool has fallen into misfortune because of his own greediness or imprudence, and the rooster here is the buffoon onomatope of Leporello and Sancho Panza. The prayer is built on wailing slides from high notes, sudden screams in high registers, and melodic passages whose design conveys the full irony of the situation [see ex. 100] As the rooster begins to lose courage, the epic tone of the line becomes more obvious, and the wails become weaker.

Example 100

Как у на-ше-го у   ба — тюшки с ма — сли — цем

The prayer is interrupted (I remind the reader that in *Renard* musical interruptions are used as characteristic ways of alerting the attention and are important formal elements) by the arrival of the rescuers. Accompanying themselves on the gusli [folk psaltery-Trans.], the cat and sheep sing a ditty to the fox (cymbalum and violins in the orchestra) [see ex. 101].

Here the rhythmic construction of the voice and accompaniment is interesting. Each word in the example is barred according to its natural accent. The second theme (beginning with "uzh kak doma li lisa") is stricter and in a more nearly regular accentuation. There results the rhythmically interesting

Example 101

combination of a dance-like movement trying to maintain rhythmic symmetry, and a comic dialogue (a sort of "game of questions and answers") which is rhythmically asymmetrical. The form of this "march" or "procession" of the cat and the sheep is based on a constant return of the first idea as a point of departure for ever more distant excursions away from it: the rondo principle, which has an improvisatory basis. We shall speak further about this connection with *Histoire du soldat,* since structures based on improvisatory principles reveal themselves especially clearly in instrumental pieces where the nature of the ideas supports similar structural principles: ideas suitable for concertizing, for being opposed to one another, for gay diversions or cautiously groping explorations followed by a return to the starting point, and other similar processes.

After a series of threats, the fox sticks out the end of his nose and asks "Who is singing? Who calls the fox?" [see ex. 102]. In reply to repeated threats of the animals, the fox begins his own lamentation, addressing himself in tones of reproach to his eyes, his feet, his tail. There is another amusing "game of questions and answers." The answers are always musically more severe and more archaic than the questions, whose song-like conformation begins each time on a higher note: the first on f^2, then on $g\flat^2$, then finally on b^2. The decisive question [see ex. 103] evokes the decisive answer from the tail: [Freely: "I got caught in the bush, and the beasts caught up with me."]

> Ya po pnyam, po kustam,
> Po kolodam zatseplyal,
> Chtob lisu zveri khvatili,
> Da zakamshili.

Example 102

Кто там пе_сни по _ ет, да уж кто там ли_ску зо_вет?

Example 103

А ты, мой хвост, гля _ ча рос?

That does it. The hostile beasts drag the fox out by the tail and kill him. (Howls.) The whole dialogue is filled with the most ingenious sounds in a "responsorial" style (leader and ensemble). The threats become successively more severe, the melodies of the fox betray his vexation, fright and rage. Thus, despite its parallelism (the rooster twice stands watch, the fox appears twice, twice the rooster is caught, and twice rescued), the action loses nothing in intensity—indeed, it gains in clarity, due to the economical use of materials and to the clever handling of the emotional and dramatic positions. The composer never quits the narrative-epic tone of the folk style. But by means of dynamic and rhythmic emphases, interruptions, syncopations, glissandi, abrupt alternations of materials, intricacies of accentuation, and other similar methods, he achieves a deeply vital expressiveness[8]—an expressiveness derived from life itself, and from the lyrical and narrative songs of peasant art which are themselves the verified experiences of masses of people. The vitality and universality of this work derive from its kinship with the experience of generations, and not from the purely personal experience of one man, no matter how deep that might be.

The action passes to the final section, the clowning dance of rejoicing by the victors, which is at the same time a grotesque funeral celebration. The dance takes its point of departure from the situation that it celebrates, that of "hitting a man when he's down." In form it is a series of rhythmically strict couplets (set to a dance-like melody) punctuated by all kinds of acid embellishments in an animated patter. The central melody, around which the others are woven, is built on five notes and is strictly diatonic [see ex. 104].

Example 104

Allegro (♩ =120)

Ли_сынь ка, ли _ си_ца! Гля _ ча дол_го не жи _ ла?

The refrain in which the patter occurs is originally confined to two notes, but it is later taken up and embellished by the other voices [see ex. 105].

Example 105

Ла_ды_ги_ны де _ ти,   хо _ тят у _ ле _те _ ти

This archaic and stylistically strict dance makes a marvelous conclusion. The ensuing "procession," during which the actors quit the stage, serves as a final decoration and repeats part of the introductory processional (the "illumination") in the same tempo (quarter note-152).

The importance of *Renard* in Stravinsky's work, as well as in the whole history of Russian music, is very great, even if it is not yet recognized by most musicians who continue to live under the spell of stylized Russian folk art as it was elaborated in the works of Rimsky-Korsakov and Liadov, as if these were final answers. Stravinsky also studied in that school, but he took away with him only what was best: technical imaginativeness, sensibility to modes, and skill in writing a clear texture. He had, however, no wish to be an epigone and go on repeating the past. He created his own new style by going back to the principles of vocal and instrumental folk material, and it now seems that he got very close to an understanding of those basic principles. Later, of course, there will emerge, from the peasantry itself, composers who will give the world a musical language as it is spoken by the people themselves. Meanwhile, the texture of *Renard* shows that Stravinsky was no mere formal and stylistic imitator. On the contrary, he had assimilated—in the fullest sense of the word—all the organic factors that could compose a music of buffoonery.

Stravinsky took laments of different kinds, cries, instrumental and vocal themes, dance rhythms, psalmody (which he treated grotesquely), humorously ironic proverbs and pribautki, and the intonations of narrative and folk tales. All these his technical virtuosity transmuted into an utterly representative (in the best sense) and disciplined work of art. The artistry of this accomplishment lies in the fact not that Stravinsky borrowed folk materials and fitted them into an alien mold, but that his work is a transmutation of the principles of musical formulation as they were worked out in the folk arts themselves. This is the important point, and in this respect Stravinsky showed himself more perceptive and more audacious than any of his predecessors and teachers from Prach-L'vov to Glinka, and from Glinka to Rimsky-Korsakov, who came into contact with folk art and made artistic use of it.

To what degree Stravinsky's music is obedient to basic principles of order and how exhaustively his intellect, once it has accepted a given principle, works out the implications of it, we can perhaps see from an analysis of the melodic motion of one episode of *Renard:* the cry of the rooster as he stands watch for the first time (pps. 3-8 of the piano score).

The vocal melodies of this passage use an archaic melodic succession spanning two octaves plus one note, that is, from F and G to g^1. I shall illustrate this succession at pitches an octave higher, since the center of attention is the tenor line that is written at that level, and since the appropriate instrumental passages can also easily be related to it.

If we take the octave g^1-g^2 and divide it into two symetrically contrasting divisions [see ex. 106] and if we join these pitches into one scale (g^1;c^2;d^2;g^2), then we can get several combinations that appear as the basic melodic contours of archaic folk melodies that have comparable ranges [see ex. 107]. These pitches can be regarded as forming two fourths separated by a second, or two interlocking fifths overlapped by the same interval. A given melodic contour may remain within one division or pass from one to the other, and it may often have the shape c^2;d^2;g^1 or d^2;c^2;g^1.[9]

Example 106

Example 107

If we take the pitch c^2 as the center of a second octave f^1-f^2 and add these three pitches to the previous ones, then the following additional possibilities emerge [see ex. 108].

Example 108

Here there are two fifths joined by a common tone, a succession of three melodic seconds, and three non-successional melodic fourths. (I note in passing that the progession of fourths g^1;c^2;f^2 characterizes one of the most important thematic elements in the last scene of *Noces* [see exs. 140-42].

Since the octave f^1-f^2 may also have a symetrically contrasted division centered on $b\flat^1$, the scale is enriched by new successions of fourth and fifths within the outer limits of a ninth [see ex. 109].

Example 109

Now there are two new sets of interlocking fifths: f^1;c^2;$b\flat^1$,f^2 and g^1;d^2;$b\flat^1$;f^2.

One can even make an analogy between certain successions of notes which emerge from these complexes of fifths, and three types of rhythms: abba, abab, and aabb (these letters designate rhythmic schemes only and do not refer to musical tones). For example, the outer fifths (g^2;c^2f^1) and the inner interlocking pair (f^2;$b\flat^1$ and d^2;g^1) form a succession that may be compared to the first rhythm; the successions of fifths and fourths (f^1;$b\flat^1$;c^2;g^2 and g^2;d^2;c^2;f^1) relate to the second rhythm; and the pairs of intervals (f^1;$b\flat^1$;c^2;f^2 plus g^2;c^2;c^2;f^2, g^2;d^2;c^2;g^1 plus f^1;$c^2c^2f^2$) relate to the third.

Crossing over from a specific division of one octave into that of another is accomplished in much the same way as the transition from one to the other of the divisions of a single octave [see ex. 107]. The transition is usually effected by means of motion through a major second followed by a fifth, or the reverse. For example, g^2;f^2;$b\flat^1$,$b\flat^2$;c^2;g^2, d^2;c^2;f^1, f^1;g^1;d^2. Jumps of a sixth are also used to go from one system to another but are immediately followed by step-wise motion in the opposite direction and a return to the first system, but on a different level of it. For example: g^2;$b\flat^1$;c^2. The jump or leap from one octave system to another is instinctively and naturally followed by motion in the opposite direction, and this type of motion has many parallels elsewhere.

On the contrary, transitions by thirds are not characteristic and are avoided, apparently because they do not contain elements that define octaves and their basic divisions, and therefore fail to provide the balance and stability that results from motion by fifths and fourths. Also avoided are progressions like $b\flat^1$;d^2;c^2 or d^2;$b\flat^1$;c^2 that suggest the archaic (anhemitonal) sequence having no major or minor connotations.[10]

Let us now proceed further to see how Stravinsky adds scale onto scale. Let us insert into the arrangement we already have ($g^2f^2d^2c^2b\flat^1g^1f^1$) a new octave with a division at $b_{\flat}{}^1$ and add its contrasting divisions ($e_{\flat}{}^2$;$b_{\flat}{}^1$;$a_{\flat}{}^1$;$e_{\flat}{}^1$). An even richer series results [see ex. 110].

Example 110

All this, however, does not yet include all of the pitches of the rooster's cry—even those of its first seven measures. Up to now we have dealt with declinations toward the dominant below, or subdominant, thereby joining each octave to the next one a whole step below. In measure 5 of the rooster's cry, the pitch e^2 breaks through in the second voice ("podaite mne yevo"); and on page 5, measure 4, the lowest voice has the pitch b. Further on, in the middle section (page 6 of the score, with the words "i nozhishko zdes' "), the tone f♯ appears (a clear indication of a dominant quality) during a development of the melodic material. The constructional scheme of this section has the following appearance: A (Exposition) plus B (a more extensive repetition with the inclusion of the dominant declination) plus C (Coda), a condensed reprise of the elements of the first section. Thus: strophe, antistrophe (development) and epode. It is the scale of C which holds together, unifies, and provides a point of transition between the two declinations (not modulations) down toward the subdominant and up toward the dominant. The declination downward approximates the character of the declination of Greek scales within the limits of the Greater Perfect System, while the declination upwards moves the pitches into the area of the dominant. The ultimate result is a systematic but synthetic scale which has begun to attract European composers with increasing frequency. If we look at the phenomenon from the point of view of its harmonic elements, then a base of C major appears to be blended with its dominant, subdominant (or dominant below), and subdominant of the subdominant ($b_{\flat}{}^1$ and $e_{\flat}{}^1$), all without conventional or solid modulations. The term "modulation" is not relevant, however, because there are no vertical chords in the usual sense, and because the broadening of the basic scale occurs melodically, by means of the inclusion of the horizontal divisions first in a downward declination ($g^2c^2g^1$, $f^2b_{\flat}{}^1f^1$, $e_{\flat}{}^2b_{\flat}{}^1e_{\flat}{}^1$) and then in an upward ($a^1d^2a^2$, $b^1e^2b^2$, $c♯^2f♯^2c♯^3$). Thus given the inner development of this scale, no harmonic modulations could occur. One can, of course, imagine a modulation from such a synthetic scale on C to a similar scale on G or F (and one can find many instances of this).

Referring again to the rooster's cry, it is necessary to call attention to the fact that all of its sections (A, B, and A/C) are based on one and the same motive: a basso ostinato on F,G,A♭,G,F. The result is a passacaglia of a sort. This "lower-dominant" bass on F finally knocks the props out from under the validity of any harmonically conventional approach to understanding the movement of voices in such music.

The sections are connected not only by this repeated bass figure but by melodic material given to clarinet and flute. Let us now see how a transference is effected out of one intonational area into another—in this case, out of the specific intonational area $g^2f^2e♭^2d^2c^2b♭^1a♭^1g^1f^1e♭^1$.

I have already said that in the fifth measure of the first section, the second voice has the pitch e^2. The ensuing clarinet melody has e^2 and a^2, and the ornamental flute counterpoint has $c♯^3$ (page 4 of the score, measure 3). In the context of the basic downward direction and declination of the melody toward the subdominant, these intonational elements are irrational and explosive, disrupting the given order but at the same time joining it by anticipation with factors that come later. In both instances their formal significance is very great and of organic importance. Why should they sound irrational to the ear, if at the same time they are fully logical? The answer is very simple: none of them (not e, not b, not c♯, not a) is included within the octaves or octave divisions of the downward declination—they merely graze certain of its elements. Let us look more closely to see just how this happens, for in so doing we shall touch upon a matter of great importance. The phrase "podaite mne yevo syuda" begins with the notes $c^2e^2d^2$, but the rest of it, instead of touching upon a^1 or b^1 (since e^2 could belong to the octave $e^2b^1a^1e^1$ or $a^2e^2d^2a^1$), slides sideways into $b♭^1$, $e♭^1$, and f^1.

The clarinet theme includes e^2 and a^2 but avoids (and this is important) d^2 and a^1: that is, the clarinet does not touch upon all the points of the octave division implied by these "irrational" pitches. Later, the flute has the pitches $c♯^3$, b^2, and a^2 (page 4, measure 3), but avoids both e^3 and e^2 (the outer octave limits of b^2 and a^2) and $f♯^3$ and $f♯^2$ (the outer octave limits of $c♯^3$ and b^2), etc. That is to say, the pitch $c♯^3$ (and the immediately preceding $b♭^2$ as well) represents an irrational moment that anticipates a later contrasting switch toward the area of the dominant. I call attention to the fact that the pitch $f♯^2$ is never sounded, though it is a close relative of the three pitches, e, b, and c♯ (I have in mind the octave divisions $b^1e^2f♯^2b^2$ and $f♯^2b^2c♯^3f♯^3$). We have before us evidence of a striking linear orderliness. The irrational or "explosive" elements make their appearance as embryos of their own systems amid a completely developed but contrasting system with a clearly expressed declination, and thus they represent the advance forces of a new intonational area and prepare the ear for it. Here we stand face to face with an illustration of the dialectical law of the interpenetration of opposites in the field of musical architectonics and particularly in the movement and interconnection of the pitches of the scale.

Therefore, the insertion of the anticipatory pitches e, a, b, and c♯ into the first system gradually expands it and paves the way for the coming of a different intonational area. The transition actually occurs when the voices sing the new melodic element $e^2f\#^2g^2f\#^2e^2d^2$ ("i nozhishko zdes' "), and when the instrumental part has its $f\#^2$ (page 6 of the score) just before the entrance of the voices. This instrumental part is thematically identical with the melody that accompanies the first section. Thus it serves as an element connecting—"soldering," so to speak—the two sections. (The tetrachord of the first section $a^2g^2f^2e^2$ is divided, in the second, between two voices, and includes $f\#^2$ and $f\#^3$. The sung parts have the characteristic motive $e^2f\#^2g^2f\#^2e^2$.

This e^2 was an important irrational element of the first section. It arises out of the octave system of g (the same one with which we began the declination toward the subdominant). If in the octave $g^2d^2g^1$ we take d^2 as the pivot, we can build the octave a^1a^2 with its two symetrically contrasting divisions $a^1d^2a^2$ and $a^2e^2a^1$. These together form the following [see ex. 111].

Example 111

It is interesting to note that the melody of the clarinet in the first section uses only the upper elements of this series, and that the voices start in the middle register ($c^2e^2d^2c^2$) before going off into $b\flat^1$ and $e\flat^1$. If we continue the series [of ex. 111], we can get $f\#^2$ by proceeding from the pivot e^2 of the octave $a^1d^2e^2a^2$ and getting $b^1e^2f\#^2b^2$ and $b^2f\#^2e^2b^1$. From this last we can also derive its dominant $f\#^2b^2c\#^3f\#^3$. But in the middle section the dominant declination upward does not receive a full and final expression because all the components of the octaves cited immediately above are not introduced, the vocal parts not going above g^2 (g^1). The epode or coda is perfectly straightforward, is joined directly to the second section, and uses the melody and ostinato of the first section.

The complete vocal system of this passage follows [see ex. 112].

Example 112

Over this two-octave span the basic direction of the pitches is downward, with a prevalence of the subdominant declination in the melodic plan. But our examination of the horizontal movements of the pitches in the body of the composition reveals the presence of intonational dynamics resulting from the insertion of individual elements of the octaves $g^1d^2g^2$, $a^1e^2a^2$, and $b^1f\#^2b^2$ into a fabric woven of the octaves $g^2c^2g^1$, $f^2b\flat^1f^1$, and $e\flat^2a\flat^1e\flat^1$.

Thus, a full comprehension of the organization of the pitches illuminates the dynamic subtlety of such a melody [see ex. 113] in which the "e," by its presence, constitutes a hybrid that contains its own element of contrast.

Example 113

We have examined one of the most beautiful examples of musical dialectic in this small section of one of Stravinsky's works. Such a technique, of course, is not rigorously used throughout the piece; it may be an element of other, larger systems of musical organization, one of many factors in the composer's musico-intonational thought. Such intellectualism is bound to provoke animosity. People are accustomed to judge a composer by the characteristic emotional tone of his music . . . by its correctness. Any widely recognized body of work like Stravinsky's elicits the cynical jeers of critics who take the diversity of his "subjects" and the stunning novelty of his methods as so many modernistic bourgeois attempts to achieve novelty at any cost,—whereas, in fact, an objective approach to such a phenomenon makes it possible, through an appreciation of the intonational processes, to understand it as a consistent system of musical thought. The labor of the mind in the creation of sound organisms—the concept of music as an intellectual phenomenon—frightens many people, especially at a time when music is reaching an extraordinarily wide public. But, on the evidence, it is hard to deny the efficacy of such labor.

The strangeness of Stravinsky's subjects will pass away. If, on the other hand, the world of his sound offers rewards higher than the music that adorns our dining and promenading, our comedies, dramas,and films, if it offers more than mere hypnotization of our feelings, then we must try to understand that what we sense as its value is a deeply intellectual phenomenon. Perhaps Stravinsky is the victim of his own fancy—I do not know—but he cannot create music except by bowing to the demands of his keen intellect. By taking the time to analyze episodes of his works, we can come to know not only much about his art and the art of his contemporaries, but also much about the folk materials themselves. However, I regard my attempts in this direction as modest beginnings only.

Notes

1. I think that the epithet opera buffa is more properly applicable to the authentic works of Italian origin than the epithet comic opera. The latter is more generally useful when applied to the opera buffa tradition in France.

2. Let not my critics find hereby any disloyalty on my part to emotional music and particularly to Tchaikovsky, whom I did and do love. But "love" is a personal matter, first of all; and second, to everything there is a time and place: here I am speaking of the inadmissibility of the emotional in the atmosphere of buffoonery and acrobatics. Observe that Tchaikovsky the emotionalist was one of the most gifted masters of the grotesque, and when he was working in this area, he never admitted purely emotional outpourings. With the exception of the observant Larosh, the critics were bored by this Tchaikovsky, just as they first saw in Chekhov only the jolly storyteller, and discovered the grumbling afterwards. I call attention to the wonderful dance of the buffoons, in *The Sorceress* of Tchaikovsky.

3. On the whole, contemporary music's characteristic concern with dance is the result of a deep, inner necessity. We can recall similar examples from other epochs!

4. The same thing pertains to the plastic theatrical movements, as was clearly seen in the production (by F.V. Lopukhov) of *Renard* at the Academic Theater of Opera and Ballet. Instead of the mannerisms of beasts being reproduced realistically, there was a clowning imitation in rhythm, movement, dance, and acrobatics. The mistake of this very interesting production, which was badly—and undeservedly so—received, was not a matter of its principles but rather the attempt to foist the dual responsibilities of singing and acting on one person. Either separate them intentionally, and sharply, as Stravinsky did, or train the singers in mime and acrobatics (a project that is of course impossible).

5. The fundamental principle of the music of *Renard* is gesture. It is not inappropriate to point out that gesture, and not description, plays the large role in the construction of Russian tales. Even Liadov regretted that he could not find in those tales poetically descriptive moments that might serve as programs for musical compositions.

6. The white notes come from the rooster's cry, and the ligatures represent divisions into pentachords. The $a_b{}^1$ appears in the accompaniment [ex. 86].

7. The tone of the devout hypocrite disappears from the speech of the fox, and the replies of the rooster are developments of his own "I sit on my perch, . . . " [ex. 90].

8. Because by these methods he "dynamites" the strictness and rigidity of the epic formulae and introduces the rhythms of everyday speech, thanks to which the texture of sounds acquires rhythmic and intonational vitality.

9. This progression is often met in Rimsky-Korsakov *(Snow Maiden, Kitezh).*

10. Very many phenomena in the field of intonational kinetics may be studied by reference to such *schema.* I am reminded of the intonational struggles waged by melodic fourths and fifths around pivotal tones in folk songs using archaic scales, as a result of which the inner divisions of the octaves are established or altered.

6

Les Noces

Russian Dance Scenes with Voices and Instruments

Stravinsky apparently worked on *Noces* in two stages. At the end of the score there is a notation that the orchestration was completed in Monaco in April 1923 while at its head stands the date 1917—that is, the year of the completion of *Renard.*

It is not enough to describe *Noces* as an original work. It is an exceptional rarity—in sonority and dynamics (the union of vocal masses and soloists with an orchestra of four pianos and percussion); in construction and form (the union of archaic musical elements with formal principles derived both from the Renaissance and from contemporary musical design); and in intonational energy—in other words, in the varied degrees of tension attained by the developing sound materials. All this evokes our lively response to the author's conception. What precisely is this conception, and wherein lies its originality? Essentially, *Noces* is a cantata, because that which is sung prevails over the instrumental texture (a texture of very subtle coloristic and rhythmic differentiations by the percussion instruments, but one which never seeks to make the vocal elements subservient to it). But as a cantata, the purely vocal and lyric elements of *Noces* are incomplete, so to speak: neither the singing nor the sheer beauty of vocal sound is self-sufficient. Both have to be understood as intimately connected with, even stimulated by, gesture, by bodily motion, dance rhythms, and ritual. The play of sound is itself the embodiment of all the scenic elements—the elements of pantomime and dance—much as was true in the time of the madrigal comedies (to which we shall return).

Being, on the one hand, an artistic transmutation of static ritual, and on the other (in the fullest sense of the word) an intonation of the body—that is, a transmutation into musical terms of the gesture and dance of the wedding ceremony—the music of *Noces* is no symphony of the emotions, no Euripidean tragedy. The presence in it of comical personages (matchmakers and attendants), and the influence at the same time of the inflexible severity of traditional ritual—these combine to make the work a theatrical ("gesture made visible") synthesis of two juxtaposed but reciprocal elements that are themselves expressions of vital principles. The first is the epic forcefulness and Aeschylean rigor of life, as expressed by the confrontation of man and his instinct for procreation. The second is the principle of knavery, escape into a world of laughter and mockery as a release from the rigors of inexorable fortune—in short, buffoonery. The authority of tradition speaks to woman: life is a burden, bear it come what may, bury your maidenhood, and with it your will. The buffoon says: life is mime, the rite of the family is theatrical farce. The chorus of *Noces,* like that of ancient tragedy, is contemplative of the action, but it may also participate in the action by expressing sympathy with certain characters or becoming party to the comic jollity. It is the comedy, of course, that pricks the seriousness with which human beings take the rites they themselves have established to celebrate the perpetuation of the race, with the reminder that the only requirements are in fact quite simple: conceive, and give birth.

The texture and action of *Noces* are therefore composed of three stylistic elements. First, the threnodial element—the grief and lamentation that are associated with the obsequies of maidenhood, for the Russian wedding rite is virtually a funeral rite. Second, the element that celebrates the invocation and excitation of the male procreative force—its whole performance, its whole energy. Finally, the humorous and buffoon element—now ironical, now undissembling. It is the laughter of buffoonery that serves to assuage the bitterness of female grief and blunt the wild impulsiveness of the male procreative energy. And it is by this same laughter—sly, inquisitive, not free of lust—that passions are aroused and orgiastic tendencies intensified.

Stravinsky compresses all this into four short, succinct scenes. The music is severe, astringent, graphic. Instrumental color is wholly subservient to the sense of the action. And if at the end of the final scene, when all the participants (after the departure of the newlyweds into the bedchamber) stand in frozen anticipation of the conceiving of new life—if Stravinsky then makes the bells ring out, this only serves to underline, to deepen and strengthen the ultimate meaning of the whole ritual: as I have said, its funereal aspect. The tragic element prevails, and with it the ironical. To foreigners, *Noces* may even seem an utter grotesque. Of course, in so far as the action is perforated by irony, in so far as the action is play-acting and not life, to this degree the whole bears the stamp of exaggeration, buffoonery, mask. But, on the other hand, there is so much of profundity in the portrayal of grief and lamentation, so much of vital male force in the portrayal of the triumphant erotic instinct, that any persuasion of the utter grotesqueness of *Noces* is unthinkable without serious reservations: if you wish, it is the grotesque of the Renaissance and the grotesque of Shakespeare, but not the grotesque of the curved mirror. And the difference is very great.

The analysis of *Noces* that I offer is nothing more than a sketch. Its purpose is to stimulate further work on the music of Stravinsky. It is always very difficult to take a contemporary work apart, and equally difficult, having laid bare its elements and their articulation, to recompose and grasp the living flux of the composition.

The music of *Noces* gives evidence of kinship with other works of Stravinsky composed around the same time: *Renard, Four Russian Songs, Three Stories for Children,* and the still earlier Pribautki (1914) and the *Cat's Cradle Songs*. It also, however, continues the development of principles that Stravinsky projected—perhaps instinctively—in *Sacre* (1912-13). The two works share common rhythms, common methods of developing material, and a similarity of intonations. But *Noces* is more intricate as a composition, and stylistically more of a whole. For all its bewitching and stunning novelty and audaciousness, in *Sacre* there is not yet a full control of the play of imaginative force, not an authentic mastery that comes as the summation of vast experience. The overflowing strength of the young artistic imagination, the fullness and richness of material, the captivating color and intensity of the musical flow, the inspired symphonic moments (like the introduction, Ritual of Vernal Regeneration, Dance of the Adolescents, and the Sacrificial Dance)— all these overwhelm the listener and make it impossible for him to stand apart from the music and analyze it coldly and rigorously. *Sacre* is a godsent wonder, the ensign of musical contemporaneity. It is fresh and raw, it has the strength of its angularity and bold straightforwardness. The difference between *Sacre* and *Noces* is one between an instinctive, irresistible urge, and a calculated, motivated action—given the same degree of talent in both cases. But the "theme" is the same for each: the sovereignty of the procreative force. In *Noces,* the music passes through the stages of the wedding ritual to the wedding feast and its culmination, celebrated amid the rejoicing and the protective assent of the community. In *Noces,* the climactic and most deeply felt symphonic moment is placed at the very end. In *Sacre,* it is at the very beginning (the Ritual of Vernal Regeneration). Stravinsky's "feast" in honor of Eros calls to mind the prologue to *Ruslan and Ludmila;* the comic elements of *Noces* suggest the *Kamarinskaya* of Glinka.

Part I, Scene 1

Striving for absolute rhythmic exactitude, Stravinsky mechanizes his writing to an extreme degree. It is necessary to mark this fact at the outset, because it provides a key to the whole ordering of the music.

The underlying metrical unit can be taken as quarter note-160. From time to time, however, the pace of the music is halved in such a manner that the total duration formerly occupied by two eighth notes is now occupied by only one—

in other words, the metronomic indication becomes eighth note-80. The result is that without changing the appearance of the notes or providing any special directions for reduction or increase of speed, Stravinsky is able to alter the musical pace and at the same time preserve a unity and strict proportion. In the middle of the scene the metrical indication becomes quarter note-120, the quality of the motion changes abruptly and becomes largely duple. This "outburst," accompanied by both intonational and dynamic changes, leads to the final section and back to the quarter note-80 or eighth-160. There are 235 vertical divisions (or measures, but of various lengths) in this scene, disposed as follows:

The introductory pentatonic lament of the bride: ten measures of varying lengths.

The speed is doubled: the opening idea is carried forward and concludes with a single measure of choral interjection. The entire section of eleven measures is repeated.

The bride repeats the choral cadence, extending it to two measures, and the attendants, taking up her musical cue, intone in a kind of psalmody *mezza voce:* "Chesu, pochesu, Nastas'inu kosu."

This refrain is used like a rondo to bind the whole section together. Here it persists for fifteen measures with a cadential solo interrupting before its end (the solo answers "alu lentu upletu" to the "a i kosu, zapletu" of the chorus).

This interruption breaks the monotonous ritual of the choral psalmody, which leads to a somewhat more extensive repetition of both sections, but with an altered termination: this time, the chorus ("goluboyu perev'yu") takes up the solo interruption and develops it briefly. Again the bride sings her slow lament (like the opening passage); but her attendants, as if refusing to pay attention and not wanting to continue the psalmody, change the character, rhythm, and tempo of the intonations and begin a fresh song of consolation: "ne klich', ne klich', lebedushka," paced at quarter note-120, with the basic 2/4 measure punctured by 3/4, 5/8 and 3/8 as the music proceeds. This whole repetition of the opening passage lasts for fifty-two measures, measure 52 coinciding with the arrival of the fresh material. This new section is very interesting from the point of view of intonational dynamics, to which I shall return later. The basis of its construction is an alternation of different arrangements and lengths of measure set forth at a steady pace (quarter note-120). It also exhibits some of Stravinsky's favorite adoptions from folk traditions: the collision of accents produced by strong beats, or a five-measure phrase divided into one plus four (the end of one phrase, and the beginning of another in a new voice).

Male voices are adjoined to female, the music rises to several orgiastic outbursts and then becomes dance-like in character. Its form is basically a set of vocal variations on the first melody. The example shows some of these variations [see ex. 114].

Example 114

The style of the development is a melodic heterophony characterized by the following: the growth of the lines is branch-like; new melodic fragments are inserted within the limits of a heretofore single melodic idea; counterpoints are added; durations are shortened or eliminated; sometimes meter is altered to conform with the text, sometimes textual accent is violated for the sake of maintaining the line; the end of one voice is fused with the beginning of another, etc. The accompaniment (four pianos and percussion) clothes the chorus in a robe of instrumental heterophony, but all the instrumental factors—harmony, color, dynamics, percussive qualities—are made subservient to the vocal line: *Noces,* as I have already said, is first and foremost a cantata. The old madrigal comedies of the seventeenth century (like the *Ampfiparnasso* of Orazio Vecchi) were cantatas in much the same sense. The music of Stravinsky's cantata, however, is completely derived from gesture, pantomime, and (at times) dance. It is for this reason that Stravinsky frequently writes lines with very emphatic rhythmic contours, like those of other vocal melodies that are instrumentally inspired (Russian airs!).

This central portion of the first scene occupies ninety-three measures, and it proceeds without pause (but with a change of tempo to quarter note-80) into the final lament of the tenor ("Prechistaya mater' ") on a new theme, over which the bride and her mother continue their own lament. After twenty-three measures there begins the final refrain of nineteen measures repeating the psalmody of the attendants ("chesu, pochesu") with the addition of a response sung by the bride (in the Dorian mode on A, with f♯). This refrain terminates the scene.

The intonational content of the scene is extraordinarily interesting. It exhibits a number of characteristics typical of the style of the traditional lament—among them, characteristic melodic contour, the psalmodic quality of certain passages, the utilization of exclamatory and wailful interjections. The lament is presented, in its various manifestations, with striking technical virtuosity and an almost lapidary severity. Nuances are shaded all the way from the dramatized groan down to the indifferently mechanical murmuring "chesu, pochesu" (always beginning with the quavering drop of a full step) that suggests a prayer spoken while going off to sleep. Characteristic of the lament are the outburst ff in a high tessitura, the rapid descent to the cadence at a lower level, and the cadence itself used as the point of departure for the following refrain [see ex. 115 b & c].

Example 115

As the leap to the lower octave suddenly contracts to a slurred major second, the bitter exclamation of grief contracts to a kind of psalmodic reiteration, as if scripture were being read over a corpse.

To this, the "consolatory" choral section that occupies the center of the scene offers sharp contrast. Just as the interval of a second (with the occasional brief admixture of other intervals) characterizes the opening section, so does the major third (frequently with syncopation [see ex. 114]) characterize the melody of the middle section. The accompaniment suggests the chiming of little bells, and the soprano and alto are intermittently harmonized at the interval of a second [see ex. 114, a].

In this central section, the volume of choral sound is gradually enlarged. The plan is as follows: The female chorus is interrupted by tenor and bass solo voices [see ex. 116]. The chorus resumes, but the bass and soprano solo voices re-enter with the opening material and have a canon at the seventh (actually, at the fourteenth). They in turn give way to the ensemble (female chorus and soprano and mezzo-soprano soloists), which has a texture of sonorous clarity. The bass and tenor ejaculations add to the general hubbub which leads finally to climactic Dionysian shrieks ("Rai, rai"), in which the male chorus also participates.

Example 116

The music is on the verge of becoming uncontrollably wild. But having brought it this far, Stravinsky gradually reduces the tension and finally returns to a simple lament (three soloists on a Dorian melody) [see ex. 117].

Example 117

These are only hints of the orgiastic excitement that is to overflow in the last scene, at the wedding feast.

Part I, Scene 2: *The Bridegroom*

From the point of view of its construction, this scene has something in common
with the first: choral psalmody, as a refrain, whose appearances give unity to
the succession of sonorities and to the action itself. There is also a gradual rise
in the intonational and dynamic tension brought about by a gradual increase in
the volume of choral sound. But the increase here is more grandiose and more
intense, and at the end widens into a colossal crescendo—a mighty, festive,
ringing of bells. The coloring of the scene is masculine, clear, spare, and rich.
The laments now become howls in the lower register and shrill cries in the
upper, like the calls of merchants in a bazaar or of the itinerant peddlers of
olden times.

Therefore, the intonational range, character, and dynamics of this scene
form a great contrast to the first. We shall analyze the construction of the
second scene. The meter is set at quarter note-120—that is, at the fastest tempo
of the first scene (as found in its middle section). Thus a connection is
established between the two scenes, and the second at once sets off at a brisk
pace. Its opening material is a kind of psalm-tone, a half-muttered incantation,
heavy, weighty, given to tenors and basses [see ex. 118] with alto, tenor, and
bass soloists entering to reinforce the ends of the phrases. This suggests a
heathen and almost blasphemous invocation of the Mother of Jesus, but it is
one quite in the style of peasant orthodox worship: "khodi k nam ukhat'", etc.
The two soloist attendants, tenor and bass, try to interrupt the psalmody with
their loud "bazaar merchant" cries set in imitative style [see ex. 119].

The forward motion is broken by the entrance of two parental solo voices
that begin a dialogue in imitative style, to which another two solo voices are
subsequently added to form a quartet. Here the coloring darkens, the tempo
becomes slower (quarter note-104), and the theme is as follows [see ex. 120].

The laments of the parents are interwoven with the melodic grotesques of
tenor and bass, and the movement is gradually returned to the original tempo
(quarter note-120) announced by a rollicking little soprano solo [see ex. 121].

This theme is adroitly doubled in the orchestra (fff), with an accompaniment of chromatic parallel fifths followed by a diatonic figuration with
tambourine ostinato. As in the first scene, the dance-like quality of the material
gradually becomes dominant, develops, branches and spreads, aided by
horizontal displacements, rhythmic and melodic variations, transpositions,
etc. In *Renard* and (especially) in *Noces,* Stravinsky released Russian lyric
melodic writing from conventional choral figurations and "variations on
Russian themes." At the same time, in folk music—in the style and
ornamentation of its polyphony, in its technique of subordinating all voices to
the central and principal melodic line—he discovered the resources needed to
create polyphonic textures of mobility and richness.

Example 118

Пре _ чи _ ста _ я мать,   хо _ ди, хо _ ди к нам у _ хать, сва _ хе помо _ гать

Example 119

Чем че _ сать, чем мас _ лить да Хве _ тись _ е _ вы ку _ (у) _ (у) _

Чем че _ сать, чем мас _ лить

_ дри?

да Пам _ филь _ и _ ча ру _ (у) _ (у) _ сы?

или то же в обращении:

Ку _ пим мы, ку _ пим мы

Ки _ нем _ ся, бро _ сим _ ся, во три тор _ га, го _ (о) _ рэ _

па _ ра _ ван _ ско _ го ма _ (а) _ (а) _ сла,

_ да,   рас _ че _ шем, раз _ мас _ лим Хве _ ти

Example 120

Ви _ чор _ са ви _ чо ру   си _ дел Хве _ тис

Example 121

Having raised the ensemble to a point of high intensity, Stravinsky breaks through with the initial psalmodic texture ("Khodi, khodi k nam ukhat'"). But this time the music is allowed to develop into an incantatory imperative. The deity is commanded, persistently and repeatedly: "Pod' na svad'bu". One has the impression that Stravinsky has laid bare the ancient heathen roots of orthodox ritual and its primitive incantatory signification (the cult of fertility and the propagation of the race).

The cries of the chorus and soloists are alternated with the exhortations of the deep basses [see ex. 122]. The harmony is derived from an archaic scale. The voices preserve a strict diatonicism. The accompaniment uses chromaticism, but only as color, as ornamental refraction. There is a second climax ff, yielding abruptly to the scene of parental benediction that undergoes a colossal and elemental intensification. Here Stravinsky has appropriated dynamic factors common to all religious services and formed them into a new ritual action. He utilizes forms of the response (leader and chorus) and of antiphony (contrasting male and female choral parts); the triumphant character of the singing suggests the hymn, and the opposition of chorus and soloists, the concerto.

Example 122

Two bass soloists establish the initial rhythms and intonations of the benediction [see ex. 123]. This passage is gradually interwoven with a dry, "business-like," fragmented psalmody of sopranos and altos, which in turn gives way to the rollicking, bazaar-like cries of the attendants (first bass alone, later bass with tenor) in the Dorian mode on the following theme [see ex. 124] (in the orchestra, piano tremolo, xylophone trills, single strokes on the bass drum, and the steady beat of the kettledrum). After a prayerful supplication by the female voice [see ex. 125] the cry "Hey," tutti, stops the movement. Then begins the benediction *("lebedinoe pero upadalo")* the soloists being introduced as cadential punctuation. Each choral phrase *piano* is concluded by a tutti *fortissimo* [see ex. 126].

Example 123

Example 124

Example 125

Example 126

At the same time, the Dorian of G major replaces the Dorian of B♭ major. A strict diatonicism is maintained throughout; the lines and rhythms are sharp, clear, severely plain. This is the Russian "austere" style, resembling that of the Novgorod school of icon painting [particularly of the late fourteenth and fifteenth centuries: icons notable for radiant pure colors, and laconic and precise outlines—Trans.] Here the singing of the chorus and soloists depicts the events of the action, as is the custom in a ritual derived from the traditions of antiquity (*viz.* the role of the chorus in classical tragedy). The development leads again to the cries of the attendants which now follow more closely upon one another (the bass echoes the tenor line an octave lower, the transposition itself affording a sort of horizontal development). This is what happens [see ex. 127].

Example 127

Without losing tension, the texture of the ensemble is broken up into a dialogue of soloists and female chorus. Again there is the tutti "Hey" which is both a conclusion and a point of departure for another, even more forceful, and more exalted hymn (of benediction and incantation). The hymn begins with a variation, in the Phrygian of F major, of the scene's opening incantation [see ex. 128].

Example 128

The development is carried on horizontally for the most part and makes use of all the principal materials of the scene. All the favorite saints are invoked with ecstatic enthusiasm: Mikita, Luke, Damien, etc., recalling the matchmaker of Nekrasov. The sound grows, widens, branches out. A huge organ point is formed: the lower octaves of the pianos, together with kettledrums, rock back and forth like mighty bells and serve as foundation and support for the branching vocal texture. In my opinion, this is the only passage in Russian music the force of whose choral energies equals the incomparable final scene of Glinka's first opera. From the seventeenth century on there have been many festival pieces that have tried to concentrate and release the mighty energies of choral ensembles. But only a composer of the twentieth century, confining these energies within a strict system of rhythms and intonations, has succeeded in attaining maximum power of expressive strength with minimum instrumental means.

The construction of the second scene, referring to its vertical divisions into measures (245), is as follows: from the beginning (the prayer-like theme used to invoke the presence of the Blessed Mother at the wedding) to the laments of the parents, there are thirty-nine measures. The initial theme takes ten measures (accompanied by two piano parts and small drum), the buffoon-like interruption of the attendants (accompanied by a small bell-like combination of piano, tambourine, and snare drum) lasts seven measures. Now four measures of the initial material follow, then the canonic calls of the attendants (twelve measures), followed by the original material and its extension ff by the tenor solo (six measures). Here the character of the movement changes, but all of this episode is the kernel of what is developed later. And not a trace of an eight-bar phrase!

To proceed: From the *meno mosso* (the lament of the parents) to the return of the original thematic material after the first climax, effected by the interplay of rollicking little vocal and instrumental melodies—there is a total of seventy-seven measures. It is worthy of note from an intonational point of view that the parental lament (mezzo soprano and tenor solo, followed by solo quartet) serves as a transition from the deep and hollow mutterings of tenors and basses gradually upwards toward a texture that is enriched and made sonorously clear by the reinforcement of its upper registers.

The lament, which occupies forty-five and one-half measures, proceeds over a monotonous "ostinato" figure in the piano which is repeatedly punctuated by sharp bell-like chords (sff in the lower registers of the piano plus kettledrums and large and small drums). There is a connective passage of eleven and one-half measures (a sort of satirical imitation of the lament) after which the first lyrical passage begins *(tempo primo)* and rises toward a climax. After twenty measures, the climax is interrupted by a return of the opening material, this time with altos added to tenors and basses. The result is a sort of grotesque monastic chorus. The development of this section, reaching a climax in the incantatory imperative, occupies twenty-seven measures. Again the pace is broken and reverts to *meno mosso,* in which the groom addresses his parents. Intonationally there is also a break here, the sound reverting to the lower, heavier registers, with the upper and lower solo and choral voices being presented antiphonally (a sort of grotesque musical "service"). The sound of this twenty-one-measure episode is marvelous. The episode leads to the scene of benediction and to a mighty climax, which yields to the cries of the attendants but returns with a final tutti in which all the material of the scene is shown in its brightest colors.

The final ensemble includes eighty measures and is divided as follows: twelve measures to the attendants, concluding with the tutti "Hey," followed by twenty measures of tutti leading to the second entrance of the attendants who have a nine-measure variation of their earlier material. (Note that the end of the tutti and the beginning of this nine-measure passage overlap, a favorite device of Stravinsky for joining episode and making abrupt transitions from one rhythmic context to another.) There is a second orgiastic "Hey" which interrupts the attendants, and then the final and gigantic climax begins over the organ point C A^1 $C\sharp^1$ A^1, a tolling of massively heavy bells (forty measures). The motion of the sound reaches a maximum intensity and then stops, suddenly, unexpectedly as if hung in mid-air.[1]

Part I, Scene 3: *Leave-Taking of the Bride*

This is the shortest scene, the most concise, and the simplest from the point of view of construction and intonation. It has only 147 measures. The development of the action is almost parallel to that of the second scene: the benediction, the invocation of deities and saints ("pod' na svad'bu"), the leave-taking. But here the sound is dominated by the female element (a succession of convulsive sobs, each an intensified expression of the wailing moan). Further, although there is a bright climax (the leave-taking), there is also a monotonous and static coda. This is the lamentation of the mothers of the bride and groom, using material from the second scene but in a different register and with a more ascetic instrumental accompaniment. The coda again stresses the funereal character of the wedding rite,[2] a quality that was expressed in the first scene but that was somewhat dispelled by the masculine brightness and glow which dominate the second. In the third scene, Stravinsky uses material from the first two scenes, especially the theme of the female chorus in which the attendants try to comfort the bride ("ne klich', ne klich', lebedushka," [see ex. 114]). In fact, the third scene opens with this melody.

This melody, repeated by the female chorus several times, is immediately succeeded by the lament of the tenors[3] and then branches out into a series of imitations by the solo quartet. The quartet becomes a passage of solo voices with chorus, and the quickly succeeding imitations are joined to another theme with a slower pace, likewise taken from the laments of the first scene [see ex. 117]. The combination of these two is effected as follows [see ex. 129].

Example 129

I cite here a typical arrangement of this same material from the first scene, where the bass and tenor soloists move in parallel fourths under a syncopated soprano organ point, and over a jazzy instrumental background (not shown) [see ex. 130].

Example 130

If one were to adduce the number of ways in which the development (by horizontal combinations and displacements) is worked out, one would almost have to reproduce the entire score! The climax of the third scene begins with a brisk and sinuous melody[4] [see ex. 131].

Example 131

И как вьет_ся хмель по _ ты- цью(у) _

The scene concludes in a rollicking style with wild choral outcries *("u,u")* set to the metallic sound of the instrumental accompaniment (piano in the upper register, xylophone, tambourine, small drum). This whole development, which occupies 102 measures, moves without interruption to the concluding lament of the mothers of the bride and groom (45 measures).

The spirit of the whole scene is pattering and lively. The opening, sounding somewhat like a little rain shower, sets the style for the rest of the movement, throughout which the eighth note remains at a constant duration (eighth-240) and is the basic unit of time here, as it was in the first scene.[5]

Before passing on to the second part of *Noces* (which contains the fourth scene alone, the most extensive and most highly developed of all), I should like to make a few remarks about the third scene as a whole. The melodic and dynamic materials of this scene have their source in the opening scene, of which this is the natural prolongation and development. The parting of the bride from the freedoms and the atmosphere of girlhood is expressed in the prevalence of weeping and doleful lament (even the richly scored tutti of the leave-taking concludes with a passage of wailing and howling) which conveys the passivity of woman and her melancholy obedience to fate. Of course, the rigidly steady rhythm does not allow the music to get out of hand. The second and fourth scenes, as contrast to the first and third, assert the power of the procreative urge and the fury of the male principle: forceful, headstrong, unrepressed, even wild, and (for all its fresh attractiveness) brutally erotic. At times, the music passes over into frenzied howls and the pantomime seems nothing less than a heathen dance over the corpse of the doomed, a kind of funereal feast. Thus, the formal and emotional plan of *Noces* relates Scenes 1 and 3 and Scenes 2 and 4, and the action moves back and forth between one emotional context and its opposite. As we shall see, all the lights are brought to bear on one focal point in the fourth scene, and the conclusion itself, although it may appear something of a surprise, is in a very profound sense logical and consistent.

Part II, Scene 4: *The Wedding Feast*

In terms of quantity of music, this part occupies a little more than a third of the whole work. In terms of quality, the music is superlatively tensile, rich, ardent. Instead of analyzing the construction in detail, I shall point out the important material as I discuss the development of the action.

This final scene contains 334 measures. The basic construction is a chain of episodes, or parts of episodes. The flow may be spontaneously discontinuous, or the end of one unit may coincide with the beginning of the next. This method of construction is characteristic of *Noces* as a whole, and especially of this fourth scene. The technique of composition is based wholly on the combining of vocal lines, producing polyrhythms and polymelodies. Chords, as complexes of color, as timbres, are utilized in the accompaniment. The interplay of melodies is brought by Stravinsky to a point of extreme virtuosity. The rich and varied dynamics and color of the sound are controlled by methods that are basically simple and long familiar, but applied in the given instance with intelligence and imagination. Male and female voices are contrasted, registers are contrasted, and the materials passed and imitated from one group to another. Furthermore, there is a purely dynamic increase and decrease of sound (without any emotional excitation or relaxation, crescendo or decrescendo) accomplished by increasing or decreasing the number of sounding lines, or their densities. And despite the chain-like construction and the uninterruptedness of the music's development, one can see, especially in connection with the turns of events, traces of sonata-allegro form or even of the form of a complex rondo with a number of inner episodes. And although the principle of development is that of the confrontation and juxtaposition of rhythms and intonations according to the interplay of personalities and episodes, there are also traces of a purely thematic development. The first forty measures form a sort of exposition whose thematic bases are the central or principal "berry" melody with its related motives, and the collateral or second "goose" melody. The first interlude or episode follows, with the presentation of the bride and the choral salutation to her mother. The development begins with a variation of the "goose" melody and seems at first to grow like a rondo (sixty-eight measures), with the "goose" melody serving as a sort of refrain. Out of the refrain there grows a new melody about the little swan, that receives extensive melodic development (a whole series of variations). The song of the little swan (twenty-eight measures), which presents the material in its original form, is the central "lyrical" episode of the development and is notable for its narrative, ballad-like quality. Beginning here, attention is transferred to the newlyweds and particularly to the bride. She has a four-measure melody that gives new direction to the development, and whose thematic importance in the reprise is on a par with that of the initial melodies and rhythms. The twenty-seven measures of dialogue (matchmakers and guests) and the cries of the attendants, form a connective to the second interlude (the warming of the bed). This passage of 105 measures is like a chain of many links. In addition to developing the connective material heard just prior to it and to making use of the bride's melody, the passage contains the essential elements of a reprise, including the reappearance of the opening dance-like theme, together with the original material of this section. The coda (the glorification of the marriage bed) serves as an extension of the melody of the bride and, together with the instrumental conclusion, occupies sixty-two measures. Thus the plan of the action of the wedding feast, as it is related to the succession of important personages, is as follows:

The chorus of rejoicing (melody "a"); salutation to the young people; salutation to the father of the bride ("Iunyv, Iunyv khodit"), with two additional melodies "e" and "f".

Repetition of the first chorus, during which the "goose" melody begins, followed by the salutation to the mother of the bride.

The first episode (presentation of the bride); further development of the "goose" melody "g", and the song of the little swan; the cries of matchmakers and attendants, and the salutation to the bride and groom, which serves as a transition to the second stage of the development. This is based on a new melody of the bride "b" and the bell-like motive of the bed-warming.

This texture becomes a kind of reprise through the interlacing of the opening material "a" and its two companions "e" and "f".

The coda has new material—a langorous song "n".

Thus the most important elements of the exposition are the melodies "a", "e", "f", and "g". The latter is the basis for the first section of the development, with the material of the little swan. This song marks an important division of the scene, after which the development is mostly occupied with melody "b", that assumes an importance equal to that of "a". When this last appears in the song of the bride, it suggests a reprise, and is followed by elements "a," "e" and "f". The whole movement is a sort of chain of episodes wedged one against the other, with attendant motives, speech-like patter, lamentations, new material, etc.

The scene begins in erotic dance-like fashion with whooping and hallooing: "Yagoda s yagodoy sokatilisya." The chorus in octaves has the principal motive. The soloists introduce a little refrain, in which the chorus joins, but this gives way later to a new melody and to other voices. The original material then returns in a richer and more powerful texture, that is interrupted by material of quite another sort presented by a solo voice, out of which a new ensemble is developed, etc.—so that the whole is a chain of closely linked, brilliant episodes. Here is the principal material "a" [see ex. 132].

Example 132

The whole choral mass, plus four pianos and percussion, hurls itself against the ear in a texture of brilliant sonorities and concise rhythms, and plunges the auditor into a world of intoxicating and ecstatic actuality. The soloists have the following refrain [see ex. 133]. The tenor solo leads off with the development of the original material [see ex. 134].

Example 133

Example 134

The solo bass *falsetto* presents a new idea [see ex. 135]. The female voices (chorus and soloists) answer him: "Pelagey Spanovich." A new motive enters, whose halting, rocking motion seems almost to disjoint the pace of the movement (melody "f") [see ex. 136].

This motive, which contrasts with the original thematic idea, plays an important rhythmic and melodic role in the development. Here it is accompanied by the tramping of the lower registers of the piano and bass drum. The chorus picks up this idea and develops it in the same rhythmic manner, but

Example 135

Ю_ньiв, ю_ньiв хо _ дит

Example 136

По_те _рял   зо _ лот перстин,   зо_лот с да_ра _ гим сы ка_ме чям

meanwhile the basses "mark time" with the original material under the syncopated choral texture. The sopranos take up the bass material, but while the orchestra carries on the syncopated idea, the quartet of soloists introduces a new counterpoint that later has the following shape as the "goose" melody [see ex. 137].

Example 137

Ле _ та _ ла гу _ сы _ ня,   ле _ та _ ла!

Stravinsky here works up an intricate combination of rhythms and melodies that suggests a round-dance of sonorities. He breaks the whole chorus out into wild hallooing, which announces a new stage in the action, with its own chain of melodies. The tenor sings a new variation of the "goose" melody, interrupted by the ecstatic howls ("hey") of chorus and soloists [see ex. 138].

Example 138

Ля _ та _ ла   гу _ сы _ ня,   ле _ та _ ла!

The groom's father presents the bride [see ex. 139].

Example 139

Вот те _ бе   жа _ наі

Then begins the ceremony by which the bride is entrusted to the groom. This is accompanied by a choral dialogue (an antiphony of male and female choral section), the lamentations of the bride's mother ("zyatik moi lyubeznyi"), and advice to the groom about his behavior toward the bride: for example, "Lyubi kak dushu." All this is conveyed by exclamatory outbursts of the attendants, the mother of the groom, and the two matchmakers. The melodic speech is clearly defined, with the vigor and clarity of gesture. This interlude is directly joined to further developments of the "goose" melody [See exs. 137, 138], while the text takes up the ceremony of offering toasts to the bride: "Boyare vstavali." The dialogue of the attendant (bass) and the mother of the groom forms a new interlude. The chorus continues the development of the "goose" melody. The mother of the groom sings a narrative ballad about the deep blue of the sea and the white swan, supported by a refrain sung at cadential points by the female chorus. The motive of the "goose" undergoes a development leading to the rising melodic progressions d_b^2-c_b^2-d_b^2-$d_\#^1$-b^1-$c_\#^2$-$d_\#^1$-$g_\#^1$-$c_\#^2$ [compare ex. 134], all of which ascend through the interval of a seventh, and out of which the narrative ballad melody emerges into the Dorian of F major [see ex. 140].

Example 140

И я бы _ ла на   си _ нем на   мо _ ри на   мо _

The choral refrain ("liuli, liuli") also flows from this introductory progression, and the web of continuity is now woven of a variety of rhythms and intonations. The remaining soloists join the soprano voices, while the male chorus underlays the female with little cries of "hey" that serve to stimulate and control a motion which gives the impression of being about ready to be set adrift. The result is a complex lyrico-narrative dialogue. But, nevertheless, the texture remains clear and transparent, the lines rounded and pliant.

I should like to quote two variations of the "little swan" melody: that of the mezzo soprano [see ex. 141] and that of the bass, with just a hint of buffoonery [see ex. 142].

Example 141

Example 142

The whole episode exhibits exceptional technical mastery and extraordinary sensitivity to folk polyphony. For all its archaicisms, it is also a uniquely serene and tender moment in an action notable for its austerity and the depth of its irony.

The next stage of the betrothal and toasting of the bride is the dialogue of the attendants and the matchmakers. I quote here the beautiful phrase of the bride [see ex. 143].

Example 143

The interlude concludes with the gay, bazaar-like cries of the tenor-attendant ("Krasnye devitsy"), accompanied by clinkings of the tambourine and bright piano figurations. Here I would like to call attention to a very important fact: from the beginning to the end, each character is a "mask"[6] with its own characteristic intonations and rhythms (that define gesture and movement), the sum of whose individualizing properties affords a better unity than could have been achieved by any logical scheme of leitmotifs with which the texture might have been encumbered. In this respect, Stravinsky follows the traditions of Bach, Mozart, and Glinka.

The next episode deals with the warming of the wedding bed. It begins with a dialogue of the female chorus and the soloists—a kind of lullaby, but one that adheres to a steady movement (quarter-120). The chorus reiterates a single phrase "d" [see ex. 144].

Example 144

There are eleven measures of this material, the beginnings of whose phrases shift to the third, and then to the second, beat of the measure. Since the accompaniment has a figure consistently coterminous with the limits of a single measure (a kind of organ point), the result is a texture of gentle cross-rhythms.

The lullaby-dialogue passes over into a song[7] in honor of the young people (female chorus, also eleven measures). This is followed by a salutation by the matchmaker and guests to the father of the groom ("sryazhai svadebku Khvetisavu"): again shades of the "berry" melody (the heavy, lumbering motive beneath) followed by the same melody in a new variation (a ᵥ) [see ex. 145] which is interrupted at the cadence by tenor secco recitative: "za stolom boyare." It is difficult clearly to describe in detail the capricious and whimsical play of motives and rhythms in this section: one is replaced by another, one flows out of another, doubtless according to some inner necessity more felt than perceived. The moment when the "berry" melody returns [ex. 145] can be considered as the beginning of the terminal section of the work. The matchmaker and guests (basses) continue to develop—now in the name of the father of the groom—their comments on the magnificence of the wedding table. The melody of the bride "b" [ex. 143] has the following form [see ex. 146].

Notice the clever canon between the two bass parts.

In this section the contrast of voices and registers plays an important role. Thus, the thick and coarse coloring of the male voices set against the undulating lullaby of the female chorus [see ex. 144] reappears with the text "vedut Nastas'iushku na chuzhu storonu." The formulation has something of the character of a stretto, the various parts of the lines (beginnings, middle, ends) being crowded one against the other. Let us designate these melodies by letters similar to the ones we have already used:

b — the melody of the bride

bᵥ — the "speeches" of the matchmakers, which make use of the same melody

Example 145

Ох, на из _ бе зе _ лья, ув ыз_бе ве _ сель _ я

Example 146

у ме _ ня сва _ деб_ка на ди_во су _ря _ же_на,

де _ вя _ ти ва _ ров пи _ во ва _ ре _ но

c — various cries and exclamations of the attendants

d — the lullaby of the female chorus

a_v — the "gala" version of the basic "berry" melody

a — the basic "berry" melody itself.

The following scheme approximates the motivic arrangement, beginning from the appearance of the bride's melody [ex. 143], whose importance as a principal connecting link is on a par with that of the "berry" melody.

$$(b + \underline{b_v} + d + a_v + \underline{b_v + a_v}) + (b + \underline{b_v} + d + a + b + \underline{b_v + a_v})$$
$$c \qquad\qquad c \quad e \qquad c$$

From the moment the bride's melody returns in its basic form, the reprise is solidly under way [see ex. 147]

Example 147

И ста _ ро_ му, и ма _ ло_му все низ_кий пок_лон

Following on the repetition of the bride's melody by the tenor (the father), the cries of the attendants "c" recommence, and the sounds become those of speech, with inflections clearly indicated. A variant of the "berry" melody emerges out of this world of speech and then disappears ($\frac{a_v}{c}$), while a variation of one of the earlier melodies of the matchmaker or the attendant (first version [ex. 135]) fails to re-establish the musical sounds. Then the halting, stumbling rhythmic motive (first version [ex. 136]) comes floating by again as a sort of accessory to the basic "berry" melody.

In the course of this intricate and complex development there have occurred the parents' reception, and the endowment of the young people, and the embrace of the newlyweds (after the words "Okh, gor'ko, okh, nel'zya pit'"). Gradually this staggering, "drunken" rhythm, supported by the "trampings" of piano and bass drum, comes to dominate the music. Through it, the attendants and women weave the original "berry" melody, but this time with new words: "Volga-reka razlivaetsya," followed by a refrain "Akh, tioshcha moya." The action approaches its goal: those who have warmed the bed emerge from the bridal chamber and lead the young people into it, with a melody which develops the bride's musical material into a kind of "Invocation of Eros" [see ex. 148]. In the orchestra there is a ringing of bells (piano, bell, and *crotales*). The great intensity and excitation which has been engendered by the music up to this point has been accomplished by essentially simple means: by

Example 148

Па_сте_ля мо_ я,   ка_ра_вз _ туш_ка   и т. д.

joining music (in the form of a syncopated melody) to spoken sounds (the impetuous exclamations of the matchmakers and attendants in a kind of measured speech), and by utilizing rhythms which seem on the point of breaking through the chain of intonations and tearing the texture asunder. One must not forget that *Noces* is the embodiment of the ancient cult of the family and of reproduction. Only among the peasants can one have a real idea of what this cult means, for the lewd elegance of bourgeois urban wedding affairs has nothing in common with the mighty and terrible manifestations of the sexual instinct under conditions of primitive cultures and heathen environments, where the central moment of the wedding rite is not the betrothal but the first union of the newlyweds, toward which the whole rite—all its orgiastic excitation and its dance-like rhythms—has been directed. In the form of the symphonic cantata, Stravinsky gave this primitive force its first artistic expression and release. Before him, the wedding rite in operas had been nothing more than a purely descriptive historico-ethnographic episode, or simply an exercise in stylization. In *Noces,* however, the approach was quite otherwise. Impressionistic stylization had been torn out by the roots, and replaced by contemporary constructivism. Its goal was to combine rhythms and intonations into lines or vertical complexes that are clear and disciplined by musical thought, and thereby to be able alternately to fire the energy of the sound to its highest point of intensity, and then release it. The longer and the tighter the process of intensification, the greater the force of the release and the deeper its effect on the listener. In the "feast" of *Noces,* in the penultimate scene, just prior to the explosion of erotic passion, it seems as if the texture of the intonations might burst under the onslaught of sensuality. But it seems so only because from the point of view of musical construction this is precisely the moment of greatest strength, when eccentric rhythms can be combined into rugged but resilient chains of textures without the slightest danger of disintegration. The aforementioned, comparatively lengthy melody "Pastel'ya moya" (in the Dorian of A major) finally asserts control; in context, and because of its archaic basis, it becomes a kind of "Prayer to Eros," like a hymn of classical tragedy. The prayer is static, an erotic choral contemplation which, amid the gradually fading sound of the bells, bids welcome to the conceiving of a new life. Noise, hubbub, dance, movement, any sound that might excite the sexual passions—all have been left behind. The people stand face to face with the act of procreation, just as they have stood face to face with the mighty vernal renewal of nature, or the processes of sowing, ripening, and harvest. *Noces* could have been written in our time only by a composer of a vast country where one can still sense the opposition of elemental forces in confrontations of nature, and feel the power of the instinct of procreation, which the bourgoisie have neither dissipated nor made extinct.

From a purely musical point of view, *Noces* shows the technical mastery of a great artist in sound, of an outstanding composer of the contemporary world. Our musical epoch is the epoch of Stravinsky. That it is, and that it will be in all future histories no matter in what ways malicious and jealous people may seek to belittle the composer's importance. They only deprive themselves of much happiness. The young generation will find in the score of *Noces* an inexhaustible fountain of music and of new methods of musical formulation—a veritable primer of technical mastery. [8]

Notes

1. Ex. 72 has a fragment of this climax.

2. That is to say, the last rite of virginity, of the springtime of life. I remind the reader of the ancient myths of Egypt and Greece.

3. Whose musical material is also taken from the first scene [see ex. 116]

4. Which is derived from material found earlier in the tutti of the first scene.

5. The first half of Scene 2 has the quarter note-120, and the second, quarter note-80. In Scene 2, therefore, the quarter is the basic unit of time, as it will also be in Scene 4, which begins with quarter-120 and concludes with quarter-80. Thus does Stravinsky establish the rhythmic unity of the whole composition. Depending on whether the quarter or the eighth is the unit of time, the character of the movement changes, and the pace of the music is set between the limits quarter-80 (eighth-160) and quarter-120.

6. Yet *Noces* is the activation of vital gesture, not just its passive embodiment. The score is no ethnographic endeavor: its essence is pure lyric movement.

7. Whose motive is a variation of the original "berry" melody.

8. In my analysis I have not touched upon one other remarkable aspect of the composition: the correlation of the sounds of the music with the sounds of the words. Never in any Russian work which has either utilized or been derived from folksong has this correlation been achieved with such wonderful awareness of, and sensitivity to, the correspondence between the textual and musical sounds and their dynamic interrelationships. The role of vowels and their various combinations and contractions merits special analysis.

7

The Significance of Stravinsky's Art

In the evolution of Stravinsky's art, *Noces* and *Histoire* together form dual summits, like *Petrushka* and *Sacre* before them. Stravinsky's extra-theatrical period (of which I shall speak later) is still not finished, but in any case it has not produced anything on a par with *Noces,* anything more complete or more whole than this most harmonious of works, where the planes of Russian melos were incorporated into a process of formulation based on principles found in ancient and primitive cultures: I think specifically of the textures of complex linear rhythms and the percussive intonations. *Noces* is a marvelously astute synthesis, like the *Ruslan* of Glinka. Therefore not at the end of this book, as one might expect, but in its center, I believe it is necessary briefly to summarize my views on the meaning and value of that phenomenal artistry which finds expression in the works of Stravinsky. The attempts to describe such artistry as epigonous are merely pitiable. Though Stravinsky began in the school of Rimsky-Korsakov, with *Petrushka* and especially with *Sacre* he turned sharply into a new path. His mentality had changed, and therefore his language changed also. Instead of a typically homophonic music with a texture of four voices and chordal voice-leading controlled by vertical progressions, Stravinsky passed on to a polyrhythmic and linear type of composition, to the use of harmonic complexes which are products of lines, and to the unconditional supremacy of principles of formulation derived from the dynamics of the melos (as that is found in folk art) and from constructive norms long ago worked out by the intuitive rhythmic sense of human beings, for rhythm is the bio-mechanics of music. In other words, under Stravinsky Russian music was rescued from the blind alley of a "school of compositional technique": the field of composition became an area for creative thought. The compositional method of the stylist is to fabricate and organize materials according to the prescriptions of an experience that has been ordered, and whose order has in turn been formulated into rules. Under Stravinsky, this procedure gave way to an organic method: to a process of thought which by refined observation is enabled ultimately to give materials a design that accords with their natural properties and with the active, flowing quality of music—for music's natural condition is one of motion and not one of abstract voice-leading that has the appearance of correctness. Technical skill, which up to that time had been the sole criterion by which a composer could be securely judged as such, came to assume its proper role as an indicator of a certain grammatical and stylistic correctness, but in no sense as an aesthetic canon. A mentality that poses this or that problem for itself, is necessarily occupied with both the technique of construction and the means of expression: it has nothing to do with ready compositional schemes that only help to produce more and more individuals who write according to the rules (by which all the exhausted sound ideas that have long ago been preserved in blessed memory are given schematic immortality). Thus, a system of composition which is based for the most part on the combining of associatively permissible units is void of sense, and the merit of Stravinsky lies in the fact that he greatly raised the level of demands on the composer by emphasizing the efficacy of intellect and artistic invention, as opposed to a passive trailing after the dictates of a school. In other words, he returned music to the basic premises common to every high intellectual activity of man. Pity the thinker who has mastered the rules of rhetoric but has nothing to think about, for whom it is not the thought that determines the words, style, and form, but the other way around.

Thus it is mentality that defines technique, and not the converse. In this respect, despite differences in endowment and in the character of their music, Stravinsky and Taneev have something in common—a common principle, of course, not a community of ideas. From the "habits" that he acquired under Tchaikovsky, Taneev went on to arrive at rigorous criteria of music as a process of thought, criteria that served as a basis for both his theoretical works and his music. Even earlier in the history of Russian music, Glinka followed a path parallel to that of Stravinsky. For Glinka, technique was precisely not the application of abstract rules to the creative process, but a living projection of mental process. Dargomyzhsky was naive if he supposed that, having familiarized himself with the contents of the notebooks given him by Glinka (that contained the rules for thorough-bass according to Dehn) and having mastered them—if he supposed that by that fact, Glinka's technique had become his. Liadov was likewise naive when, pointing to the score of *Ruslan*, he once said: "Why look further, when the ideally beautiful technique may be found here?" True, the technique is there, but only as the fruit of Glinka's mentality and not as an eternal law. All musical thought has in common certain premises and bases, but the inferences to be drawn from them, and the practical application of them (technique) do not follow automatically. Glinka was no eclectic, he was no academic drone buzzing from flower to flower sampling musical nectars. Therefore, his music exhibits those general principles of musical formulation found in the works of Mozart, Cherubini, Gluck, Beethoven, and Berlioz, without evidence of borrowing, or repetition, or servile stylization. He could write the *Spanish Overtures* and the marvelous *Kamarinskaya* without fear of stylization, simply by using his artistic imagination to penetrate to the soul of those nations that had created the original material.

Perhaps, indeed, one may perceive a direct path from the *Kamarinskaya* of Glinka to the *Noces* of Stravinsky. In pointing out the upheaval that Stravinsky caused in the area of compositional thought and technique, I by no means imply that he alone was the creator of the tremendous movement of renaissance in Russian music. He was a child of his epoch, of course, but he was older than the rest, and more perspicacious. In addition, I re-emphasize that what interests me in Stravinsky is not the individual who writes the music, but the general phenomenon, the great artistic and cultural enterprise in which are concentrated the designs and hopes of the pre-revolutionary and revolutionary generation of musicians. The upheaval derives not from the art of any individual, but from the aggregate experience of an epoch, an experience that was first and most clearly visible in the art of Stravinsky. If so, it is not difficult to understand or assess the importance of this composer's work. The fact that he established his reputation in the theater and continues to do so, does not diminish this importance. Whether Stravinsky can successfully "translate" himself into the purely symphonic field, only the future will tell. If he does not, others will. Let us also not forget that the social role of the theater in our time gives it a significance akin to that of the Greek theater and puts it in this respect ahead of the concert stage. It is not surprising, therefore, that a "pioneer" of musical contemporaneity should have made such a brilliant reputation in the theater. *Sacre* and *Noces,* two of his greatest accomplishments, are both tragedies: tragedies of race, not tragedies of destiny. But we need to remind ourselves that these two works cannot be fully comprehended on this narrow theatrical level, that their chief importance lies in their structure as symphonic music. Very likely we shall have productions worthy of these great creations of the human intellect only when the theater will have "symphonized" itself (and a trend in this direction is already discernible): that is, not just when music may be present only nominally (an orchestra in the pit or behind the scenes), but when the whole action, the text, the tempo of the spectacle and its construction will have been disciplined and inspired by music. Thus, from Stravinsky the path of evolution leads not only toward symphonic music but toward a new and newly profound theater.

There is something else of importance. If our most gifted young people, after studying Stravinsky's works, can learn to distinguish the essential (his thought and his methods of formulating it) from the superficial and the transitory, then they will have gained full confidence in the fact that facility in the use of scholastic devices is not yet technique and does not establish canons of correctness, that without profound and serious intellectual growth the contemporary composer can never get beyond emotional improvisations artfully got up in ready-made designs. And I might add that the complete isolation of school composition from life, from the evolution of the other arts, and from musical materials themselves, has reached the point where our theorist-composers, for all their technical facility, have positively no idea of what the contemporary opera theater demands of them. Any intellectually alert and cultured regisseur can formulate the problems of the opera in more concrete terms than any composer of whatever degree of talent. On the other hand, this situation, far from being peculiar to the domain of the theater, is widespread, finding an echo in all areas of musical activity. It is only by versatility and finesse that composers can hope to work productively; lessons in the abstractions of voice-leading will just make matters worse. This is not the time for a genteel academicism and the passive use of outmoded methods and skills. He will be no Raphael or Velasquez who can only assimilate their manner or imitate their techniques. But only by studying the great masters closely can he understand that their techniques were the creatures of their unique mentalities. That is the lesson that Stravinsky has to teach us.

Yes, you may say, but does not all this serve to confirm only the specifically musical significance of Stravinsky's work and not its broader social significance? I, of course, believe that any widening of artistic horizons and deepening of the musical mentality of the artist is a fact of enormous social significance, since thereby the composer is led out of the laboratory of technique toward life itself. But one must frankly state that the great mass of people can be scared away from his music. And it is not just a question of the pungency of the sound. Without objection, the public "swallows" combinations of sounds not less (though not more) audacious, if only they produce some kind of emotional hypnosis (for example, the whole history of Scriabin and his works, which achieved popularity within a brief time and despite critical revilement). What makes Stravinsky's music very difficult to grasp are the sharpness and iron discipline of Stravinsky's musical mentality. Any listener, no matter how conservative, can adjust himself to the most audacious sound-combinations if he is not called upon to do more than listen and enjoy. But if he must grasp an idea and follow it in the process of formation, then he finds himself at an impasse, hounded by a pack of critics yapping after the false scent of musical evolution. There is nothing new in all this: the consequence of Bach's "dry" intellectualism and the incisiveness of his musical mentality is simply that his work still lives and nourishes contemporary musical thought, while many "musics" that appeared to have answered the sensual and sensible needs of their own times, many wonderful shoots, and flowers of musical fantasy, have faded forever. Stravinsky is not Bach—he has not Bach's range or depth, but the strength of his music derives from its relatedness to life and from the creativeness of his musical mentality with respect to this, not from rational mastery of rules or schemes or the raw expressions of his own private experiences. If you please, Stravinsky's musical thought is soulless and extra-personal, just as his music is extra-sensual (but not sensual-less or life-less): in a word, it is like any philosophical or artistic work in which the dynamic of the intellect controls the musical flow. In the wide world of music there is room for everything: for the spontaneously passionate explosion of strophic song, where the moment of minimal purely musical interest may coincide with a maximum intensity of impassioned utterance expressed in music whose simplicity is in reality utter refinement, as well as for the highest and most intricate manifestations of musical thought, like the *Art of Fugue* of Bach or the technical virtuosity of the Netherlanders. Does not philosophy encompass everything from the simplest everyday philosophizing to the mightiest systems? Does not poetry include everything from the ephemeral emotional lyric to *Faust?* Only nobody takes it into his head to say that Goethe or Kant must come down to the level of the Philistines. But it is just these same people who are suspicious of music, who ask that music be accessible to all, who consider blameworthy a preponderance of intellectuality in music, and who question the right of independent musical thought. The inventions of Bach may be "trifles," but the strength of their effect is irresistible just because they are the expression of intellect and not just ephemeral emotion. Stravinsky is now being sarcastically called a contemporary "Bach-er." If Stravinsky himself really senses his affinity to Bach—not Bach as a specific composer but as a supreme phenomenon of colossal energy who incarnates the musical mentality of the Enlightenment—then he is profoundly correct. Indeed, only by pursuing this line of reasoning may he surmount certain harmful propensities that prevent a deepening of his thought and the unfettered exercise of his great endowments (I am thinking of a touch of aestheticism and a haughty self-conceit). The attitude and conduct of the pre-war era (during which the art of Stravinsky developed) was so aimless, skeptical, and pusillanimous that one could not help being concerned for their effect on him. But if Stravinsky's creative efforts never rise above the heights of *Sacre* and *Noces,* the significance of his entire career (not only the artistic reputation of single works) will in no way be diminished. That which he has already created will steadfastly answer for him.

This said, however, there is no denying the directness with which Stravinsky's music touches the senses of listeners and their imaginations. In spite of the presence of irony and occasional satirical tendencies, the basic tone of the music is zestful and optimistic. Of course, Stravinsky is never undisciplined, never gives himself up to the simple flux of emotions. Rhythm, which disciplines his whole musical mentality, also permeates the entire fabric of its sound. The best of his works are not "reflections" of life—rather they incarnate the drive and appetites of life affluent in living beings, crowds, masses, and the poignant attachment to life felt by the unfortunates and the "captives." Vitality, actuality, and strength of character are also made manifest with extraordinary intensity in the dynamics and kinetics of Stravinsky's music. True, Stravinsky is no psychological dramaturgist like Tchaikovsky, Verdi, or Musorgsky. It is not the inner subjective experiences of people that fascinate him, but the styles in which people display themselves. Stravinsky's music embodies the motive forces of life and the rhythms that give life its organization. The music also brilliantly and fascinatingly conveys properties and characteristics of human nature as they are summarized in various types of human beings. In so far as Stravinsky's art is firmly grounded in principles inherent in folk art, so for the most part it remains extra-personal and supra-individualistic. The style of the music is individualistic, but its roots and "subjects," its actions and character do not express the experience of an individual personality. They express, rather, the energy of life manifest in natural and human phenomena, as that energy is perceived by humanity as a whole. The highest attainments of Stravinsky's "serious" style are essentially supra-individualistic "actions" (*Sacre* and *Noces); the highest attainments of the comic style are "masks" and "mimes": *Pulcinella* and *Mavra*. *Pulcinella* revives Petrushka, who has escaped the clutches of the magician; in *Mavra,* Stravinsky gives new life to the masks of vaudeville comedy. And everywhere there is life, life, life. The renewal of spring, the violence of the carnival, maidenly languor, masculine rage, ceremonial games and dances still aglow with the savagery of heathen attitudes, the frenzy of festivals, the debauchery of brute force, sparkling laughter and mad rejoicing, languid nightingale songs and somber incantations, the diverting proverbs and tales and impudent fun of children—is all this really not enough to let us recognize, behind a body of work which has opened our ears to so much new and unusual music—to let us recognize the depth of its social significance?—not only in the sense to which I have already alluded (that of musical mentality), but also because it embodies life's riches and vigor in all the variety of their manifestations, because the most diversified materials have been transmuted into art?

Nevertheless, there are people who hold, with the light literature written by his lightheaded enemies, that Stravinsky's music is nothing more than whimsey, or a highly refined grotesque. According to this, for a good part of his life Stravinsky must have supposed himself either a kind of freakish sideshow for the Parisian public, or a reincarnation of Cagliostro, the master hoaxer [Alessandro, Conte di Cagliostro (1743-95), charlatan, magician, and adventurer—Trans.]

Stravinsky, first and foremost, is a master, disciplined, astute, sound, and supremely skillful. At the same time, he has no fear of fun and games. The grotesque is also part of his world, without question. But there are many kinds of grotesque. Stravinsky's grotesque is nourished by a deep sense of irony, the same irony that is found in all great masters, all "great designers." Leonardo knew it, and, to all appearances, for his own contemporaries he was a representative of the grotesque. The Encyclopedists knew it, for all their worship of *ratio*. Even Goethe knew it. I am not comparing Stravinsky to Goethe (but those who are afraid to praise an art not already drowned by the applause of tens of generations should be the last to smirk). I assert only that Stravinsky, like any "designer" who has mastered all the secrets of his trade, has his own irony, an irony that is also present in other "magicians"—magicians to the outer circle of spectators and listeners, that is, not to the experts themselves.

Whence comes this irony? From lassitude? From boredom? Oh, no! There is nothing of Byronism in it, nor—if you please—of Oblomovism (in Goncharov there is also irony and the grotesque). It seems to me that the irony of Stravinsky, like that of many others, proceeds both from pity and from envy (yes, envy) for the great number of people who, like children, can still find amusement in various games and toys because of the secret mechanisms that make them operate. The curious child breaks the toy open, but he does not uncover any secret thereby: the expert knows that there is no secret, but simply, for example, a spring adapted to a form. He pities the child and wants to laugh. The great representatives of every epoch have always embraced the cosmos as it appeared to them, in full, as if there were no room for any further secrets. Thereupon, new ones have floated into sight. Every master's life and art give him ample grounds for an ultimately ironical point of view on either of two grounds: either because he understands that there are no unknowns, and innocence is therefore out-of-date, or because he sees that to know everything is impossible, the final "secret" (the "ultimate cause") making its escape, like sand through the fingers.

We take pride in our firm belief that everything is reducible to simplicity and clarity: that the laws of nature and a universal energy control matter (indeed, one is a form of the other); that life is a mechanism; that death is a natural and normal phenomenon; that reflexes determine our whole behavior in the material world; and that economic and industrial considerations condition all our creative work. Such is the truth of the contemporary world, and music follows in its train. Music becomes entirely constructivist, for, as one of the phenomena or transformations of energy, music is first and foremost material for cultivation, for the organizing and refining powers of human cognition. A music rationally and efficaciously organized does not, by denying belief in a self-sufficient psyche or in the fiction of inspiration—does not become less distinctive or less significant, because the intensity and content of the vital sensations have not been attentuated thereby. Feeling remains feeling. It is one thing, for example, to know that death is a normal and natural phenomenon, and quite another thing to have felt it as such. And even if music ceases to be emotional, it retains its strength nevertheless. It can be dynamic even if extra-emotional; it can remain deeply vital, the bearer of mighty energies, even if it rejects an animism that shrouds the world in its own shadows. Stravinsky, by nature a rigorous realist, knows the contemporary truths about life and composes beautiful music, music that is true to life and its premises at the same time that it comments ironically on the "children" amusing themselves with their illusions. Music expresses everything of which life is composed, the totality of life's relationships. The phenomenal world of music is a mechanically exact world, and it is rhythm, made manifest in the motion of sound patterns, that activates that world. Rhythm gives organization to the materials of sound and to their most intricate and fanciful crystallizations, for rhythm is the vital force of music, its pulse and its constructive principle. The music of Stravinsky leaves no room for emotional interpretations; everything is written as it sounds, and there is no need for arbitrary accelerations and retardations. All is mechanized; through all there runs the rhythm of the machine, for our pulse and our heart are also machines, and life is one of the forms of matter. For those who understand this, life does not thereby become less expressive. And neither does music.

Such are the bases of irony in Stravinsky's music. Irony is its soul, and the grotesque, a natural consequence. One need only look for a moment at the antics of man himself, a tiny mechanical consequence of the rhythmical collisions of particles of matter! Watch him suffer, watch him revel in suffering, grapple for the truth, and perish from the horrors that he creates. The essence of things is not altered a whit thereby. Gaiety and grief are only phenomena of the energy of sound raised to different powers; it is we who perceive and identify the specific qualities as such. Basically, energy is nothing but the play of atoms—like the world.

Despite its irony, however, Stravinsky's music is soundly optimistic. Rhythm, song, and instrumental color live a full life and, like all living things, obey certain general laws of development. The source of irony in Stravinsky's music is less often a sense of malicious ridicule than it is pity for people who seek the essence of things where it is not, and fail to find it where it is. Example: *Petrushka*. But pity can pass over into chagrin and the sarcastic grotesque— and give rise to the sharpness of *Soldat*, in comparison to which *Renard* is just a jolly little buffoonery.

Soldat is one of many variations on an old theme: in this case a soldier who, by common sense, wins out over the wiles of the devil. Actually, at the end Stravinsky's soldier is defeated, but the moral is clear: like Faust, the soldier has lost his powers of sagacity. Despite the essentially syncretic plan (the union of narration, pantomime, dance, and music), *Soldat* is chiefly a musical composition. Such is the fate of all attempts at artistic synthesis in the presence of music, itself the art of the movement and transformation of the energy of sound: music immediately begins to dominate. Therefore, *Soldat* is first and foremost a musical score, a great musical score of the contemporary world that exhibits logic and strength, that makes a brilliant and profound use of the expressiveness of the instruments individually and in ensemble, all this with a maximum economy of expressive means. (The orchestra is composed of violin and contrabass, cornet-a-pistons and trombone, clarinet and bassoon, and a battery of percussion.) There is a complete absence of musical garrulousness, of any kind of superfluous or decorative diffuseness, and an absolute rejection of sentimentality—as if to release the listener's fancy from dependency on habit and make it possible for him to sensate independently. *Soldat* is half symphony and half suite. The presence of plastic and motor-muscular formulations (pacing, dance) is characteristic of the suite; symphonism expresses itself in the energy of the music, in the dynamism of the material, in the presence of dramatic contrasts, and in the intonational and thematic cohesiveness of the musical sections.

Soldat, which was written in 1918 after the sketches of *Noces*, is a complete contrast to *Noces* in one respect: In *Noces*, the vocal element is dominant; in *Soldat*, the instrumental. But they have also basic premises of construction in common: pantomime and dance are, in both, the stimulants of the music, and both exhibit an inventively idiomatic treatment of the percussion instruments. Virtually throughout the work the percussion instruments assert their musical leadership: they are an actual element of the action, it is they who ordain the rhythmic and intonational vitality of the work. They are treated as virtuosos, and not as lifeless antique ornaments or pendants of the score.

The following purely musical analysis of necessity does not exhaust the interesting details of Stravinsky's score. It can only deal with those of principal or more obvious interest.

8

Histoire du soldat

To Be Read, Played and Danced

Part I

Introduction: The Soldier's March

The tempo is set at quarter note-112. The section contains ninety vertical divisions, or measures. The rhythm is crisp and strict, like military discipline. The pace is confident and masculine. The double bass beats out its "organ point"—one, two; one, two—steadily, and almost without interrruption [see ex. 149].

Example 149

The cornet and the trombone set the tone of the entire first part of the march, which is also embellished with rhythms and characteristic melodies of clarinet and bassoon. The percussion is for the moment inactive. The first tutti arrives at measure 50, only to yield quickly to a fanfare-like coda of the bassoon (ff). At measure 64 there is a new and more extensive accumulation of sonority and a powerful tutti that leads, in measure 84, to an unexpected bassoon solo pianissimo. Thence the march proceeds to its final cadence, which imitates the introductory measures. The two dynamically saturated moments "collect" the segments of sonorities that are elsewhere intentionally fragmented, for the lines of the march are often broken by pauses. Only the pace is unchanged, despite the moments of silence—the rhythm is not silenced, and there is virtually no interruption of the basic movement.

The soldier's head is full of random recollections—flashes of barracks life and other details of soldiery—that find their musical equivalents in motives from military calls and intonations of commands, fanfares, and snatches of march melodies. The memories of the barracks have not left him, but they are on the point of doing so. However, he has not yet related himself to the freedom of the world around him: the man is still very much a soldier, and from time to time he rouses himself and begins to march, exactly as he was marching in his company not long before. It is amazing how Stravinsky pieces all these fragments and scraps into one uninterrupted (despite the pauses) line—into one mood, but with varying degrees of tension. He who looks in this march for a "song form with trio" with its usual formal periods and outmoded styles, will miss the basic point: the dynamics of the march *qua* march, and its rhythmic discipline.

The material of the march is very important for the future course of musical events. I therefore quote the basic melodic elements, which are in essence variations and outgrowths of one or two basic motives [see ex. 150]. The last of these later plays an important role in the formal organization of the Little Concert.

Example 150

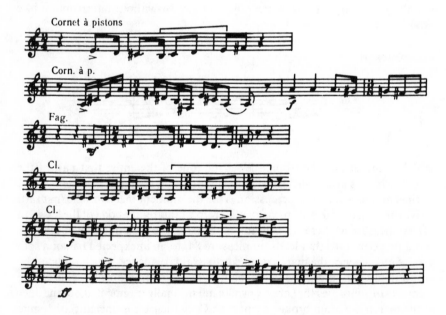

Music for the First Scene

(The edge of a stream; the soldier has sat down to rest; he is playing his violin.) The tempo is now set at quarter note-100. This section contains 106 vertical divisions, or measures. From the "vertical" point of view, as in the march, everything is completely chaotic and arrhythmic, for the vertical divisions themselves are of varying lengths (2/4, 3/8, 5/8, 6/8, 7/8, 3/4) and recur in varying sequences. But from the horizontal point of view, everything seems simple and logical. The whole movement of the concertizing voice (the violin) is ordered according to the principles of improvisation: starting out from a center, the voice comes gradually to establish a wider gravitational field around this central point. This is at one and the same time in an ancient and a modern principle of musical formulation. In this case it takes the following form: the violin melody establishes the melodic center, over an ostinato bass [see ex. 151].

Example 151

First the violin plays alone. There follows a passage of four measures which includes a brief new melodic fragment, and a return to the initial point. Later there is a second excursion further afield that develops elements already present and culminates in the arrival of a new idea as striking as it is surprising [see ex. 152].

Example 152

Stravinsky knows that the character of music that is idiomatic to the violin displays the patterns of moving fingers that have been so trained to explore the geometry of the fingerboard that they seem to keep discovering new designs almost instinctively. This second excursion occupies seventeen measures, not counting the basic melodic element. After a trip so far afield and the discovery of a new melody, Stravinsky returns to a variation of the opening material whose rather extended repetitions suggest that the player is now temporizing in search of new ideas. The bassoon offers a suggestion that is taken over by the clarinet and made over into a typical clarinet idea ("the appearance of the devil")[1] [see ex. 153] The violin continues to improvise, playing variations of its own material and groping for new ideas. Out of all this there emerges a kind of game of instrumental sonorities in which the clarinet is joined by the bassoon, cornet-a-piston, and trombone. This instrumental dialogue is supported by the basso ostinato—the fragment I have already quoted ([ex. 151 b] contrabass pizzicato).

Example 153

(Le diable parait)

The whole music sings. Its rich folk ideas and improvisatory character make it continually attractive and intriguing. The sonorities are fascinating, fresh, full, without the slightest fault or blemish. The passage concludes with a violin "flourish" [see ex. 154].

Example 154

Music for the Second Scene

Lento (quarter note-48). A lovely, picturesque episode of an improvisatory-pastoral character (first bassoon and clarinet, then cornet-a-piston, and ultimately bassoon and clarinet again, over sustained notes of violin and contrabass). In places, the melodic line recalls the song of the fisherman in *Nightingale.*

Music for the Third Scene

A shortened variation of the "soldier's violin."

Part II

Introduction. Variation of the Soldier's March. The Royal March

The Royal March is a remarkably constructed, brilliant episode, a model of exceptional grasp of instrumental technique and knowledge of Spanish rhythms. The tempo is set at quarter note-112. The metrical changes, to the eye, seem capricious, but to the ear the music sounds flexible and beautifully proportioned, and the texture of lines is composed with extraordinary precision—something like looking down from a great height onto a street or a square and seeing the various streams of people, trams, and automobiles compose themselves into a harmony of movement, where from below there is only an impenetrable chaos. The Royal March is a synthesis in musical movement of a great many rhythm-intonations (fanfares, dance themes and their accompaniments, rhythmic motives of the street, of soldiery, and of the formal dance). Although the rhythmic beat reigns supreme, there is at the same time an instability that may vary from one moment to the next as the regular correlations of strong and weak beats are dislocated to form zig-zag sequences [see ex. 155].

Example 155

In contrast to the first march, the texture of this one is much more complex, terse, tightly knit. The lower instrumental parts are freed of the burden of reiterating the organ-point: before the soldier now stand the allurements of a life of freedom. The form of the march is determined by the statement, variation, and repetition of a number of similar thematic elements whose units may succeed each other, or one of which may be incorporated into another. The principal materials are that of the opening (trombone) [see ex. 156] and the material of the cornet-a-piston already quoted [ex. 150]. The third important thematic element takes initially the following form [see ex. 157].

Let us designate the opening motive as A, the musical twist of the cornet-a-piston as B, and that of the example [ex. 157] as C (or A_v, as a variant of the opening), and the fanfare as F. The scheme of the march is therefore as follows (the numerals designate groups of measures):

Example 156

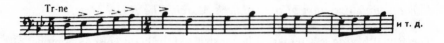

Example 157

A (10):	B (5):A$_v$ (7)	: F (3)		
	B (5):A$_v$ (12)	: B$_v$ (14)	: F (4)	:B$_v$ (6)
	B (6):A$_v$ (19)	: F (5)	: C (6)	
A (4) :	B (5):A$_v$ (16)	: F (2)		
A (10)				

In all, there are 139 measures.[2]

One must also notice that in the majority of cases, the measures flow into one another in such a way that the end of any one period may coincide with the beginning of another. Actually, any schematicization by measures can only be approximate. There is also a paradox: this march, which can be perceived as a strictly vertical composition, is at the same time linear and polyrhythmic and—as if that were not enough—still further complicated by extraordinarily intricate accentuations. The organization of the movement can be approached by grouping the elements in any one of three ways: by motive, by accent, and by rhythmic phase (in the perception of which the vertical coincidences of the elements will be a factor). It is also useful to notice, from a formal point of view, that the two episodes of the "Spanish" march (B$_v$ (14) ; B$_v$ (6)) are supported by an ostinato from the opening march of the work.

Little Concerto

This is a competition of concertizing instruments. The tempo is set at quarter note-120. The violin takes the lead and dominates the whole music. The cornet-a-piston and the clarinet—and later the bassoon—are introduced as rivals. As in the first march, a tutti also appears toward the end as a logical result of dynamic accumulation, and the tutti is followed by the final moments in which the three concertizing instruments (violin, clarinet, and cornet-a-piston) again have the field. The sonorities and form of the movement are the consequence of a brilliant concourse of technique and expression. The movement is, strictly speaking, the high point—the summit toward which the action is drawn and by which it is given a center. Material from all the preceding episodes is used and brought to a point of high intensity. Motives alternate with one another, cross-fertilize one another; pieces of motives are intermingled with other motives; motives are compressed, extended, or shortened. I cannot keep from referring here to Stravinsky's frequent use of oblique vertical displacement, resulting in a texture of strong beats disposed to look like slanting rain, and creating an irregular pattern of cross-rhythms. For example, the treatment of motive B in the Spanish Royal March, or two similar places in the Little Concerto [see ex. 158].

Example 158

We can see in this example how the rhythm immediately begins to decompose, so to speak, how the thematic elements are splintered and measures broken apart, and how the strong and weak beats and the vertical divisions themselves clash against one another in zig-zag fashion. These are two of many similar illustrations that might have been adduced. The equilibrium of such a texture, which lasts in this case nine measures, cannot be established until a new texture (also syncopated) makes its appearance [see ex. 159]

Example 159

By virtue of the way it combines and disposes a variety of motives and melodic elements, the Little Concerto offers us an exemplary model of Stravinsky's motivic technique—the technique of mosaic. His teacher Rimsky-Korsakov approached this technique most clearly in the intricate inter-minglings of vocal and instrumental forces in *Tsar Saltan*. Here the technique is a purely instrumental one, of course. It reveals itself both in the subtle design of the "improvisatory" competition of the solo instruments, and in the alternation of these passages with a tutti (7 players) that has distinctive richness and clarity. As a result of all this (and also because of a certain similarity in the principle of design), the Little Concerto emerges as a complete concerto grosso in miniature. Even Liszt, in enclosing a "cycle of movements" within a sonata of uninterrupted duration, used as a principle of formulation a technique of variation which also produced a mosaic style. It is extremely interesting, with the aid of the melodic materials already quoted, to investigate the construction of the Little Concerto and establish the formal inflections and dynamic phases of the piece.

The first twenty-eight measures are composed for clarinet, cornet-a-piston, and violin in three parallel lines. The materials are developed from the music of the first scene [exs. 152, and 153]. The clarinet fragments which were originally heard at the initial appearance of the devil [ex. 153] play a very prominent role. The beginning of the concerto takes this form [see ex. 160].

Example 160

The chromatic progression of the clarinet (a^1, $a\#^1$, b^1, c^2, b^1, $b\flat^1$, a^1, $a\#^1$, b^1) serves as a thread joining the first episode (twenty-eight measures) to the second, in which the contrabass has an organ point suggesting the opening of the piece. The clarinet and cornet play in thirds, alluding rhythmically to the element A ᵥ from the Royal March, while for eight measures the violin takes over the chromatic thread [ex. 158a]. There is a development of the opening material of the concerto [compare ex. 160 and its variation ex. 158b]. The rhythm of A ᵥappears again, this time highly syncopated, and the final typical clarinet "flourish" brings the whole episode (eight plus nine plus eight measures) to a suitable close [see ex. 161].

Example 161

The cadential use of such an instrumental flourish is one of Stravinsky's wittiest devices.

The third, or instrumental-dynamic, phase of the concerto is marked by the appearance of a new melodic element, but one joined with violin and clarinet materials from the music to the first scene. This new melodic element, feminine in nature (a princess?), introduces an important factor into the music of the concerto: the cornet-a-piston [see ex. 162].

Example 162

Here there is an interesting development of this material, which will later exert a strong influence on the structure and motion of the music. The initial eighteen-measure treatment of this "princess" theme (as we shall call it) is a lyrical dialogue of beautiful clarity. This dialogue is cut off by rhythms from the Royal March, which in this concerto plays the role of refrain, breaking and changing the character of the movement (five measures). Now the violin itself takes over this melody and passes it for variation to the cornet and bassoon. The texture is a beautiful interlacement of melodic segments, which comes to rest after eighteen measures on one of the motives from the Soldier's March [ex. 150, the last fragment][3]. For a while, the likeness of the princess disappears. The whole episode, from the arrival of the new melody through its working out and the interruptive interludes, lasts fifty-five measures (forty-one plus fourteen), measures of unequal length ordered with the fullest vertical asymetry.

The violin next introduces a second, parallel version of the "princess" material. Here are the two versions, side by side [see ex. 163].

Example 163

With this second version there sounds one of the themes from the Soldiers's March [ex. 150, third fragment]. Again the "princess" material is veiled in march rhythms. There follows a brilliant, martial tutti, which concludes with a coda of fifteen measures, also fortissimo, composed of the trilinear texture of the opening in a slightly altered version. The end of the concerto is a sharp, clear break. With the coda, the entire episode lasts forty-one (twenty-six plus fifteen) measures. The scheme of the whole piece is as follows:

The beginning of the composition (a version of the "soldier's violin," the rhythms of the Royal March, continuation of the concerto and new, more persistent intervention of the march rhythms, syncopated): twenty-eight plus eight plus nine plus eight, $28 + 8 + 9 + 8$, totalling fifty-three measures.

Second stage: the presentation of the "princess" material with rhythms of the Royal March: eighteen plus five, totalling twenty-three measures.

Third (principal) stage: two parallel presentations of the "feminine" melodic material (the violin takes the lead in its working out), both being concluded with rhythms and intonations from the Soldier's (and not the Royal) march. The first section is thirty-two measures, the second, more positive and concentrated, lasts twenty-six measures.

Coda (which also serves as reprise): fifteen measures. There are 149 measures in all, at the pace of a quarter note-120.

In form, the "concerto" approaches the sonata-allegro of the synthetic or Lisztian type, because throughout its course it clearly opposes various types of actions and various characters and moods. The first two stages of the concerto compose the exposition. The third stage is the type of development in which use is made of the improvisatory principle of repulsion—that is, (in this case) two parallel but different developments of one theme taking off from a single point of departure. The constrasting rhythms of the "violin" and the two marches set up a tension that seems to carry forward the musical development of the tale. The soldier has finally met up with the love and beauty he has so much desired. Despite a whole series of trials and tribulations,[4] despite the disappearance of his relatives and friends, he still has not lost his will, his courage, or his physical bearing. He himself achieves his own happiness by understanding that daring is half of winning. I repeat, the "concerto" is the center and summit of the action. From this moment the soldier begins a new life, whose first step is winning the love of the princess. Stravinsky describes the course of the romance in a suite of three dances.

Tango

The pace is set at quarter note-80. There is a suggestion of the "theme of the princess" in the violin melody, which also has the improvisatory quality of the "soldier's violin." There is a virtuoso percussion accompaniment (bass drum with cymbal, and side drum without snares). The principal theme [see ex. 164] is developed through thirty-three measures and passes over into the dance of the princess, a dance based on a now familiar motive (accompanied by clarinet) and giving rise to a beautiful bi-tonal passage of eight measures. There follows a varied and compressed repetition of the principal idea (eighteen measures) and a second appearance of the princess theme joined to a coda and occupying in all fourteen measures. There are in all seventy-three vertical divisions, but of course the whole plan of the development flows in horizontals, for the accompaniment (the harmonic basis) has reduced itself to rhythmic intonations of percussion instruments and to a clarinet ostinato accompanying the motive of the princess [see ex. 165]. The melodic line of the dance (played by the solo violin) is remarkable for the technique of its development, which is like a gradual unwinding of a thread knotted with fragmented ideas. Again Stravinsky uses a principle derived from motivic improvisation: from a given starting point, the violinist gropes his way into upper and lower areas of sound, with frequent return to the melodic ideas which have taken root in the digital technique and memory of the improviser. At such moments Stravinsky forms his melodies by a technique which exactly parallels the way in which melodic lines are grown in the musical art of the "oral tradition," where the accumulation and ultimate crystallization of the material is the termination of a process which begins with experimental improvisation and the formation of elementary intonational patterns that imprint themselves on the memory and gradually grow into precise and (now) familiar sequences.

But the melodic element of this tango is not its only interest. There is also the accompaniment, the rhythm-intonations of the percussion. I should like again to point out that both in *Noces* and in *Soldat,* Stravinsky uses the percussion section not as a supplementary group, but as a unit organically

Example 164

Example 165

rooted in the conception of the composition. Not only do the percussion instruments mark the rhythm—they form an organic fundament, a rhythm-texture. In *Soldat,* with even more thoroughness and virtuosity than in previous works, Stravinsky makes use of the elements of percussion in the greatest variety of ways: there are independent rhythm-lines (rhythm-themes), there are rhythm-harmonies (rhythm-complexes), there are layers of poly-rhythm. The percussive "apparatus" becomes highly intricate. One performer must direct the movement and dynamics of an entire "rhythm-texture," using two drums (without resonating snares) of different sizes, a military drum with and without snares, a bass drum, cymbals, tambourine, and triangle. Through the making of detailed differentiations by size, register, timbre, and character of stroke, Stravinsky is enabled to have combinations of exceptional excitement and novelty at his disposal. He is not making background "noises" characterized by percussive strokes that delineate accent, nor is he firing rhythmic "shot." He is creating a sphere of intonations with its own vocabulary of shades and shadows and moods of differing degrees of intensity. In the tango, for the first time in *Soldat,* the potentiality of this vocabulary fully reveals itself, and the variety of timbres and registers makes itself felt with striking sharpness and clarity. The possibilities implicit in the jazz band are here converted into a rich texture of sound-forms of extraordinary luster and exhibiting a masterful degree of differentiation. This is a fully European art. Thus did Mozart in his time convert "Janissary Music" into the sounds of the *Abduction;* thus did Liszt give form to the improvisatory style of the Hungarian gypsies.

Waltz

The tango proceeds without interruption into the amusing little waltz. The pace is set a quarter note-184-192 (the quarter equivalent to the eighth of the tango). There are 114 measures. Only five instruments play: violin, contrabass, clarinet, bassoon, cornet-a-piston. The waltz has something of the familiar *Petrushka* element, but it is more refined. The music is a very clever imitation of the street ensembles of itinerant musicians, combining suggestions of the mechanical restraint and captivating clumsiness of marionettes with a youthful enthusiasm and slyly playful humor. The charming ornaments, delicious accents, and rhythmic irregularities, the surprises of the layered melodies, the motivic fragments arching from register to register, the amusing contrasts of timbre—all these factors compel the ear to an attentiveness that permits not the tiniest ingenuity to escape. The violin remains the leader, and its line the guiding thread. The waltz proceeds without interruption to the Ragtime, and its final twelve measures prepare for the transition by containing the (duple) improvisatory rhythms of the Ragtime within the tripe beat of the waltz: four measures of the waltz melody contain three of the Ragtime (that is, 4 X 3/4 equals 3 X 4/4). Naturally the scoring adheres to the 3/4 measure.

Ragtime

The tempo is lively and cheerful (the quarter note of the waltz equals the eighth of the Ragtime). The smart, sharply syncopated opening motive is given to the violin, accompanied by percussion and contrabass [see ex. 166].

Example 166

The next section is announced by a gay violin theme, out of which there grows a distinctive motive that plays an important role in the following movement (more about this later) [see ex. 167]. To this, the bassoon improvises an ornamental counterpoint [see ex. 168].

Despite the iron grip of the basic rhythm, there are a number of extemporized instrumental excursions, each one more witty and effective than the last. Fragments of old as well as new melodic materials form themselves into fanciful and unexpected combinations and series. Nevertheless, the plastic and resilient line of the dance and its basic motion make themselves constantly felt. A characteristic rhythm figure (dotted sixteenth and a thirty-second) gives

Example 167

Example 168

unity to the different sections of this "broken" dance. The percussion "apparatus," inactive in the Waltz and almost completely so in the concerto, plays a large role here, as it did in the Tango. The form of the Ragtime is similar to that of many old sonatas and can be designated as A + B + C + B + A, section B including one of the important elements of the texture, a violin figure which plays a large part here, and in subsequent phases of the table, and which grows out of the smart opening theme. This figure also bears a relationship to the motives that appeared during the statement of the "princess" theme in the Little Concerto [see ex. 169].

Example 169

The Ragtime takes on an agitated and orgiastic character toward its end. Besides Stravinsky's usual sharp dynamic shifts to and from marcatissimo, sf, p, leggiero, secco, and pesante, short and sharp crescendi and diminuendi (often glissando) also figure importantly here.

By reference to the Little Concerto that precedes it, the Tango also seems made up of a series of dynamic jumps and glides. In place of long emotional intensifications and broad crescendi, Stravinsky habitually prefers sforzando and subito—that is, sudden alternations, or very brief and impetuous changes of intensity lasting a few notes at most, plus glissandi or similar passages idiomatic for individual instrumental technique (like the little "flourishes" that we have already met). Dynamic gradations in Stravinsky's scores of recent years have been very throughly considered and have been ordered with the same exactitude that any composer would give to the usual considerations of voice-leading and the durations of tones. Inasmuch as Stravinsky has no sympathy for the spontaneous, emotional dynamics added by the performer that supposedly give a composition its "animation," preferring rather to build his dynamic intensities into the sonorities of the score, he must of necessity give detailed attention to accentuation, to caesuras, to the disposition of the strengths of sounds, and to the degree of sound saturation. His extreme carefulness in these matters is an important element of his art and must be recognized.

I have already said that the Little Concerto, preceding this suite of dances, is the focal center and summit of the action, dynamic plan, and drama of *Soldat*. Now I shall go further. Analysis of the concerto and the dances that follow it, shows that the whole of this music forms a complex *symphonic circle* composed of: the dramatized sonata-allegro of the concerto (with exposition balanced against development and recapitulation-coda), the Tango as the lyrical slow movement, the Waltz as scherzo, and the concluding "sonata"—the dance-like display of the Ragtime. Thus, if the initial march of the soldier and the improvisatory music of the first scene ("the soldier's violin") present the kernel of the material from which the remainder of the development grows, the "Concerto with Dances" is the central episode in the soldier's "romantic adventure." Logically, the "Concerto with Dances" should be followed by its consequence—a hymn, symbolizing the union of the lovers. So will it be when the chorale arrives, but before this there will appear the devil in his final dance of ecstasy, wherein his furious rage exhausts itself and him, leaving him without force, spent. The stage direction refers to the victory of the soldier and the recovery of the princess[5] and permits the inference that this particular triumph of life over the impersonal forces of evil is yet another variant of one of mankind's cherished illusions. The sharply grotesque dance of the devil also casts a certain doubt on the sanctity and stability of the subsequent marriage. We shall see that the chorale turns out to be the height of irony.

Dance of the Devil

The Dance of the Devil cuts directly across the course of events that is approaching its denouement. It is a brilliant dance, completely without restraint and full of impudence and mockery. "Concerto" elements in their sarcastic, Mephistophelian refraction play a prominent role. The pace is furious, the movement characterized by thrust and counter-thrust, the patterns of accentuation clearly derived from gesture. The dance is allegro, quarter note-138. There are seventy-three measures. The opening has the following appearance [see ex. 170].

Example 170

After an eleven-measure statement of this theme, there begins a "development" consisting of the alternations of variations of material drawn from the two marches and the little concerto. Here are the basic elements of the passage [see ex. 171].

Example 171

a) 2 measures 5/8 = 1 measure 5/4.

b) Over the pedal

c) V-no

And finally

The final link in the chain of dances forged by the devil leads to an abrupt pause: the movement then concludes with a violin glissando and the outcries of trombone and percussion. During moments of great dynamic excitation in Stravinsky's music the impetuous thrust of the sounding lines often endeavors to break through the fetters of the meter, much as in Beethoven's music the element of violence is felt in the struggle between syncopated rhythms and the measure, or in the combat between duple and triple. In the Dance of the Devil, the impetuosity of the movement is greatly intensified by the power of the very accents needed to hold it in check, with the result that the musical stream that is finally released has the force of an arrow or a rocket. One of the elements of this dance that contributes significantly to the force of its energy is the following [see ex. 172].

Example 172

As a whole, the dance is a precise and polished work in which, as in no other place in this composition, the energy of musical thrust makes itself felt.

The Little Chorale, which follows on the Dance of the Devil, signifies the happy uniting of the lovers. The devil offers ironical comments in a flat, metered speaking voice, his couplets accompanied by violin and contrabass ostinato and punctuated by the phrases of cornet and trombone. He prophesies the soldier's sudden doom, but the lovers have thoughts only for their happiness in one another—they have no ears for his threatening. The soldier cares for nothing except what he has and what he has attained; he has no reason, therefore, to be afraid. At this point the "big" chorale begins, signifying the triumph of a virtue that has welcomed the regency of love, is grateful for small favors, and wants for nothing else. The chorale moves in a Largo, quarter note-54. The clarinet, bassoon, cornet-a-piston and trombone form four voices over a background of tremolo violin and contrabass. The chorale is self-contained, it sounds rich and substantial. Stravinsky has been a keen auditor of everything that is most characteristic of the ordinary, traditional singing of the Protestant community and has transcribed it into the sounds of this chorale. The most amusing aspect of this grotesque is the attention that the cadences draw to themselves by virtue of their style: they seem to be saying that everything comes out well in the end, because they always succeed in bringing together into the most innocuous consonant chords, lines that have been moving toward the limits of individualized utterance. Seven such cadences, with fermatas, certainly signify peace and contentment. But the eighth is left hanging in the air by an unresolved 6/4 chord. The earth itself has dropped away from under the feet of our happy hero! It is happiness that has finally wearied him, in truth, and lured by the memories of his native land and the mother whom he has abandoned, he again sets forth toward new adventures, like the indefatigable Faust.

It is interesting to note that shortly after *Soldat,* the figure of Faust was resurrected again in the opera of Busoni—not the Faust of Goethe, but no less interesting for being more antiquated, since each generation of necessity leaves the imprint of its own experience on the favorite issue of its collective imagination. The sixteenth and seventeenth centuries did it, as did the eighteenth, and nineteenth, and the twentieth is doing it also. It is noteworthy that the "devil" in Stravinsky's tale is as multi-faceted as the Mephistopheles in Busoni's opera *Faust.* Two of the most powerful synthesizing intelligences among the musicians of Europe, each giving collective unity to a heterogeneous aggregate of cultural traditions, arrived almost simultaneously at similar conceptions, however different may have been their outcome. Humanity still loves its "adventurists," restless, discontent, eternally alert. In truth, the distance that separates the "Russian soldier" from the old Doctor of Alchemy is not so great. There is less sulphur, less fireworks, but otherwise the essence of the Faustian theater remains unchanged.

As a story, *Soldat* seems to come to a very natural conclusion: every person who is dissatisfied with what he has done and who refuses to sit contentedly at home, will find his destruction in some adventure or other, just as the soldier finds his. Earlier, we might have been confident that the devil would carry the soldier off into hell, and the text of *Soldat* even concludes with this prediction. But is this what his music tells us? Call it hell, or give it any name you wish, at the end of the very expressive triumphal march of the devil (the last episode of *Soldat*), the soldier actually vanishes—that is, his soul, his "I," vanishes, whereupon all the live instruments, all those possessing "voices," gradually fall silent. Only the violin in the hands of the devil continues to "fight for its life." At the end, the percussion instruments remain alone, beating out their steady rhythmic pattern.

The grotesque chorale is followed by the triumphal march in order to provide *Soldat* with a theatrically more convincing finale, because it would scarcely have been worth the complexities of the rhythms and intonations of this piece only to convey at the end the rather vulgar thought that the fulfillment of any life properly animated and free to follow its natural course is the attainment of constant, habitual domestic bliss. The splendid tutti with which the march opens, presents one of the motives from the Royal March, which is grotesquely "inflated" in order to convey by exaggeration a caricature of diabolical power and might [see ex. 173].

Example 173

But this lasts only three measures. Then the motive disappears, almost as if it has been ripped out of the texture. Balance is restored by the sharp, clear military fanfare, which is followed by a sort of route marching theme with a firm beat. The violin then recalls one of its improvisations from Ragtime [original in ex. 169]. Fifteen measures of the march have now elapsed.

The pathos of the opening measures is reinstated (the same theme, almost literally repeated) and is again broken off after three measures. The violin then plays a sarcastic variation of the "princess" melody [see ex. 174].

Example 174

The whole episode lasts twelve measures, after which the first motive once again enters triumphantly for two measures and then yields to a ten-measure ironic variation of the "princess" melody that in its turn is interrupted by the fanfare. The opening motive now appears for a fourth time, and in its original form. This fourth statement of the opening measures signals the beginning of a repeat of the entire first section but *without* the martial interruptions. After the fanfare has again been reached, the first episode is partially restated again, but this time without the introductory march measures. The new form of the large repeated section occupies forty-three measures.[6] The terminal episode lasts twenty-nine measures, of which the final fourteen are given to percussion alone. The plan of the ending is the gradual extinction of the convulsive motions of the violin that still tease the ear of the soldier with the motive of the princess. The march motive, almost unrecognized, passes quickly by. Only the percussion is left. Again a short, convulsive movement of the violin—its last. No living figure remains. But the rhythm of life does not change—it goes on quite as before. However, the melos connected with the figure of the soldier, and reflecting his feelings, his reactions to life—the melos vanishes, since there is no longer a sentient being. How unlike this are the splendors of Isolde's last moments, or the finale of the Sixth Symphony [i.e. of Tchaikovsky—Trans.]! Death in *Soldat* is more laconic, more simple, and, by virtue of its simplicity, more tragic. The March of the Devil recalls the many ways in which the "Dance of Death" has found expression in the legacy of the fine arts. Stravinsky's "engraving" of the final fascinating moments of his tale might have been entitled: The devil plays his violin before the soldier, beckoning him to follow after. Neither in conception nor in fulfillment is Stravinsky inferior to Holbein. Only the irony of Stravinsky is deeper and more sophisticated.

Can it really be maintained, on the basis of such an ending, that Stravinsky is a pessimist? or that his art is nothing more than the regrettable outcome of a century of decline? One can, it seems to me, find just as firm a basis for maintaining the exact opposite—namely, that Stravinsky, born a joker and a fabulist, and looking around for something with which to shock the bored Parisians, simply hit upon the idea of concluding this work with the sound of drums, and nothing more. Let us leave such fantasies. As composition, this work is so intricate and at the same time so organic that it is impossible not to treat it with full respect, even though every innovator must wait a long time for even a primitive (from the cultural point of view) respect to come and replace the baseless nullifications of the critics whose decisions are reached according to the principle: my taste is final. Stravinsky's ending to *Soldat* is right. Don't forget that *Soldat* was written during a period of frightful carnage when there was plenty of justification for pessimism. But there is no pessimism in *Soldat*. There is pity for a departing life, there is irony, and there is, if you will, skepticism: Stravinsky seems to be asking, when I am no longer a sentient being, will there be any future me in eternal change, eternal transmutation? or is all life just a rhythmic pulsation in the noisy roar of eternity? Perhaps so. There was the same irony in Rabelais, in Cervantes, in Leonardo da Vinci. Have those who have concluded their tales with gay wedding feasts never really felt pity for life, or never sensed the irony of the inevitable sadness which is the outcome of all such revelry? It would be sorry so. Their art would have benefited from such depth of feeling. The art of Rimsky-Korsakov, for example, shows this, in the contrast between the formality of the concluding gloria of *Kitezh* and the finale of *The Golden Cockerel*. But it would be laughable, for any such reason, to count Rimsky-Korsakov among the pessimists and to say that because his art does not convey the joy of life, it is therefore socially harmful.

I see in *Soldat* the affirmation of life, just as I saw it in *Sacre* and *Noces*—but a life of severity and enormous power, a life that moves mechanically like a machine, a life which is self-sufficient, and which destroys the unruly and the weak. The primary law of all life is rhythm. Rhythm proceeds from movement and controls all movement. All our senses are rhythmic, and especially our sense of hearing, for outside of rhythm it is difficult to conceive the nature of the material of sound; without rhythm, that material remains scattered and unordered. Since rhythm is most directly perceived through motor-muscular sensations, the most abiding intonations are those that have been most closely connected with such sensations—through gesture, movement, and dance, and finally through the sound of words. Dance is the primary agent of form and movement in Stravinsky's art.

The score of *Soldat* is saturated with the rhythms of intonated movement (gesture, pace, dance) from beginning to end, without surcease or failure. It is march rhythm that activates this specific work. There is no place here for indifference or indolence, for cold or passive contemplation—only movement, only a constant and inevitable changing of aspects and phenomena. Life is thus, reality is thus. Do all our aspirations and "adventures"—the pursuit of the pleasures of love, the struggle for power and fame, for riches and creativity—do all these therefore become less inviting? But even if they should, nothing would be changed: man has no power over the machine of life. His feelings and his consciousness are mechanisms activated by springs, wound up when he is born. People refuse to see this, and create such illusions as the affections, "good and evil," "free will," etc., as countervailing antitheses. Stravinsky's thought is developed amid the constant and deeply contemporary antagonism of theses and antitheses themselves the products of his creative imagination, of his penchant for critical thought on the one hand and for the romance of the fable on the other. One might have thought that at a time when much had been clarified and when the whole life of the mind had come to be regarded as nothing more than a private conceit—that at such a time there would be no place for such antagonisms. But man separates himself from his illusions only with difficulty, especially so from the illusions of "good and evil." Kashchey, "sorcerer," "devil"—these are all images conceived by the imagination of the composer, and one of the most significant manifestations of contemporary musical thought is the very existence of these images. Even our direct sensual perception of phenomena is weighted with similar superstitions to the same degree: without them, man's life becomes "empty," at best a machine, propagating imponderable values. Is this not really the kernel of Stravinsky's skepticism?

Notes

1. This theme plays an important role in the "Little Concerto."

2. 140 measures in the piano reduction, because the measure (3/4) before the final statement of the opening material is divided into two (2/4 and 2/8) for the sake of a strong accent.

3. This chromatic motive is related, of course, to the clarinet "thread" that is later taken over by the violin [ex. 158a].

4. The devil has succeeded in acquiring the soldier's violin in exchange for flattering and rosy promises. The soldier overstays his leave and becomes lost. When, after the passage of many years, he returns to his native place, no one recognizes him. A lonely figure, he seeks forgetfulness in wealth, but finding neither happiness nor peace, he renounces everything and becomes a beggar again. Chance now brings him, a fugitive, to a land where fortune and love's happiness smile on him.

5. Here is the stage direction: After the dance, the devil, exhausted, falls to the ground. At a sign from the soldier, the princess grasps the devil by the paw and they both drag him into the wings. When they return, they fall into each other's arms. The music plays the chorale ("le petit choral").

6. The improvisatory principle of construction is also present: each new development moves off from a starting point of its own.

9

Pulcinella[1]

Stravinsky's reversion to the formal models and intonations of the seventeenth and first half of the eighteenth centuries points to a search for a firm basis for the erection of deeply contemporary constructions. Just as in architecture there is a constant search for the "eternal" material, of great solidity and durability, and just as today the contemporary iron-and-concrete building has achieved a classical monumentality and universality by virtue of its constructive clarity, the sober simplicity of its form, and the degree to which it exposes the qualities of its materials, so Stravinsky's art remains strong, healthy, and rationally organized no matter where it goes for its materials, and it does not fear to assimilate everything that is useful to its growth. The enemies of Stravinsky have tried to depict his music as decadent, as a fabrication pandering to Parisian taste, and as having the impermanence of a seasonal fashion. All this, I repeat, is a batch of lies and slander promulgated by those whose expectations Stravinsky did not live up to. Of course he did not live up to them—he surpassed them, first of all, and then went on to become his own dictator of standards and taste. He was the one who first borrowed materials, assimilated them, and gave them an unique newness unknown before him. He did this with the technique of the "Belaiev School," then with the techniques of impressionism and the jazz band, both of which were in turn left far behind after *Noces* and *Soldat*. It was he who broke ground for contemporary composers, and they who followed him,—not the other way around. One could not have been alive, and still have failed to hear—even in the Octet—intonations that are strong, vigorous, and full of a confident creativity.

In this light, I regard *Pulcinella* not as an intermediate step in Stravinsky's creative career, but as a completely natural attempt by a Russian master who has gained his place on the universal musical stage, to turn, like the artist Ivanov, to the monumental forms of the past that survive to our day, for a fundamental and solid basis for all his later conceptions. Those forms have endured because they so clearly comprehend inalterable and extremely economical principles of construction that have a general relevance. Whereas in *Soldat*, Stravinsky utilized the greatest variety of intonations and created an universal "histoire" out of a Russian theme, in *Pulcinella* he imposed severe restrictions on himself and, without losing his own identity, borrowed musical materials that had already been utilized by the great Italian G.B. Pergolesi (1710-36). These materials he reproduced in a new setting, but one appropriate to their simple graphic clarity. The resulting suite, or chain of musical statements, makes in its turn new use of classical Renaissance principles of musical formulation.

But *Pulcinella* is not stylized or arbitrarily archaic to the degree that one might at first believe. Despite obvious identity of material, Stravinsky's fragrant music is neither repetitive nor slavishly imitative of Pergolesi. In *Pulcinella,* as in any genuinely contemporary work, there is economy—even asceticism—in the choice of expressive means, and a continuing attempt to speak not in the intricate schemes of abstraction but in an unaffected musical language that is melodic, alive, and heart-warming. The forms that articulate the musical speech are clear and easily grasped, and compose a succession of pieces danced and sung. But the principal delight of *Pulcinella* lies in the fact that again (and again, moreover, by a Russian composer, following the lead of Glinka and Tchaikovsky) the beautiful plasticity of Italian melody—eternally alive, eternally fascinating—is treated with love and tenderness. There is always present in European music some element borrowed from the fund of inexhaustible energy created by Italian melody. For the music of Europe, indeed, the legacy of Italian melody constitutes a kind of universal reserve—a sort of musical "central heating system." No matter what the attacks on the "hostility" of the Italian style, the public has never successfully been delivered from the clutches of this alleged enemy. When, from time to time, a composer from any country comes into contact with that source of radiance, heat, and health, and when he starts to drink deeply of it and convert its potential energy into active force—such is the beginning of radiant works. Very few of the great masters of music have escaped the Italian influence, and those who have, have been the losers. Among those who have not escaped—besides Glinka and Tchaikovsky—I can mention Bach and Mozart, Berlioz and Bizet, Wagner (alas, yes—and from whom? Bellini!—and where? even in *Tristan!)*[2] and Richard Strauss. This recurrent contact with the Italian melos has thus borne fruit in every epoch, and the principal significance and value of *Pulcinella* lie in the way the Italian melos is refracted to produce a contemporary work of art.

I think that, as a source of stylistic refreshment and refinement, contact with Italy has an importance for Stravinsky's art equal to that of the poetry of Pushkin. The Italian influence is evident, for example, in the lean, graceful, plastic lines of the Octet, just as the irony of Pushkin inspires and sharpens the spirit of the grotesque in Stravinsky's *Mavra*. Essentially, *Pulcinella* is, like *Mavra,* also anecdote and also vaudeville, but the principles and methods of the Italian commedia dell'arte which the composer came up against in

Pulcinella are more general, more basic, and more pervasive than those of the traditional vaudeville-opera in Russia. These principles, of course, had their own influence on flexibility of form and expressiveness of language.

Characteristic of *Pulcinella* are the austerity of its construction, rigid economy of means, and a classical control of compositional techniques. The design is clean and has the clarity of an etching. There is a basic diatonicism, expressed in the great number of tonics and tonic-dominant harmonies, and in careful attention to the forms of the perfect cadence and to conventional uses of the leading tone—meaning an absence of the troublesome "German" dominant [i.e., the German sixth f-a-c-d♯—Trans.]. The instrumental color is transparent and lyrically expressive: the "soul" of every instrument and the character peculiar to it may be heard in every phrase. To a greater degree here than in *Petrushka* or *Renard,* and not less than in *Soldat,* the instruments are treated as characters in the gay comedy. They are the doubles of the figures on the stage, and their music is the mirror of everything that goes on there.

The musical content of *Pulcinella* is extraordinarily simple. It is, as I have said, a chain of episodes danced and sung, related to one another according to the principles of the suite, and distinguished from one another by a great variety of technical contrast. Rhythm, meter, tonality, timbre, tempo (speed and character of the motion), dynamics (force and intensity of the motion), design, chordal complexes, the varied relationships of melodic lines—all the elements, in brief, that make up a composition, are used as actual "concertizing" factors in each comic incident. In essence, Pulcinella is one continuous dialogue of instrumental lines, because whenever a given dramatic situation may pose the confrontation of conflicting elements, the various musical articulations and contrasts that provide material for the musical organization of the scene are not just simple formal methods, but ideas that activate and rule the very dynamic of the action itself. Pieces differing in style and character follow one another according to some preconceived plan and constitute a chain of causes and effects, statements and counterstatements. The links of this chain are logically and organically so ordered as to produce a constant dialectical intensification that ultimately permits the disengagement of a unified musical content out of the widest variety of materials. I shall have occasion to speak further about this point, which is basic to the principle of "concerted" music. I broach the subject here in order to show how the episodes of *Pulcinella* are related and in what sense they are mutually interdependent. Let us not forget that here, as in the madrigal comedies of the sixteenth century, the sound of the human voice is added to the instrumental texture. One might even say that the whole work refers simultaneously to the instrumental suite and to elements of the intermezzo or cantata. Certainly, the moments of vocal and instrumental "concertizing" dialogue, and the alternation of solo episodes with tutti, play a role of basic importance. The score shows the typical concerto grosso differentiation between the string tutti and the solo string and wind instruments, and the use of these and other typical devices permits Stravinsky to show both the universal relevance of the old forms and the flexibility of contemporary technique. The aspect of Stravinsky's genius that enables him to expose the universality of these formal and technical interrelationships is, I might add, a hallmark of Russian genius and Russian culture. In this sense, there is a relationship between *Pulcinella* and the little Boldino tragedies of Pushkin. [*The Covetous Knight, Mozart and Salieri, Don Juan (The Stone Guest),* and *The Feast in the Time of the Plague,* all completed at Boldino within a period of two weeks in the fall of 1830—Trans.]

Having looked at the general plan of the music of *Pulcinella,* let us turn to the details. The whole composition is divisible into a few large sections, each with its own subdivisions. The ballet begins with an overture or symphony (G major, allegro moderato, 4/4). The principal theme, an idea whose "pompous" character befits its position at the head of the work, is presented three times in keys that are related according to classical principles [see ex. 175].

Example 175

The overture is followed by a melancholy and charmingly tender serenade (tenor solo, larghetto, c minor, 12/8). This is a typically Italian cantilena, the solo oboe first announcing the tenor melody, whose vocal phrases are punctuated by the "dry" splashing of pizzicato strings that form the ritornelli. The oboe melody begins in this way [see ex. 176].

Example 176

The airy sonorities of this piece are among Stravinsky's most remarkable accomplishments. The strings, flautando and in harmonics, are wonderfully combined with "quivering" cello harmonics on the open fifth c^1-g^1, doubled by the flutes. There is a masterful use of the different registers of oboe and flute (here, as in *Sacre* at the beginning of part two, Stravinsky uses flute harmonics). One texture is overlain with another in a marvelously transparent way. There are also inner chordal trills, and pizzicati used to imitate percussion instruments, a favorite compositional device at once old and eternally fresh. All this combines to produce a deeply poetic atmosphere. In my opinion, this piece can rank with the serenades of Mozart (and particularly from the *Abduction)* as the best and most typical examples of such pieces.

The serenade is immediately succeeded by a light C-major scherzino in 4/4 (a series of dialogues: oboes and violins, soli and tutti strings, and others). The first section of the scherzo is joined by a brief episode (poco piu vivo, 2/4) to the gay and frisky allegro (A major, 3/8), where the concertizing solo violin plays the leading role. The music is led on by a short connective episode to a typical pastoral dialogue of exquisite tenderness (andantino, F major, 2/4). Here the principals are solo violin, horn, flutes (again with harmonics) and finally bassoon, all over a transparent background of strings and winds. A brisk and highly humorous allegro (B♭ major, 2/4) succeeds the intimate pastorale and in its turn is followed by a coquettish canzonet (D major allegretto, 4/4) sung by the soprano. Up to this point the prevailing "tone" had been bright and clear, only occasionally shadowed over by brief and beautiful melancholy phrases that recall the chromaticism of Mozart.

The canzonet's melody has unwound itself and is about to stop, when the mood is suddenly exploded by an allegro aria (c minor, 3/8), grotesque, willful, capricious, and stormy. This is a violently "dynamic" episode, built on a strongly rhythmic, hot-tempered, and volatile theme, and making maximum use of the sharp shock of chordal attacks. Frightening though these attacks may be initially, their violence portends more noise than action, for the music tends to spin around in one spot, and at its close returns to the opening chords.

The following allegro (G major, alla breve) has an amusing melodic idea wedded to a stumbling, almost staggering, rhythm. The orchestral introduction first presents the material that is later taken up by the bass solo and made into a grotesque aria, one of the brilliant vocal episodes of the ballet. Here is the beginning of the melody [see ex. 177].

Example 177

After this buffo-aria, the character of the music is sharply altered and passes on into the sedate calm of the largo (E♭ major, 3/8). This slowly unfolding movement has a majestic Handelian quality and a peculiar gentleness that combine to make it a perfect complement to the grotesque music that has preceded it. A vocal trio (soprano, tenor, and bass) joins the orchestra in development of the original idea, which passes from the sunny brightness of Eb major to the gloomy darkness of Eb minor and the tenor's lament on the theme of the serenade. The duet that follows (soprano and tenor), passionate and agitated in character, terminates this group of pieces. The two voices in octaves lead the way through the contrasting key of F major to the chirring bustle of the orchestral scherzo (d minor, alla breve), whose musical idea is shortly taken up by the tenor. This "patter" song, whose rhythm suggests the comedy of a cinematic "chase," is abruptly cut off by one incisive chord composed of the A major triad over the open fifth Eb-Bb. There is a moment's silence, and then the doleful gloom of the lament returns (largo, 6/16). The repetition of this episode not only fails to restore the musical balance that was upset by its first appearance, but as a matter of fact the repetition actually increases the intensity by being inserted between the runaway presto and the new episode (allegro, G major, alla breve) that follows.

Thus, beginning with the bass buffo aria, the musical movement is more volatile and subject to more violent changes than was the case in the first section of the work. Indeed, the changes of tempo and rhythm begin to resemble the chain-like constructions of the finales of the old Italian comic operas, where the episodes are threaded one after another onto music that rolls toward its denouement in an increasingly animated whirl of ideas.

Returning to the g minor episode (allegro, alla breve), we see that it is a self-contained whole that acts as an intermezzo, as an eddy in the flow of the musical action. It begins with an octave motive of majestic, pompous severity, the second part of which is a descending sequence. Here is the beginning [see ex. 178].

Example 178

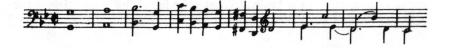

Stravinsky's technique, of course, enables him to handle a monothematic development of this type, and in *Pulcinella* he does it not without success.

The playful gaiety and friskiness of the tarantella (allegro moderato, Bb major, 6/8) cover all traces of the haughty fugato, and stand in sharp contrast to the ensuing soprano aria of Pergolesi, the famous "Se tu m'ami, se tu sospiri" (andantino, f minor, 2/4) ["Se tu m'ami, se tu sospiri sol per me, gentil pastor," aria for soprano, now attributed to Alessandro Parisotti (1855-1913)—Trans.], whose sad mood is dispersed by the bright impudence of the following toccata.[3]

The toccata (allegro, E major, 2/4), is in a style that recalls Scarlatti, and transforms the mood of the work into a final one of bright cheerfulness. The piece is almost entirely played by winds (the trumpet, freely imitated by the bassoon, directs the movement), the strings being used as accent, or to carry the movement from one register to another. Here is the way the movement begins [see ex. 179].

Example 179

The charming gavotte for winds (allegro moderato, D major, 4/4) is one of the gems of *Pulcinella* (the other being the serenade). The gavotte melody [ex. 180] serves as a theme for two variations, also for winds. The first is an allegretto, D major, 6/8, and the second an allegro piu tosto moderato, 4/4. The lines of the oboe, horn, flute, and bassoon are woven into a tasteful pattern with occasional touches of decorative humor. The next episode (vivo, F major, 2/4)—the "duel" of trombone and contrabass—is a rough and raw grotesque, and the freshness of its sounds is strikingly effective. The music is clearly plastic, laden with gesture, as if it were itself the impersonation of an illustrious buffo, some gay character out of the commedia dell'arte who is an old hand at the repertory of comic routines. The concertizing instruments perform with enormous gaiety and impudence a parody of a typical comic scene in the Italian style. This duet is succeeded by a minuet, sedate and flowing, but with a suggestion of pretense and bourgeois provinciality that are alien to the court style. The music affects a simple artlessness (minuetto, molto moderato, F major, 3/8), and the instrumentation is partly serious, partly amusing. The horn carries the melody at first, and then the strings. The character of the bassoon counterpoint is obviously buffo, and its humor sets it off from the string accompaniment. When the opening motive is repeated, the bass, tenor, and soprano participate in the texture as the principal melodic elements. The comparatively placid and stately mood of the minuet is broken into by the loud commotion of the final gay C major rondo with its two contrasting themes (finale, allegro assai, C major, 4/4). Amid the rhythmic hurly-burly of noisy salutes, with the tutti chords crying bravo in advance, the music concludes its witty stylistic commentary. As always with Stravinsky, the festive elements, once they have gained the foreground, are handled with brilliance and temperament. Here is the theme of the minuet and the two themes (a and b) of the concluding rondo [see ex. 181].

Example 180

Example 181

The music of *Pulcinella* adheres to strict tonal relationships as a unifying principle. In this work, Stravinsky almost never departs from the principles of construction that are expressed in the classical relationships of major-minor and tonic-dominant. There are tonal surprises that break this classical pattern, but these can easily be explained by the fact that the proper connectives have been elided to produce an effect of tonal contrast. Each of the "surprises," furthermore, is subsequently heard as logical within the general plan. C major (c minor) and G major are the principal tonalities, and they give rise to dominants and to parallels above and below.

The whole work is notable for the kind of simplicity that is the reward of great effort and long experience, for rhythmic flexibility, for mobile melodic lines that are notably clear and clean, and for extraordinary transparency of sound. The suite has the same dynamic basis as the instrumental suite (concerto grosso) and the old operatic finale. The quality of the music is buoyant throughout. Of course, one should not expect the music to be a slavish imitation of Pergolesi. Clearly, Stravinsky's intention was to rid Pergolesi's melody of the sentimental excrescences of the salon arrangements of the second half of the nineteenth century, excrescences that imposed on his ardent and passionate music the stamp of a deliberate effeminacy wholly out of character with the vigor of Italian melody, a melody that is not, so to speak, erotically individualistic, but expressive of the broad sentiments of a whole society. Pergolesi died at the age of twenty-six. He loved life, and women. He was a warm, sensitive man, a hard worker who made his own way with exceptional energy and pertinacity. Along with pages of charming amorous tenderness and intoxicating lyricism, Pergolesi wrote music full of the strength and vigor of the sap of life, and brilliant passages where humor, youthful energy and deviltry, and an irrepressibly lighthearted gaiety, are given free reign. It is just these elements of Pergolesi's style that Stravinsky's music has so brilliantly refracted.

The Suite for small orchestra from the ballet includes the following episodes: (I) Symphonic Overture: (II) Serenade; (III) Scherzino, allegro and andantino; (IV) Tarantella; (V) Toccata; (VI) Gavotte with two variations; (VII) Duet (trombone and contrabass); (VIII) Minuet and Finale. The Suite for piano and violin, also drawn from the music of the ballet, is so well-proportioned and organized that one might have thought it wholly original. I shall speak again of this.

Notes

1. This essay was adapted, with several changes, corrections, and additions, from my article in the collection "Igor Stravinsky and his ballet *Pulcinella*" (Leningrad, Academia, 1926).

2. Alfredo Casella had the wit to remark on this in his good and valuable work *L'evoluzione della musica a traverso la storia della cadenza perfetta.*

3. The designations "scherzino," "tarantella," and "toccata," are not found in the piano score. I take them from the score of the orchestral suite.

10

Mavra

Comic Opera in One Act, after Pushkin. Text by Boris Kochno.

This opera, dedicated to the memory of Pushkin, Glinka, and Tchaikovsky, was written in 1922 and had its first performance in Paris in the summer of that year. The character of the conception and the style of the music are greatly influenced by the three individuals to whom the score is dedicated.[1] Pushkin, Glinka, and Tchaikovsky were all great Russian artists who maintained the closest relationships with their environments. Never did their works—even those of the highest artistic quality—fail to reflect the dynamics and details of actual life. For them, life in all its aspects and fullness—its energy, its activities, its roots and traditions—was material to be converted into various systems of rhythms and intonations where were themselves added enrichments of that life.

Let us regard *Mavra* as a way of combining rhythms and intonations such that rhythm itself is the plastic basis of the musical form that prevents the scattering of the intonations, and the intonations are brought into existence to act as the dynamic and emotional "soul" of rhythm, each sound, sung or played, presupposing precise muscular effort or the controlled expenditure of breath. No matter how severely rigid the construction of any piece, a change in the disposition of the particular dynamic arrangements will create the sensation of a change in intensity: no such music, no matter how strict, can ever be completely without feeling. Rhythms and intonations, of course, are normally quite as inseparable from each other as pulse beats are from the filling and emptying of the body's vessels with blood. It is only mechanical instruments, in the playing of which human breathing has no part and where "acoustical pulsation" (change in oscillation) is controlled by the flow of extra-human energy—only such instruments can be used to make a music completely abstract, of cosmic severity, and—like nature and the machine—"indifferent" to human emotion.

Thus the area in which organizational schemes are simplest is that which is the plain expression of ordinary life and its emotions. But in the area of expressivity that is the result of artistic organization and of a rational choice of materials (rhythms and intonations)—in art music, that is, there is usually generated a permanent conflict between a bias toward emotionalism and a bias toward intellectualism. In extreme cases of the latter, indeed, one reaches quite a different area—that of musical constructionism and extra-emotional energetics—music without a soul, in the sense that philosophical concepts, mathematics, and machines can be said to be without souls. Here music pretends to the status of pure thought and becomes wholly intellectual. To some, this kind of music seems void of vitality and vigor, and it was precisely under such a conception that the emotional nineteenth century came near to excluding from the history of musical development whole epochs of so-called abstract contrivances (for example, the fifteenth-century Netherlands school), though it had the grace to recognize their validity as "preparatory exercises" to any worthwhile musical accomplishment.

Stravinsky's development, like that of any great, sensitive artist, cannot pursue a rationally determined straight line. He now stands on the border between two worlds. Having opened up new paths for "pure" music, and having experimented in his latest purely constructionist instrumental works with a new kind of dynamic symphonism, he has now returned to the theater (with the opera *Oedipus* and the ballet *Apollon*).

In *Mavra,* he was still moving directly toward ordinary life, choosing to approach it through the little grotesque story of Pushkin that sparkles with the humor of everyday "truths."

Mavra is an old Russian vaudeville dealing with an incident in the Thirty Years' War.[2] Both the vaudeville itself and its musical version are original, coherent, and organic works. The character of the musical rhythms and intonations is determined by the nature of the work and the materials appropriate to it, the work itself being a typically Russian petit-bourgeois lyrico-sentimental romance with music of the same type. One can get into endless arguments about its merits—whether it is "bad taste," "pseudo-Russian style," a kind of "gypsy music," just plain vulgar, etc. But the fact is that ever since the 1820s this style has been the favorite everyday musical language of the petit-bourgeois segments of our society—the language that they have used for spontaneous musical expression. Glinka, Dargomyzhsky, and Tchaikovsky were not afraid to come to grips with this language and convert it into artistic speech, without loss of freshness or vital warmth. Neither was Stravinsky, and the fact that he used different methods of formulation gave the material even greater chance to remain true to itself and retain its natural qualities. In *Mavra,* Stravinsky does not imitate or stylize.[3] He gives this everyday musical language a formal expression that enables it to reach a full bloom. Far from doing violence to its natural qualities, he utilizes them to the full.

This petit-bourgeois melos has absorbed many of the scale formations of Russian folksong, many of the emotional intonational patterns of gypsy music (how much of the "Russian East" comes from just that source!), and a host of "Italianisms," from Bellini and Rossini to Verdi. The "St. Petersburg Teutonic," so picturesquely drawn by Pushkin in *Onegin,* has also made its contribution to this intonational "potpourri" in the form of couplets, little songs, and sentimental romances out of old Singspiels and from Weber. One has only to glance at popular collections of vaudevilles and other Russian pieces of many kinds to find elements of this so-called "pseudo-Russian" musical language derived not only from Aliabiev, Varlamov, Gurilev, and Verstovsky, not only from Tchaikovsky, but also from Glinka, Dargomyzhsky, and Musorgsky. The melodies of everyday Russian music have a quite striking cleanness and suppleness, they are plastic, expressive, unaffected. These are qualities that do not just appear by themselves even in the melodies of the "art" song. They have been fashioned through generations of big composers and little composers, of unknown improvisers and singers, each of whom made his contribution to this musical and emotional language. And if we forget aesthetic prescription for a moment and look at the simple facts, "sentimental Russian melos" and "gypsy elements" and "Italian elements"—these are enormously valuable musical factors that no strong composer has ever feared, that all strong composers have really loved, because they knew that life itself sang in those terms. Of course, each composer utilizes them according to his own style and purposes.

The texture of *Mavra* is that of the familiar vaudeville, brim full of the many emotional and melodic elements to which reference has already been made. Stravinsky, by dedicating his work to Glinka, Pushkin, and Tchaikovsky, points to the range of his imaginative efforts, to the limits within which his imagination worked, to the area that formed the background of his work. He does not want to say that *Mavra* belongs only to the epoch of Pushkin, but that the material that has gone into it, dates from that time and has been kept alive through succeeding generations. It is still alive, even now, as I have said. In terms of the range of its materials, therefore, *Mavra* is a synthetic work, but from the particular choices that Stravinsky makes, there emerges a complex of great intricacy in which melodic elements from Glinka, Dargomyzhsky, and Tchaikovsky are intermixed with "cruel" love songs for voice and guitar, with the sentimental middle-class merchant lyricism of brides and their confidantes out of Ostrovsky, with the rollicking gypsy songs of all sorts of bohemian types—officers, actresses, literary figures—and even with snatches of "military music."[4] The choices are made by the skillful hand and the cultivated ear of a musician who knows, understands, appreciates, and loves his material and is completely at home in it. At the same time, *Mavra* is a little grotesque quite in the style of Pushkin or Glinka. There is no trace of the later horrors of Gogol, or the hallucinations and anguish of Tchaikovsky's *Queen of Spades,* or the humor of Chekhov's world, whose petit-bourgeois inhabitants find themselves in blind alleys they know not how. The expository style is compact, laconic. Each person sings only as much as is absolutely necessary to convey with the utmost clarity "type," character, and feelings. There are four "types," and not individual personalities: soprano, mezzo, contralto, and tenor. The result is an ensemble in the style of Mozart, where the writing for each voice exhibits precisely those qualities that characterize the "type."

Parasha (soprano) is a young maiden, bored, looking for a fiancé, and ready for any kind of "adventure." She offers little resistance to the voices of nature, but her submission is less corrupt than it is naive. Her character is revealed in the music written for her—music in the style of the sentimental love song of the 1830s and 1840s, but always less affected, more genuine. Many Russian maidens have poured out their love in melodies like this—and still do [see ex. 182]. This passage is charmingly expressive of her coquettish mistrust [see ex. 183].

Example 182

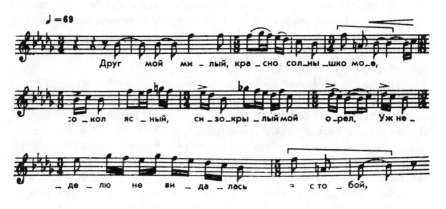

Example 183

The melodic models seem to be Glinka's Antonida and, in several places, Dargomyzhsky's Natasha, but the vocal line is richer and more florid and its emotional content truer to life, in the sense that Stravinsky succeeds in combining the music of everyday speech with the rhythm of the conventional song to make a unified, coherent whole. Parasha speaks as she sings and sings as she speaks: she is sincere, trustful, loving—and in the presence of her mother reserved and cunning without loss of artlessness. Only the extraordinary insight of the composer could have produced a pattern of musical "speech" of such touching simplicity and seductive tenderness.

The hussar (tenor, who is also the cook Mavra) is a complete contrast. Not because his music is artful, or resembles the studied speech of the theatrical *ingenu.* Nothing of the sort. This hussar is genuinely amorous and romantically disposed. But whereas Parasha tends to regard her love for Mavra as an eternal commitment, the hussar treats the whole affair as a happy accident. His boldness is utterly natural, not mischievous. He is self-assured, persistent, passionate, impatient, wholly free of vulgar charm or sensual nastiness. His intentions are pure spontaneity. Here are a few characteristic passages, somewhat gypsy in style, having the character of melancholy elegies that partake of the poetical moods of Polezhaev and "tearful" improvisations with guitar accompaniment, in the style of Apollon Grigor'ev [see ex. 184].

Example 184

The music given to each of the characters of *Mavra* is designed to convey temperament, character, habits, manner of speech, and general appearance. Parasha's melody, for example, does not utilize disjunct intervals or "temperamental" rhythms. It has a smoothly gliding line and lightly playful melodic ideas with occasional decorative leaps—suggesting sometimes a lullaby, sometimes the spontaneously flowing song of the skylark. The hussar, on the other hand, is always trying to stun and overwhelm Parasha, to catch her up in the shocks and floods of his spontaneous ardor. His "entrances" are bold, and his cadences passionate, with a final little ascending run that halts the melodic motion for a moment, just before the final notes. That is his style in dialogue with Parasha. Left alone, he becomes a little more dreamful, if not less ardent. His lyric monologue—the elegy before the shaving scene—is his most remarkable musical moment and one of the best passages of the entire work. Never in Russian opera has the ambiance of the love song with guitar accompaniment, or the character of the person who sings such a piece, been portrayed more accurately, more truthfully, or with greater art. In spite of the many times this type of ardent and passionate wooer of maidens' dreams has been portrayed in Russian literature and painting, no one before Stravinsky has so well grasped and conveyed his essential qualities. This song is the classic example—the complete and finished characterization—of this species of musical lyricism, in which the improvisatory and stereotypical constantly reinforce one another to produce an emotional effect that is inseparable from the formal design. The disappointed seducer, found everywhere in Russian life and art, has here been given its ultimate musical definition.

Together with its instrumental introduction, this song has a duration of 101 measures, in slow tempo (lento, quarter note-80, poco rubato). The vocal line is strung out through eighty-nine measures without interruption or pause. The first eight measures of the melody are its "kernel," its point of departure, always to be kept in mind and, after an amazing development, ultimately to be revisited. The following eighty-one measures pass without even a momentary break in the developing melodic intensity. The melody blazes up, glows, and dies down, forming a line which rises and falls in graceful arcs. The rhythm of its delicate design is suddenly broken—as easily, it seems, as one would break the delicate stem of a flower. But no, the lightest of accents restores the motion, and thereby gives the interruption the quality of a pause for breath, a pause which itself becomes an integral part of the musical statement. After the best of Glinka, Dargomyzhsky, and Tchaikovsky, I know of no other more completely "virile" melody of this kind that so typifies the songs from which it is derived without in any way being a deliberate stylization of particular folk elements. The form of the elegy's line is, of course, highly organic. Its range is from f^1 to a^2. I will try to describe the process by which it unfolds, because I think that understanding its movement and growth may be the key to a contemporary understanding of form.

The first eight measures ($b\flat$ minor), the "kernel" of the melody, form a line within the limits of two conjunct tetrachords with a center on $b\flat^1$. The basic direction of the line is downward [see ex. 185].

Example 185

The center does not remain on b♭^{1}, however. It moves to a♭^{1}, and a further development is evoked. In the course of a further variation of the basic idea, Stravinsky arrives at a♭^{1} a second time. In similar fashion, each of the successive arching developments is a variation of the first ten measures.

Here is one variation (immediately following the preceding example) [see ex. 186]. Comparing this to the "basic" form of the theme, we find that the absence of the phrase "Ya zhdu pokorno, drug" also leads to the omission of the corresponding sixteenth-note motion. But, as the following example shows, it is only the position of the sixteenth-notes in the phrase that has been changed, for they ultimately appear as part of a new development of the idea [see ex. 187].

Example 186

Example 187

So far the movement of the line has been continuous, and it remains so, passing on into a middle section that now and then suggests the music of Glinka's Ratmir. The figure of the hussar is thereby given a new poetic dimension, and the subsequent denouement an added subtlety.

The structure of the middle section is determined by the manner in which the original material is developed, a fact that examination of the music quickly reveals. Only a composer who was a natural melodist and sensitive to the horizontal could have achieved such melodic coherence. Here Stravinsky shows himself to be a master of the organic development of supple vocal melody. I quote almost all of the "middle section," up to the return of the opening sounds [see ex. 188].

Example 188

The range extends up to a^2, thereby continuing the line's gradual ascent through $e\flat^2$, f^2, $g\flat^2$, $a\flat^2$. Looking closely, we see that the basic unifying thematic element is a two-measure descending motive (motive "a" [ex. 185], of which motive "b" is an imitation). There are other variations of the same motive [exs. 186, 187].

Of especial beauty is the appearance of the key of b minor in measures 5-7 [ex. 188], the way in which the line descends to a^1, and the grand arc (a sort of "rainbow") that rises up and over from this point [see ex. 189]. The form of the arc was prefigured in the motives for the textual fragments "Ya zhdu pokorno, drug" and "Vozniknet pervaya zvezda vo mgle." The following smaller arc ("i dnei nedavnikh vozdykhan'e") has the wonderful effect of moving the tonal

Example 189

center from b minor to b♭ minor and leads naturally to a variation of the earlier ascending run. The device of permitting the tonal center to slide down a half step in this manner may be frequently found in later works of Stravinsky, beginning with *Soldat*, and there may be earlier examples that have escaped my attention. Obviously, the technique of lowering the level of the central linear pitch turns the tonality into an unexpected area. This is not a modulation in the usual sense, but an original and particularly beautiful way of refracting the course of the line so that it suddenly finds itself in an intonational sphere different from the one in which it began. One result of such refraction is that the implications of the melody are deepened and enriched. Stravinsky drew on the experience of life itself for this technical device. In my opinion, the source of the device may have been his observation of pitch slides in the singing of unaccompanied choruses and individuals—slides that often take place without knowledge of the performers themselves. It may be this kind of observation that he has converted into an artistic device. Referring to one of the instances of its use in *Soldat* (the "Marche royal"), the conductor Ernest Ansermet kindly suggested that the impulse for it may have come from the wavering and sliding pitch level of the gramophone. Thus, though I may be wrong about the specific origin, my opinion seems confirmed and even strengthened: that the device does illustrate how details of sound behaviour in everyday life can be converted by an artist into valid technical procedure.

But the melody does not come to a stop in b♭ minor. It moves on to trace a new outline and further to develop motives that are already familiar [see ex. 190]. Only after eighty-one measures of such development do the implications of measures 7-8 of the original idea find complete expression and bring the piece to an end.

The sources of this melody go back to Glinka and his times, but some of its qualities seem derived in part from a later style more characteristic of the genre in the 1850s and 1860s, the details of which have not crystallized even in our time, although the creative forces that originally evoked the style were products of a society that is no more. This is often the case in the evolution of intonations: they develop in a given milieu and are sung and played by people who find in them wholly adequate means of expressing their experiences and feelings. When the society that produced the intonations is replaced by another with equally firm traditions, the development continues, but in a different direction. Generation after generation will remake its musical inheritance after

Example 190

its own spirit—some of that inheritance, but by no means all of it. Part of it becomes stereotyped, crystallized, ossified, giving expression, so it seems to some "median" emotional tone common to great numbers of people, and sometimes continuing to serve as a vehicle of expression through several epochs. It is in this way that those thematic-melodic fragments have been formed, that persist and reappear in a variety of melodic contexts. The memory seizes on them as familiar combinations of sounds, as intonational prototypes, and the creative imagination makes use of them as the foundation and starting-point of its improvisations. These, it seems to me, are the basic premises of the development of melody and of linearity in general. In music of the "oral tradition," instinct, memory, the processes of association, and an aural conservatism (which clings to the familiar) play much larger parts than in an intellectual, rationally based, musical tradition. In the former, it is premises similar to the ones I have mentioned that are the basis of musical formulation and that must be reckoned with by anyone who wishes to develop a sense for linearity and thereby root out one of the basic qualities of music: melos, and melodic development, the processes by which melodies are formed and what conditions are favorable to their propagation.

If we keep our eyes only on the peaks of musical and intonational development—on individual works of major significance—and if we concern ourselves only with metrical matters, for example, then we divorce musical evolution from everything that gives it life, from everything that makes it a real language of the emotions. By ignoring the sound, in other words, we ignore the very factors that determine the plan of construction and the form. The techniques of *Noces, Pulcinella, Soldat, Renard,* and *Mavra* are the richer and more organic for having embraced the rhythmo-intonational experience of the whole of human culture from the moment when the elementary ranges and sequences of sounds were fixed in the human consciousness, and not just forward from the late Renaissance through the Enlightenment and the nineteeth century. Through the poetry of Great Russia, *Noces* makes contact with the most basic intonational patterns of rural life. *Noces* is, essentially, outside of history. *Renard,* being a comical—sometimes even farcical—buffoonery, deals with a world of intonations that is closer to us and evokes, in spirit if not in detail, the whole world of "plays" and madrigal intermezzi. *Pulcinella* relates to the commedia dell'arte, the intonational sphere of the late Renaissance. *Soldat* utilizes intonations of enormous scope, ranging from the primitive rural improvisations of village life down to our contemporary constructionist urban dances, its intonational model—the march—thereby being given a variety of styles and genres. In this music Stravinsky prefigures the road he will take into the extra-theatrical world of his more recent work. But of all these pieces it is *Mavra* (with *Pulcinella,* of course) that opens up historically the most specific and the most self-contained spheres of intonations: the romantic song of the urban culture of the 1820s, which formed a musical style that still lives in our time.

Thus the whole constellation of musical intonations, the combinations and organic conjunctions of sounds played, sung, and intellectually conceived, is of an infinite richness and multiformity. It contains within it the sum of society's experiences, though its qualities may be differently perceived by different social groups. To ignore or to be indifferent to the totality of its details for any reason would, for the investigator, be tantamount to reading pseudo-history. Does the naturalist refuse to recognize a species of flora or fauna just because he does not like it?

The dialogue of the other two characters of *Mavra*—the mother (contralto) and the neighbor (mezzo)—constitute a sort of narrative mémoire that utterly contrasts with the love songs. They talk about the weather, about friends and old times, and they gossip, gossip, gossip. The intonational speech is full of interrogatives, salutations, injunctions, admonishments, expressions of surprise, "ohs" and "ahs," etc., etc. Stravinsky here lovingly and wittily continues a long tradition in Russian opera: his prototype was Larina, and one of the basic melodic ideas of Parasha's mother is almost identical with a phrase of Larina from *Onegin,* and with the music of the song "Evening" *(Vecher),* one of Tchaikovsky's charming evocations of rural life [see ex. 191].

Tchaikovsky in his time was much upbraided for his bad declamation: incorrect accents, ungrammatical word-couplings, pauses in the wrong places, metrical confusion, etc., etc. The given models were Dargomyzhsky, Musorgsky, and the salon speech of Cui. We can leave Cui to one side, but we must deal with the general reproaches made to Tchaikovsky, because in the declamation of mother and neighbor, Stravinsky readily and obviously used as models

Example 191

Из _ ба _ ви бог при _ слу _ гу, дочь мо _ я, те _ рять:

or:

Где взять ку _ харку? Сведай у со _ седки, не зна_ет ли? Де_ше_вы_е так редки.

Tchaikovsky (Larina, the nurse), Dargomyzhsky (*Rusalka,* and not *The Stone Guest),* and Glinka (*A Life for the Tsar,* and some of the songs). Standards of correctness and incorrectness have nothing to do with the matter. The central problem is to define the music of speech—speech that differs in style according to epoch, rank, the organization of society, and the personality of the individual. Speech may be narrative, it may be filled with interjections, exclamations, interrogatives, declarations. The problem is to catch its whole excitement and explosive violence without loss of continuity. Therein lies the key difficulty in writing dialogues and vocal ensembles.[5] In addition, reproaches of the kind I have mentioned are also compounded of stimuli from reading, and the intonations of written style, on the one hand, and on the other from the pathos of theatrical speech. When we listen to a foreigner whose language we do not understand, it is easy for us to catch the musical sense and emotional tone of his speech, its melos, its continuity, and it is just those things that we have stopped attending to in our own native language environment, where we have been schooled to listen only to the meanings of the words. In the ariosos and recitatives of Russian opera there are several "manners" of declamation that can be distinguished. As far as their impact on the ear is concerned, they can be reduced to these four: (a) broad melodic declamation characterized by singability and a clearly prominent and almost continuous melodic line in which purely grammatical musical punctuation plays no part, the interruptions either having a purely emotional basis or being arranged for the necessary intake of breath; (b) an explosive speech, full of accents, vocal jumps, and intonations characteristic of such a style: a broken line, no continuous melody, a desire to emphasize every word and every thought; (c) in the first case, we must make a further distinction between folksong and composed music; (d) in the second, we must also take into consideration the genre and character of individual speech, as well as the degree of grammatic formality, the influence of poetic line and meter, and the influence of the pathos of theatrical declamation. With the exception of Marfa, Musorgsky's music is dominated by the "explosive" style; and if there is melody, it is carefully designed to convey one particular genre and character. Dargomyzhsky's music touches on all types. In many respects, I cannot rate his *Rusalka* below his *Stone Guest*. But the style of his music is not so highly particularized as Musorgsky's—the intonations are synthetic, the musical language is that of the cultured St. Petersburg nobility of the 1840-60s, but minus the full-bodied folk element. One can find obvious traces of the speech of the intelligentsia, and much of the affected salon speech of the merchant bureaucracy. It is this species of intonations that Cui enthusiastically adopts and mixes with the lyric poetry of the French salon to arrive at stereotyped formulae.

Let us now look at Tchaikovsky's declamation in the light of these comments. All of it is wholly synthetic melody, but without much differentiation with respect to genre. This material comes from gypsy lyricism, from Italian melody, and from the songs and romances of the urban intelligentsia. Its particular style, however, derives wholly from the music of the speech of the Russian middle class, a speech which at that time had neither turned fashionably literary nor begun to show signs of violent nervousness. It is a type of speech that can still be heard in the provinces. Words pour out in unbroken melodic lines, commas are ignored, breaths are taken not where grammar dictates but simply where they can be caught—with the result that it is emotional tone and its nuances that take splendid precedence over sense. There is no trace of theatrical pathos here. It is probable that Tchaikovsky's close friends and acquaintances talked like this, especially in Moscow and in the little country seats where he so liked to live. The "St. Petersburg" intonations in his music are of quite another sort.

In writing *Onegin* and in trying for simplicity, Tchaikovsky was instinctively led to convey this simplicity in musical terms via the ordinary intonations that he was accustomed to hear in the speech of those around him. Actually, these intonations were not far removed from the language spoken by the rural and urban intelligentsia in Pushkin's time. The busy and bustling landladies and mothers, the nurses and housekeepers unmindful of the "world" outside, the wives completely absorbed in the details of daily living and reacting to the events of life in purely emotional terms—these people intoned their emotions in a sing-song speech which, when it became narrative, moved within the limits of a smallish middle range. I well remember hearing this speech in capital circles in the 1890s, spoken by the lower classes of civil servants and the small intelligentsia. Any musician-philologist who wants to understand the evolution of melody and is interested in the relationships between that melody and the intonations of speech, will find inexhaustible materials in the literature of Russian vocal music. Then, perhaps, we will begin to have a real appreciation of Tchaikovsky's *Onegin* and begin to see why this opera was so loved by more than one generation, despite the contempt of many arbiters of taste and critics of art.

I have so far discussed only the beginning of the musical speech of mother and neighbor. After Parasha has been sent off, the mother gives herself over to recollections of the deceased cook Fekla and her various virtues. It is a charming narrative elegy (f minor) with just the right touch of self-pity to convey the regret always felt by older people for days that are no more. The middle section of the song (F major) is a bright, agreeable pastorale, charmingly ornamented by its instrumental accompaniment. Throughout all of *Mavra,* the accompaniments are striking. Their wit and fascinations derive from the way in which they reflect emotional sensitivity and portray masterful characterizations within the context of a seemingly "mechanical" motion. This is accomplished by the most "casual" scattering of accents, turns, thematic fragments, codettas, ritornelli, intentionally shuffled sequences of chords, etc. There is nothing extravagant or queer for its own sake, nothing coarsely grotesque, but the greatest latitude is utilized to provide striking settings that still convey the characteristic qualities of the love songs and other intonations. Whether sounding alone or acting as accompaniment, the basic content of the instrumental texture always sounds familiar and comfortable. Its design is austere, clean, laconic, severely tailored to situation and mood.

Let us take a closer look at the episodes of the opera.

A charming overture in B♭ major makes clever use of four very characteristic melodic types [see ex. 192]:

- a. a slow, archaic diatonic theme
- b. a typical urban song melody, resembling *"Vdol' da po rechke"*
- c. a lively instrumental dance
- d. a folk-like dance melody

Example 192

After statements of these themes, the overture again takes up theme (b) and afterward a melody distantly related to theme (a). The overture concludes in the style of Glinka: with chords like harmonies of the first opera, and with scalewise progressions up and down. The overture is followed directly by Parasha's song, the B♭ major of the overture changing to b♭ minor. Then comes the hussar's song: "Kolokol'chiki zvenyat" [ex. 184] that, by means of an abrupt change of key and tempo (from B♭ minor to b minor, and from quarter note - 69 to quarter note - 120) evokes the quite different mood of gypsy ardor. After giving the hussar a chance to declare his extravagant attentions, Parasha tries to dampen his ardor by suggesting a slight change of subject:

U pesen vsekh slova odni
Skazhite mne zamesto pen'ya,
Kak proveli vy eti dni
Ot seredy do voskresen'ya.

Her attempt is serious and coquettish at the same time. For a time the hussar lowers both his emotional tone and his register, but he suddenly gets carried away again and moves into a more lyrical style [see ex. 193]. This arioso evokes further coquettish objections from Parasha, set forth in the characteristic rhythms of the vaudeville couplet, with a suggestion of the style of Dargomyzhsky's *Rusalka*. From this moment on the dialogue becomes more intense. The hussar seizes the maiden's phrases and enlarges on them [see ex. 194]. The music becomes more passionate, the texture filled with syncopations and chromaticisms. Finally both voices cadence together, and there follows the love duet (g minor), quite in the style of the conventional love song with a theme typical of the 1830s [see ex. 195]. The end of the duet is inconclusive, like twilight: G major alternates with g minor. The melodic line then becomes a busy recitative [see ex. 196].

Example 193

Ах, Па_ра_ша, при_зна_ю_ся, я то_бо_ю по_ло_нен.

Example 194

Бе_лой гру_ди ко_лы_ха_нье, снег зат_мившей бе_лиз_ной.

Example 195

Example 196

Left alone, Parasha again resumes her "bourgeois" melody in b minor. But the mood changes: the music becomes more narrative and begins to treat conversational trivia. The mother (whose musical style is illustrated [ex. 191]) brings the conversation around to the servant problem and asks Parasha, without paying her much mind, to seek the advice of a neighbor. Parasha's retort to her mother is handsomely stated and beautifully accompanied. We spoke earlier of the recollections of the deceased cook. The neighbor Petrovna (mezzo) interrupts these [see ex. 197].

Example 197

The gossiping begins. In all respects, this dialogue of mother and neighbor stands in complete contrast to the love music. Its character is different, and its "subjects" as well—weather, God's will, the servant problem, high prices. Bits of Glinka, Dargomyzhsky *(Rusalka),* Tchaikovsky (the duet of Tatiana and her nurse), and various airs and songs of less well-known composers find their way into this conversation. Like Mozart in the *Abduction,* Stravinsky takes what seem to be the most stereotyped and hackneyed intonations and transforms them into a brilliant and persuasive music. He adds new lustre to the currency of sound. He seizes on what others have long since discarded, and demonstrates that any of these intonational patterns can be made to radiate the smile of life, that all these intonations contain hidden sources of musical energy. The whole of *Mavra* is like this. The conversation of the neighbor and mother is rather lengthy. It is characterized by a duple measure and a rhythm like that of the couplet and pieces of that genre. Here are the most important themes [see ex. 198].

Example 198

Mavra is full of such syncopated, arching melodies (found also in Dargomyzhsky and Rimsky-Korsakov). The texture of these curving lines, ornamented with little flourishes and broken only by exclamations and protestations, gives to the conversation a deliberately naive character. The neighbor occasionally breaks out into unseemly cackles [see ex. 199], but Parasha's mother soothes her with the weight of her authoritative replies.

Example 199

до _ ро _ же с каж_дым   ча _ сом   вновь...

The appearance of Parasha with the cook puts an end to this play of musical ideas, and to the endless succession of trivial comments on events of no consequence.

Then begins the amusing scene of the hiring of the cook. Strictly speaking, this is the central musical episode of the opera, since all the characters come together to form the large ensemble—the quartet. The voices are so disposed that the cook (the hussar in disguise) carries the principal melody [see ex. 200].

The other three voices are variously grouped and given rather independent rhythms, but they pursue the "ideas" of the cook, commenting on them, developing them, imitating them, being generally sympathetic and commiserative. It is interesting that the principal key of this piece is the "pathetic" c minor,

Example 200

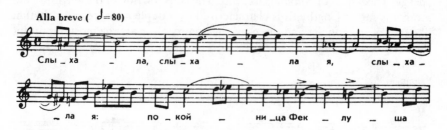

and even the departures from it (d minor, g minor, c minor, G major) serve to reinforce the grotesquely ardent character of the cook's music. For all its complexity, the quartet's texture remains clear throughout. Here is one of the "labyrinths," or, more accurately, entanglements from which Stravinsky easily extricates himself [see ex. 201—a continuation of the cook's melody quoted in ex. 200].[6]

Example 201

The last phrase of the new cook *("sluzhila vam userdno desyat' let")* is taken from a phrase of the neighbor in the previous dialogue [see ex. 202]. This is repeated by Parasha twice *("Ya govorila mnogo ne voz'met...," "Ya dumayu, polezen byl moi trud").* The bracketed phrase in the mother's line [ex. 201] also repeats the initial motive of the whole ensemble—the music of the mother's question to Parasha when she reappeared with the cook: "What took

Example 202

а це _ ну вы у _ знай _ те на _ пе _ ред

you so long?" (page 41 of the piano score). Thus the characters are all caught up in a web of intonational strands that winds itself first around one, then around another. And a network of rhythm is fashioned in the same manner. I should like to call attention to another fact of importance: the disjunct intervals that characterize ex. 202, and especially the melodic progression of the minor seventh. As the *Stone Guest* of Dargomyzhsky shows, the interval of the minor seventh is used in dialogue to express surprise, an unforseen result, doubt, or the desire to lead a conversation astray, and it sometimes connotes a didactic declaration. Notice that in the previous dialogue of Parasha and the hussar, there was almost no instance of the melodic minor seventh occuring without its third and fifth as well.[7]

The seventh begins to be important in the dialogue of the two older ladies and is used to express amazement and surprise [see ex. 203].

Example 203

О _ де _ ла божь _ я бла _ го _ дать   Не забы _ вай _ те   и не _ дуг

The organic character of Stravinsky's musical speech is illustrated by the following: Parasha, fearing that the cook may not be hired, and overhearing the neighbor's comment about wages, twice uses the neighbor's musical idea herself as she emphasizes the "reasonableness" of the new servant's demands. And the cook, in turn, observing that the neighbor is acting as counsel in the matter, reiterates the same melodic idea.

One more observation, and then we move forward. The material for the principal melodic idea given to the cook (hussar) in the quartet is derived from Mavra's answer to her mother's question: "What is your name?" [see ex. 204]. Again, the music of the mother's question to Parasha, "What took you so long?" [see ex. 205] is inserted almost literally into the texture of the quartet [ex. 201]. In other words, the materials of the ensemble are prepared in the hiring scene, and the following ensemble collects, combines, and assimilates these materials and thus brings their development to a logical climax.

The fragment of the quartet's texture quoted in ex. 201 virtually terminates its first section, which serves to establish the fact that "the deceased

Example 204

Example 205

Fekla gave ten years of loyal service." Now the three female voices develop the thesis of "devoted service" with a new motive sung at the unison and octave [see ex. 206].

Example 206

The great significance of this motive for the later development of the ensemble resides in the fact that it introduces an element of mock-heroic pathos that considerably deepens the grotesque character of the situation. The march-like rhythm of this motive in pompous iambics is enormously amusing and places all the other material in a new perspective. Against the background of the established c-minor, this flash of d-minor stands out in very amusing contrast, made doubly so by the fact that the key cannot maintain itself and immediately begins to disintegrate. Thanks to the A♭, the original tonality can be easily reasserted. But after the introduction of a new textual idea—"she never once broke her word"—the texture of the quartet again becomes saturated with sound and reaches a new level of intensity: beyond all possible shadow of a doubt, Fekla was a paragon of staunchness and valor. The music almost becomes a hymn in honor of her virtues. Dramatic upward flights of the voices, momentous pauses, emphatic unisons and octaves—in a word, every device that could confirm the earnest seriousness of the moment is made part of this "funeral feast" in honor of the deceased cook. After this climax, the neighbor does her best to sustain the operatic pathos of the pompous military iambics by exhorting the new servant "in every respect to follow the example of the old." She is joined by mother and daughter and receives the obliging response of the cook (hussar): "I hope all will be satisfactory" [see ex. 207]. This concludes the hussar's participation in the ensemble. There follows the G-major coda, in which the neighbor sings a new melody that is taken up by Parasha and her mother in turn:

Nu kak, zabyv raschety i dela
Ne skazhesh' pryamo, chto ona mila.

Example 207

На _ де _ юсь, все   ос _ та _ нут ˙_ ся   до _ воль _ ный

A short larghetto in the rhythm of a Siciliano serves as a transition to the love duet: the neighbor excuses herself and departs; Parasha's mother gives her a few parting instructions and also leaves. The action returns to its starting-point: to bourgeois lyricism, to the dialogue of Parasha and the hussar, and to the original tonality (b♭ minor). At the initial joyous outburst (con moto, quarter note - 110) the music boldly assumes the character of a Russian gypsy song. One of the melodic fragments that undergoes extensive development is very typical of its time [see ex. 208]. The duet proper begins as follows [see ex. 209]. Here Stravinsky walks in the footsteps of Dargomyzhsky and, occasionally, in those of Tchaikovsky also. The movement and melodic outline of the duets in both the first and second acts of *Rusalka* were also in their time literal representations of the (Russo-Slavic) musical life of the era.[8] Here is one more typical, and still different, combination of melodic elements [see ex. 210].

Then an episode meno mosso recalls Parasha's song with which the opera began (the first bit of recapitulation). The quicker tempo returns and sweeps the lovers along in a flow of familiar melodic elements that is punctuated by further brief passages of recapitulation and occasional new materials. The hussar's ardent melodic idea [ex. 208] takes on a more pensive aspect and forms an eddy in the musical movement [see ex. 211]. "But you never told me," replies Parasha. The character of the music undergoes a sharp change: the key of f♯ minor is introduced, with the characteristic triplets of the accompanied ballad song. A "romantic tone" is established—I am reminded of the f-minor Fantasy of Schubert [see ex. 212].

But the anxiety and doubt are resolved into resolution and faith. The final climax, in the best tradition of operatic rejoicing, confirms the victory [see ex.

Example 208

Example 209

Example 210

Example 211

Example 212

Example 213

Те_перь   то _ ми _ тель _ ный   за_прет   на _ ру_шен,   те_перь то _ ми_

213]. And the epoch reasserts itself: instead of a hymn-like finale, the finale is in fact a "Hymn to Cupid" cast as a lyric waltz. After the joyous outbursts, the exchanges of vows, recapitulation of earlier anxieties and a climactic and grotesque operatic "credo" ("Our happiness shall have no end"), the arrival of the waltz abruptly restores the atmosphere of domestic "adventure" and acts as preparation for the concluding episode.

Stravinsky's duet is completely successful. He uses the vocal couplet as the technical basis for the ardent dialogue of the lovers and varies its flow with changes of mood, including amusing allusion to romantic dreams and heroic pathos. His final sentimental lyricism à la Weber is the natural consequence of all that has preceded it. When the lovers have come to an end with the traditional sixths, and when the C-major triad has been heard in the accompaniment, the mother's voice sounds from behind the scenes in a new tonality (e - c♯): the spell is shattered! "Mamasha" begins her domestic chatter anew, to familiar material [ex. 191 and others].

I have already spoken about the hussar's elegy (sung after the departure of Parasha and her mother). I repeat: the whole composition is magnificent, the melodic line is perfection itself, the style is beyond reproach (no slavish imitation of the past), and the accompaniment by wind orchestra, suggesting the military band, is an amusing commentary on the situation.

The hussar's song ends with the transference of one of its themes to the accompaniment. The music soon fades away, and the mood changes from a poetic to a more neutral color: "Perhaps this is the time to shave." The shaving scene is announced simply, by this phrase [see ex. 214].

Example 214

По _ жа _ луй, вре _ мя на _ сту _ пи _ ло по _ брить _ ся

The denouement (coda) is built over a continual organ point and an unchangeable rhythmic pattern of the following type (horns) [see ex. 215].

Example 215

The ending is short and unexpected. Stravinsky asks that the accompaniment by played *piano* right down to its last note, except for occasional little sforzando shocks that break the machine-like rhythmic regularity like the sounds of a misfiring motor. The hussar's situation is desperate and beyond help ("Good Lord, help me escape!"). Over the regular rhythms of the horns, Stravinsky's voices—now sung, now spoken—are like little bursts of lightning, little exclamatory flashes that illuminate the neutral rhythmic background. There is no crescendo, no accelerando, nothing resembles the usual comic finale. The characters are half dumb, they can only utter little cries, they get in each other's way—and not knowing what to do next, they make a great fuss of doing nothing. Any other kind of comic finale with the customary racket, singing, and endless intrigue, would have been false. Here Stravinsky feels the primary need to convey the nonsensical absurdity of the whole anecdote, the atmosphere of casual confusion caused by the sudden weight of disaster that collapses the carefully constructed plan.

> Togda potuplennye vzglyady
> Zazhgutsya plamenem lyubvi,
> I ty do utrennei prokhlady,
> Vnimaya zamysly moi,
> Moi lyubovnye priznan'ya
> I dnei nedavnikh vozdykhan'ya
> Uznaesh' vse, sklonyac' ko mne
> V blagoslovennoi tishine.

And suddenly, in place of this: "the cook is shaving!", "scoundrel! thief!", "God save us, quickly!", "Stop, thief!", and the wails of Parasha leaning out the window: "Vassily!"

There is no sort of extensive terminal music. The mother faints, the hussar jumps out the window, the neighbor is completely bewildered, and the maiden bids her dreams farewell. The logical development of the action has been utterly frustrated, and Stravinsky's music ends with a mechanically repetitious rhythmic pulsation.

Mavra is an opera of extraordinary originality. Stravinsky took the urban, sentimental, "cruel" love song, the normal vehicle of dreams and tears, and gave it new color and life. He also used the songs and couplet forms that were the favorites of the lower middle class world. He brilliantly continued the ironic tradition of Dargomyzhsky, giving his figures and characters a new illumination and a sharpened outline, and he did all this with the love and tender sympathy of a great master. Passing over the sinister and fantastic grotesque of Gogol and Dostoevsky, he turned back directly to Pushkin and combined the principles of contemporary constructionism with sharpness of observation and an artistic treatment of domestic life. The value of *Mavra* resides in the fact that the ingenuousness of reality finds a new and authentic musical utterance.

Notes

1. I have already had occasion to speak about this in my article in "Igor Stravinsky and his ballet *Pulcinella,*" (Academia, Leningrad, 1926)

2. Compared to *Sacre, Noces,* and *Soldat,* both *Pulcinella* and *Mavra* are good examples of deliberate stylistic declination. This was also true in Pushkin's case. See the biographical essay on Pushkin by B. Tomashevsky (*Pushkin. Sochineniya.* Leningrad: Gos. Izd., 1924).

3. Unless, by style, one means the manner in which Pushkin wrote this tale, in which case Stravinsky "stylizes" in the same sense.

4. This very interesting score gives the impression that the music of the opera is supplied by a military band—that is, an orchestra of winds of the kind one hears on the streets and boulevards and in the public parks—or outside the windows of the "Little House in Kolomna." The strings are reduced to celli and basses as a foundation (also trumpet and others) and to two solo violins and solo viola, which only occasionally join the otherwise almost exclusively wind sound. Horn chords, for example, accompany Parasha's first song, and often perform the functions of strings in the middle register. The trumpet plays the ritornello preceding the lyric romance of the hussar-cook. In general, it is this orchestral accompaniment, composed of sounds one hears in squares and on the street, in barracks and on parade grounds, that is set against the sentimental petit-bourgeois melodies and the musical settings of everyday speech. It is brass instruments in a military style that accompany the hussar, and woodwinds that form the background for the songs of mother and neighbor.

5. Here I call attention to the celebrated dialogue of Tatiana and her nurse in Tchaikovsky's *Onegin.*

6. These measures have an accompaniment based on the note G.

7. One or two exceptions only serve to prove the rule. In ex. 184, measure 21, the hussar sings a melodic seventh, but the interval occurs not within a single phrase but as a leap to the beginning of a new phrase at a higher octave (on the words "shirinochkoi to mashet"). Also, at

the words "v barabanchiki to b'et" [ex. 184, measures 13-14], there is a typical ninth between g^2 and f^1, with its three other intervals sung as well.

8. Dargomyzhsky was writing *Rusalka* during the twelve-year period 1843-55, but there is no doubt that the score contains allusions to music of an earlier time.

11

The New Instrumental Style

In the years following the appearance of *Mavra,* there was a clearly noticeable shift in Stravinsky's interests away from the theater and from vocal music toward instrumentalism in its "pure forms," and more particularly toward that area of instrumental music where the dialectic of formal organization can most clearly be seen in action: the area of the concerto. The basic principles of the concerto cannot be sought within the narrow confines of a "contemplative" virtuosity: the principles are more serious, and more pervasive. I cannot dwell at length here on my notion of the concerto; I do it elsewhere. But briefly: the significance of the "competitive" element is not confined to virtuosic superiority (control of the instrument, ease in overcoming technical problems). At issue is perfection of dialogue, and its expression. The two, or more, concertizing instruments start from the same premises, but they discover different principles that demand different courses of development. Each instrument, therefore, takes its own course and develops its own point of view, at the same time being constantly alert to the necessary coexistence of the principal idea with the contrasting idea that it has itself engendered. The masters of Italian instrumentalism (Domenico Scarlatti and the great "violinists"), Handel, Bach, Mozart, Beethoven—all these men continually worked on materials with these principles in mind. The fugue, the variation, the sonata—each of these various "aspects" of music could be dialectically reworked to make a concerto. But in the concerto itself, the dynamic of the dialogue becomes an independent force that determines the dialectical organization. Dialogue and dialectical organization are inseparable. In music, the principles of dialectical organization are most clearly revealed when the instruments are given musical ideas that contrast specifically as thesis and antithesis. These ideas contrast not merely in the sense of being thematically different, but in the sense that their differences are striking for being distinctive and complementary at the same time, a fact that it is up to the musical development to make clear. It is a mistake to think that sonata form must be a vehicle of musical dialectic. In so far as the sense of the sonata is to be sought in the contrast of two opposing themes, there need be no dialectic. Contrast is not dialectic. But the converse: that dialectic implies contrast—is true.

It is equally erroneous to think of the concerto as something definable in terms of mode or manner of performance, or to hold that each of its many and various manifestations is either formally vague or a special case of the application of sonata form. To hold such ideas is to show ignorance of the history of the concerto's development and its many transformations. Further, and still worse, it ignores the organic formation of the concerto, it loses sight of the fact that sonata-form is one phase in the development of the musical mentality, and that as such, the form owes much to the concerto. Indeed, one might think that sonata-form had been created in one glorious instant by an academic deity who had finally reached the conclusion that it was the most perfect musical scheme, and that there remained nothing further but formally to acclaim it as the eternal model of all musical virtues. Let the academics, alas, have their deductions, their didactic and theoretical fabrications. In the meantime, the evolution of sonata form (and other forms as well) proceeds apace. And as a matter of fact, the origins of the form owe a great deal to the earliest concerted forms—to the aria, and the symphony (overture) also. This fact is confirmed by the latest scholarly researches (see, for example, in *Archiv für Musikwissenschaft*, April 1925, the article of Helfert entitled "Zur Entwicklungsgeschichte der Sonatenform.") The operatic aria was related to the concerto not because of superficial virtuosic display (this kind of excess comes in a period of decline), but because it afforded a medium for the dialectical exposition of mood and character. The oldest Italian operas (both seria and buffa) were dialectical in character, being themselves products of one of the most brilliant dialectical epochs in human history—the Renaissance.

Characteristically, the most discriminating composers, in their search for means of expression adequate to the great social problems that face the twentieth century, neither use as models the works of Beethoven or Bach or Handel nor write in the style of the sonata or fugue. They go back much further—to the later Renaissance, to that gigantic laboratory where the forms of symphonic music began to take shape. They are not looking for ready-made formal schemes, but for the principles of formulation out of which the later developments proceeded, the principles that themselves produced the impro- visational and variation forms, and subsequently the fugue and the sonata. One of these basic principles is that of concerted music—the musico-dialectical principle. And until the implications of this principle were made explicit in various manifestations (of which virtuosity *an und für sich* is certainly one), European music was unable to produce extensive and cohesive forms on purely musical grounds (as distinct from those of poetry, painting, dance, etc.). Most importantly, in fact, music was unable to arrive at an idea of musical development per se. I call attention again to a significant contemporary fact: simultaneously with the growth of dialectical awareness in all fields, all the basic efforts of the leading musicians have been directed toward the mastery of the concerto idea and toward the development of the principles that follow from it. This is a fact that is difficult to deny.

I consider that the contemporary concerto[1] has widened and deepened the principles and methods of musical development. This has been accomplished by the dynamic intensification of thematic development itself, by the way in which impulses contained in the material (be it theme, thematic element, or fragment) are, by means of instrumental dialogue, made gradually to disclose their full potentialities. The same might be said of the sonata or, more exactly, of the sonata principle. But the sonata itself grew out of the concerto idea and, having broadened the resources of development as such (the ways ideas are handled and extended) now returns to the mainstream—not to the primitive concerto of the Renaissance, of course, but to the more highly developed forms of much later epochs. The development section, which occupies a special location in the standard scheme of the sonata, became, as a technique, the locus of historical activity, and gradually this technique, which is essentially dialectical, began to pervade every part of the whole and ultimately became indistinguishable from it. Beethoven reduced thematic material to an extreme of brevity and terseness—to its "kernel." Liszt brought the variation into the sonata, and Reger, the fugue and canon, though both had been anticipated by Beethoven. Contemporary music is taking the last step: the instruments themselves and their idiomatic materials are the bearers of the dialectical development of the musical idea and convert the potential energy of the musical material into a musical movement which reveals the dynamic of the sonorities themselves. In all this there is no preordained "spirit," or *ratio,* or scheme. Logic was not the intellectual begetter of thought, but just the reverse—thought, as it developed out of the struggles of existence, created the norms of logic. So, in the sphere of musical evolution, it is the potential of the sonorities that determines development. It is out of the cumulation of trial and error that the canons and principles of musical formulation emerge.

But I have digressed. The contemporary concerto is first of all notable for having provided a field for the union of conventional development and dialectic, wherein the idea becomes the active force, musical movement the action, and the concreteness of each voice (each instrument, that is, and not the abstract "voice" of the academic style) the bearer, or, more exactly, the "agent" of the development. Development itself ceases to be something imposed on the music from the outside: it is the sine qua non of its existence and actuality, the raison d'être of the style. In the work on musical form that I am preparing for publication [*Muzykalnaya forma kak protsess,* Moscow, 1930 (Book I), 1947 (Book II)—Trans.], all this is treated in detail. I have gone into it here only to establish a few principles necessary for the analysis of Stravinsky's later instrumental works and also to indicate a particular connection between this chapter and the one on *Soldat,* a work which, despite its obvious theatricality, is built on the principle of the concerto.

The sequence of the instrumental works is as follows: Ragtime for eleven instruments (1918); *Piano Rag Music,* concert piece for piano two hands (1919); Three Pieces for Clarinet solo (1919); Symphony for Wind Instruments in memory of Claude Debussy (1920); *Five Fingers,* eight easy pieces for piano two hands (1921); Concertino for string quartet (1920); Octet for wind instruments (1923); Concerto for piano and winds (1923-24); Piano sonata (1924); Serenade for piano (1925); Concert Suite from the ballet *Pulcinella* for violin and piano (1925).[2] This list is impressive, and of consequence. It shows that Stravinsky was one of the first, if not actually the first (the chronology is hard to establish) instinctively to turn in the new direction. It is possible that he took this new turn because he had passed beyond the need to compose for the theater. If so, the fact that he turned to instrumentalism, to instrumental constructionism, takes on an added significance, because the instrumentalism of the end of the seventeenth and the first half of the eighteenth century (which also developed by taking up problems connected with the concerto) was in many respects the logical consequence of having passed beyond the need to compose vocal music, and represented the development of the melos of vocal music in a new area. There is no necessary relation between the music of the theater, on the one hand, and vocal music on the other, but historically, a parallel suggests itself.

By always choosing the course of greatest resistance, by never stooping to imitate others but, on the contrary, embracing new and ever newer problems, Stravinsky is rightly esteemed as a musical master and an incisive intellect. Note that the idea of the concerto is intimately associated with the principles of improvisation. *Pulcinella* (1919) relates itself to the commedia dell'arte (the hearthstone of improvisation), and the musical construction of *Soldat* (1918), which is based on the idea of the concerto, also makes extensive use of the principle of development through improvisation. The configuration of the musical texture (the musical syntax) organizes the musical movement in such a way that the sounds are constantly propelled further and further away from a starting point—a basic musical premise, that is—and also constantly attracted back to it. Thus, by a process of groping for the extraction of new intonations from already established materials, Stravinsky produces a continual development of the music in a dialectical sense. In *Soldat,* the dialectic is the product of the "dialoguing" instruments, and there is a strikingly logical (in the philosophical sense) development of consequents from antecedents, without in any way risking abstraction or estrangement from the specific nature of the musical materials themselves. Ragtime for eleven instruments, the Symphony for Wind Instruments, the Concertino for string quartet, and the Octet all carry forward the development of these principles. These are no classical ensembles in the ordinary sense—there is no single dominant emotional current, nor do all the instruments take part in the development of themes that have been presented solely for that purpose. Stravinsky's ensembles are not divided into important sections, on the one hand, and, on the other, "empty" passages that no running figuration can ever fill. The constructive principle that utilizes every technical device to develop a musical texture as an activity concentrated around a specific point, rejects as incompatible the use of casual musical materials as filler between poles of attraction. In the course of a musical texture that develops dialectically, each instrument must gradually disclose and display all its unique and peculiar sound characteristics, because only then can the energies contained within the original concentration of material be fully revealed. Therefore, the ensembles of Stravinsky never contain a unity that is purely architectonic and that results from the conformation of heterogeneous elements without regard to nature or quality, nor the (more frequently encountered) unity resulting from the subordination of all voices to some rational abstraction accepted a priori (the canons of consonance, of 4-voiced texture, of thematic relationships, of symmetry, etc.). No, on the contrary: this unity is a synthesis of opposites, a synthesis of sonorities of instrumental lines, each of which develops a given idea to its fullest, in accordance with the nature of the instrument. But this is not the kind of synthesis that declares itself at the end of a work, or by any convention of the "perfect" cadence, or by any system of acceptable vertical arrangements, or only because exposition and development may be clearly contraposed. This is a synthesis that embraces the whole sound process—every moment, every stage, every element. It is a unity synonymous with the whole of musical movement, felt in the intensities of the dynamic of sonorities, and perceived dialectically.

Ragtime begins with its musical material stated and developed by flute, clarinet, horn, cornet-a-piston, trombone, first and second violin, viola, cello, cymbalum, and a group of percussion instruments (small drum "with" and "without" snares, bass drum, cymbals.) The cymbalum plays an important role: as in *Renard,* it acts as a unifying element, "cementing" strings and percussion instruments. The rhythmic aspect of the basic material is detailed with exceptional mastery. The piece demands extraordinary accuracy and attention from the players, who must perform like workers at instruments or machines the functioning of which depends on absolute evenness and complete accuracy of movement. This piece has been considered a joke: it was so unusual a work that no one took it into his head seriously to object to it, or seriously to attend to it, either. But even if music again descends to the level of romantic emotionalism and a saturated lyricism, these experiments of Stravinsky in using rhythm as a formal agent of musical material cannot be without consequence, because one feels in them the iron discipline of the will and submission to the rhythms of work. Ragtime is a wholly linear composition. Out of the principal rhythmic materials and with the help of rhythms and intonations characteristic of each instrument, Stravinsky composes a continuous line of sound. It abounds, of course, in rhythmic transpositions and displacements, interruptions, couplings and enchainments of various kinds, but never in abstract combinations, always as logical extensions of particular details of the material itself that delineate the palpably stimulating melos whose combinations of rhythms and intonations express and define the essential Ragtime.

The Concertino for string quartet is more complex. Here the basic rhythmic framework is not derived from the dance, and the perception of the line as a synthesis of musical components is not aided by changes in movement or by improvisatory deviations (apparent deviations, that is, that actually only serve to call attention to what is essential), but lineation is nevertheless an important stimulus of the motion and its dynamic basis. In this latter respect, the Concertino is a continuation of the trend projected in the three Pieces for String Quartet (1914). But in the Concertino, the dynamism of "quartet-edness" is more pervasively and more basically stated—even if, perhaps, less tersely, less intensely, and in a manner that is less obvious at first hearing. In the Concertino there are two principal rates of movement: half note-84, and half note-58 (andante). The violin and cello open the work by playing the ascending scale of C major through the interval of a ninth. This scale is accompanied by its "shadow"—a scale beginning on c♯ (and derived from B major). The opening moment introduces immediately, therefore, an element of antagonism, and it also reveals the full range of the overtone "content" of the basic scale: all twelve semitones appear in the course of the ascending motion, with notes e and b common to both scales. The principal theses are exposed by three "themes" that also act as agents of the ensuing action. Here they are in brief outline [see ex. 216].

Example 216

At first the exposition moves in little jerks: the horizontal statements of the thematic material are repeatedly disintegrated by verticals sforzando. These dense chords block the course of lines that are thrusting forward, striving to unwind, to convert their potential energy into the sound of actuality. The percussive pizzicato and the syncopations only accentuate the unexpectedness and obstinacy of the initial obstacles. This is the impression of the opening. Gradually, textural coherence begins to assert itself. The verticals have not disintegrated the lines, it seems—they have only served to propel them forward. In measure 29, the outer lines ascend scalewise from d to a♭, and in measures 40-41 from d♯ to the octave above, this time accompanied by the viola's diatonic octave of unaltered pitches (beginning on d, with e and b, therefore, still the common tones). Here the sequence of ascending scale fragments is again interrupted, and there is a return to the opening, with its jerks and sforzando verticals.

Do the first forty measures of the movement succeed? Are the implications of the opening intonations and combinations made explicit in some way? Undoubtedly so. The opening ascending scale, which is almost immediately dissipated, is by degrees reconstituted again, and now in an aspect enriched by what has preceded. The movement then continues the segment of ex. 216 (b), but at other pitches. In measures 52-53, after a few false starts, the ascending scale returns. Now it rises from C, and with Dorian pitches (e♭ and b♭). The accompanying "shadow" in the viola starts from C♯. Again the movement is stopped by sforzando jolts, but even this short passage displays the thematic material in yet a new light.

An andante begins at a slower pace (three measures), then three measures of Tempo I, then the andante again—all composed of vertical sonorities. The motion has been "braked," and the progressive energy present in the first two elements of material [ex. 216 (a) and (b)] is no longer utilized. Stravinsky's instincts now lead him to explore the development of the material by introducing a cadenza, a moment of improvisation. The result is a quite singular intermezzo, in which the leading role belongs to the first violin, which describes a flexibly curving line ascending in pairs of notes from d^1/a to $c\sharp^3/g^2$. This beautiful interlude, "at anchor" over an organ point (as if to put a restraint upon the motion), serves as the composition's slow movement. The melodic line reaches up and grows like the stem of a strong plant gradually rising up and out of its seed. Having let the line ascend to $c\sharp^3$, Stravinsky breaks off the movement (Tempo I, half note-84) to reintroduce the opening material [ex. 216 (a)] starting on d, followed by the segment [ex. 216 (b)] in canon. The jolts of the vertical chords can no longer restrain the energy of the ascent that is contained in these "themes" with their upward leaps of fifths: the forward movement assumes full control. The material here is largely that of ex. 216 (b) and (c), which reveals very interesting intonational possibilities. At the very moment when the thematic segment (b) finally crystallizes in the upper voice (first violin), the movement, without interruption, enters its last section—the finale. The music moves with fire and intensity toward its terminal point—toward the return of the original scale formations (C : c♯ : C / d² : d♯¹ : d) whose final ascent "takes off" into a cloud of percussive sforzandi. In this section of the piece there are three moments when the material of segment (b) of ex. 216 is dominant. This is its basic form [see ex. 217].

Example 217

sub. meno   *e sempre staccato*

The first time it is "resolved" into an extra-thematic and extra-melodic complex of "tonic-dominant" chords, which are sharply accentuated rhythmically and dynamically. The second time (beginning on D♭ and then on D in the bass) the material dissolves into a sparkling new theme of dance-like character. The same melodic sequence f♯:f:d is retained, but E♭ now appears in the bass. Here is the new motive [see ex. 218].

Example 218

и т. д.

The manner in which it is presented, constructed, and developed has much in common with the dance-like finales of Tchaikovsky and also with a few moments of *Renard* and *Noces*.[3] The dance appears and disappears like some alien element, but the pitch sequence out of which it grew (f♯:f:d) continues and is even emphatically set forth in the stubborn, percussive chords. One characteristic of this method of writing—the rearrangement of melodic material into a sequence of heavily accented chords—was cleverly utilized by Tchaikovsky time and time again (for example, in the exposition and recapitulation of the Third Symphony, last movement, and by Stravinsky himself in *Petrushka*). Here the vertical complex that contains the altered C-major scale is ultimately rearranged into an horizontal form like that appearing at the very beginning of the piece. This scale-wise movement is dissipated, and the motion is topped by the convulsive sforzandi, exactly as in the beginning. Then the andante appears again (half note-58). The first violin makes a smooth and gradual ascent from b to b_b^2, remains in this register for a few moments, and then with equal smoothness (and playing vertical pairs of pitches) descends to c#. In this one gesture the final sequence of events finds its completion, as does the cadenza, the original horizontal statement, and the development as a whole. The composition betrays no weakness.

Stravinsky's Concertino is a very severe piece, but its methods are very convincing. The piece is clearly and consistently dialectical by virtue of the way it logically derives its own substance from its principal materials, whose dynamic potential gradually becomes the active motion of the musical texture. It would seem that even the most violent denigrators of the coherence of Stravinsky's music would have to admit that, in this instance, Stravinsky shows himself to be a constructionist composer of great intellectual force and consistency. Naturally, by having spoken almost exclusively of constructionism, dynamic, and dialectic as properties of the particular nature of this music, I do not mean to deny the depth and strength of music's psychological effect or of the wealth of personal reactions and impressions that compel us to assert that one piece is music, and another is not. I have not spoken of these things here only because I wanted to confine myself to the study of musical language as an "instrument" of expression, as a complex of expressive means, and to the expressive "manner" characteristic of one composer. It is from this domain, indeed, that one can proceed to define the composition and character of the psychological effect and content of music.

The Octet for two trombones, two trumpets, two bassoons, clarinet, and flute, continues in certain respects the line from *Soldat* through Ragtime. The concerto idea and the dialectical principle are not expressed in the conventional way—as a display of particular sonorities; rather does the form express—and derive from—a grouping of the sonorities into five categories or "branches." The particular tone-color and expressive qualities of each branch thus form the basis of the musical material itself. The Octet has two parts: I, Sinfonia (E♭ major); II, Theme with Variations, leading directly into a Finale. The sinfonia is patterned on the old overture, with a slow introduction (the first part of the movement) followed by a gay Allegro (the second part), which opens and closes with its principal theme. Traditionally, the opening largo, lento, or adagio is composed in such a way that the restraint of the motion produces a very high degree of tension, after which the following allegro, which acts as a release for this long accumulated energy, comes as the logical dynamic consequence. One can cite an exceptionally brilliant Russian example of this method of composition—the *Jota Aragonesa* of Glinka, where the entire E♭ major allegro sounds like a triadic synthesis acting as the "resolution" of the colossal tension of the introductory grave. In the opening lento of the Octet, Stravinsky reaches no such degree of tension, because he has selected a different kind of freely flowing material. But the element of contrast is present, because where the opening lento has been predominantly a texture of flowing, rounded lines, the entire allegro moderato is built out of sharp, fragmented materials whose rhythmic configurations are sometimes amusingly grotesque. Here is the opening "Russo-Italian" theme—bright, brisk, and gay [see ex. 219].

Example 219

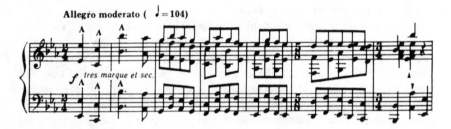

The whole first part of the allegro shares this spirit. The design and intent are precise and clear, the statements are tersely made, and there is a wealth of syncopated figures and imitation. The next theme (here quoted without its polyphonic setting) has this appearance [see ex. 220].

Example 220

The second part of the allegro is composed of clever combinations of this fragmented line with new formations, some of which are drawn from it, and all of which are in harmony with the logic of the movement's course. The theme of ex. 220 makes three appearances. The rhythmic regularity of the bassoons (in eighth notes) balances and controls the pace. In its feeling for line, the whole composition betrays the professional hand of the engraver, but one is made constantly aware of the relationship between the design itself and the timbres, dynamic qualities, and rhythmic formulas that characterize each kind of instrument. A canonic statement of the opening theme closes this first movement, notable for its precision and conciseness.

The character of the theme that Stravinsky has selected for the variations (andantino, quarter note-92) nicely counterbalances that of the preceding allegro. Because of the alternations of the pitches c♯, c, b♭, and a, this new theme has a somewhat shadowy, crepuscular quality. It is stated first by the flute and clarinet two octaves apart, and then by trumpet followed by trombone [see ex. 221].

Example 221

The melody seems "tinted" with several shades—that is, the ear hears polytonal implications (in the line alone, without accompaniment). Observe also that the progression c♯:c:a:c♯ is similar to the progression f♯:f:d:f♯ in the Concertino. From *Firebird* on, Stravinsky has shown a fondness for the "shimmering" colors of alternating major and minor thirds and has made frequent use of this device in a variety of contexts. Remember the introduction to *Firebird* [see ex. 222] and the eighth Sonata of Scriabin, etc.

Example 222

In the first variation (eighth note-126), the tonal possibilities of the theme (stated by the trombones) are explored by "scales" of bassoons, clarinet, and flute that move fleetingly above. In the second variation, at the same speed, the melodic design is developed in a style resembling a street march, played first by trumpet and then by flute and clarinet, over a grotesque bassoon accompaniment. The march concludes with a fanfare and passes directly to a repetition of the first variation. In the third variation, the material assumes yet another aspect: that of an amusing waltz, in a familiar style. The prototype may be found in *Petrushka, Soldat,* and the Three Easy Pieces for piano four hands (as well as in the Little Suite for orchestra). The flute (supported by the clarinet) plays a sinuous solo melody that is amusingly unsuited to the doll-like rhythm of the accompaniment (ben marcato). The trumpet playfully inserts its own theme. The waltz passes on to the fourth variation, which has the amusing character of a galop (quarter note-189). The theme is converted into something that sounds a little like the famous paraphrases on the *Dog Waltz* [Chopin, Op. 64, no. 1 (D♭)—Trans.] Shadowed by a clarinet counterpoint, the bassoon carries the melody, which is overlaid with the thematic fragments of trumpet and flute. The variation begins as follows [see ex. 223].

Example 223

The waltz and the galop together form the Octet's very humorous scherzo. Music of this kind has its roots in a genre that has almost disappeared—the music of street and itinerant musicians, and the improvisatory music of the fairs. Its configurations suggest the pencil drawings of the great caricaturists, in which every detail of pressure and stroke is visible, and the whole is neat, graphic, incisive, and (above all) gay in a completely harmless and inoffensive way. Nowhere does Stravinsky's irony—an irony of a Pushkinesque order—refract the details of real life so brilliantly as in this kind of music derived from the most everyday sounds—the music of the salon dance, of street and fair, of country and city life. The dominating figure, of course, is that of Petrushka (both the traditional Petrushka and the Petrushka of Stravinsky). After the waltz and galop, the first variation is repeated, allowing the whole movement to partake of the character of a rondo. Then comes the fifth variation—fugato—whose subject has the following form [see ex. 224].

Example 224

The theme is answered by the clarinet. The trumpet and the flute-clarinet then present subject and answer in a texture now complicated by the presence of new voices and a countersubject. After the trumpet has taken up the theme again, orderly development ceases. Following a two-voiced texture of clarinet and flute (subject and countersubject), the flute in its turn is left alone with a solo variation of the theme in inversion (moderato, quarter note-116). The bassoons take up the rhythmic "skeleton" of this passage and lead into the finale of the variations and of the whole octet. The theme of the finale (bassoon) is a merry one [see ex. 225].

Example 225

The second bassoon accompanies the first—these instruments act as "masters of ceremonies" in all the grotesque episodes of the Octet. The theme undergoes extensive development. For purposes of sharp contrast, the next piece of material is coarse and grotesque, but even it stays well within the confines of the Italian "rural" style—like certain moments in *Pulcinella* and typical Italo-Russian passages in Tchaikovsky [see ex. 226].

Example 226

The whole exposition is repeated. Concertino trumpets open the development pp staccato and take the theme into a new tonal area (D♭). Then comes a section of "trio"—flute, clarinet, and bassoon. The flute, taking over from the trumpet, plays a variation of the material that the bassoon had had earlier [see ex. 227].

The "trio" yields the development of the ideas to trombones and trumpet, which share a bassoon counterpoint. Clarinet and flute re-enter with a syncopated fragment of the theme, and the resulting development—a spectacular fugato—reaches its climax with the entrance of the trombones playing the principal theme of the finale in augmentation. This is answered by the second trumpet, whereupon the first trumpet, imitated by the trombone, takes up the theme in its original C-major, to the accompaniment of thematic figuration in

Example 227

the woodwinds. This whole third section of the lively and spirited finale is remarkable for its clarity and dashing gaiety. It is quite natural that the trumpets, having opened the development, should also terminate it. Having worked the thematic line gradually up to the trumpet pitch b^2, Stravinsky breaks the ascent with a pause, and his final twenty-seven measures (introduced piano subito and continued pp) bring the line back down from c^3 to c^1. The trumpet theme passes to clarinet and flute and then back to the trumpets. Here is an outline of this descending line [see ex. 228].

Example 228

The Octet as a whole impresses as a lively and beautifully proportioned work, and a work whose architectonics are very carefully calculated. Obedient to classical *principles* of form, but not to ready schemes, Stravinsky has disclosed new intonations and new colors; he has happily avoided the pitfalls of repetition (in the reprise), but he has nevertheless brought the basic ideas brilliantly down through all phases of the development. I should like to draw attention to an important stylistic feature: Stravinsky's sensitivity to the interval as an expressive thematic device (the interval, of course, always being given a precise rhythmic and dynamic setting). In the first part of the Octet, the seventh is the important thematic interval. The variations are characterized by the alternations of major and minor thirds. In the fugato these thirds are inverted into sixths, and in the finale, the ;hematic ascent is accomplished through seconds and sevenths. The choice of a specific rhythmo-intonational complex to characterize a given link in a chain of linear construction is found in all melodico-polyphonic music and is a legacy of music of the "oral tradition," where notes were grouped around a central point, and the resulting complex acted both as a unifying device and as a basis for permutation and transposition. It is interesting that the use of intervals in a specific context as elements of expression and characterization is also found in opera (particularly in recitative and dialogue). There it is used both to define the identity of the personalities involved, and to give the "emotional tone" of this or that personality its characteristic utterance. The more linear the opera and more dominant the role of melodic dynamism in it, the more logically and consistently do these qualities reveal themselves. In the *Stone Guest,* Dargomyzhsky makes impetuous use of the interval of the fourth to convey the violence and temperament of Don Juan, and the descending leap of the seventh to characterize the counterpoint of cunning and open-mouthed astonishment that typifies Leporello.

In instrumental music, of course, pitches and rhythms are not used to compose sound complexes that have precise emotional connotations. Nevertheless, choice of material must be made, and that choice inevitably produces an inner logic of its own and a precise sonorous image—or, more exactly, a unique complex of intonational "gestures," by which the character and pace of a piece are defined. Our senses and imaginations accept those sonorities and gestures as representing the "musical thought" of a given work or section of a work, and we form an association between them and other optical or motor-muscular sensations. Otherwise, memory would have nothing to cling to, and there would be no basis for retraining impressions. It is precisely on such plastic factors, and not on abstract prescriptions about the conventions of voice-leading, that are based both the actual perception of music and the strength of the impression that it may leave in any given case. The "plasticity" of Musorgsky's harmonies and the associations evoked by them make such a deep mark on the psyche that no protestations about his technical faults can persuade listeners of the so-called "bad" qualities of his music—in its uncorrected form, at least.

The Suite for Small Orchestra (1921) is made up of works originally found in the two sets of Easy Pieces for Children (1915-17) about which I have already spoken in my chapter on Stravinsky's transitional period.[4] This suite contains four dances: march, waltz, polka, and galop. Nowhere in contemporary genre music are there more witty instrumental inventions. Over the harmonic (clarinet) and rhythmic ostinato, the march sets forth two themes. The trumpet plays them both (the horn echoes the trumpet in the second), and the flute, oboe, and bassoon utilize fragments as a basis for a contrapuntal "commentary." Despite the brevity of the work (forty-two measures), the composer says everything that need be said: his ideas are stated incisively, and their martial "content" is set forth dialectically through the fragmented interpretive "commentary" of the instruments. The result is a witty and lively dialogue. Stravinsky also made frequent use of the device of "commenting" by way of instrumental dialogue in *Soldat* (and also in Ragtime and the Octet). Thanks to it, the center of interest is not on statement per se—exposition and reprise—but on dynamic development. The developmental process as a whole acquires an organic unity, because this process, which utilizes fragmented interpretive commentary, exposes, without in any way exhausting, the rich resources of the material. In such a context the reprise is superfluous, because it cannot in any case act as a synthesis: it can only block the developmental process by returning everything to the original thesis. In place of a reprise, the conclusion of a work is formed either by a coda that summarizes the movement, or by an emphatic full stop consisting of the movement's most characteristic rhythmic pattern or intonational formula—sometimes even its initial element or period (the first idea). This is the way the march ends. Concerning the waltz, I need add nothing to what I have already said about Stravinsky's waltzes—this one is another elegant and playful grotesque, whose melody is borne by flute and piccolo, with bassoon, oboe, and trumpet contributing running commentary.

There is a splendid polka. The statement of the melodic line is shared by trumpet, clarinet, and flute, each contributing its own characteristic intonations. After the "trio," there is no mere mechanical repetition: the trombone contributes important decoration built out of the most ordinary motive of a type like *"Chto tantsuesh', Katen'ka."* But the galop is the most remarkable part of the suite by virtue of its impetuosity, brilliance of sound, richness of invention, and the innovation of utilizing the most hackneyed and exhausted devices (such as, for example, the "musette-like" ostinato of fifths in the bass). The highest praise, in my opinion, that one could give this suite would be to compare its use of musical ideas of the most common currency (*Allerweltsmotiven,* to quote the neat expression of Abert) with that of Mozart.[5] It is amusing to see how worshippers of the classics sometimes pompously extol the virtues of themes that were in their times wholly banal and perhaps even vulgar, while they contemptuously reject materials of like coarseness in the works of contemporaries. It is also strange that people who like dance music reject Stravinsky's suites and similar pieces as comparatively coarse and lacking in wit. Probably the absence of an obvious sensuality is an important factor explaining this attitude; brilliant imagination and a sparkling wit being no compensation for many people. But just as Mozart's Don Juan in his violent and temperamental "champagne" aria soars far above the level of vulgar sensuality, so does the trifling galop of Stravinsky, and for the same reasons.

The Concerto for piano and winds (1923-24) is a work of the greatest interest and curiosity, but the novelty of the intonational conception makes it difficult to analyze. The difficulty arises, of course, from the strangeness of the whole texture, though it is just this strangeness that points to the heart of Stravinsky's accomplishment: the refraction into a wholly new timbral spectrum of both the concerto idea and the dialectical development of the musical themes. The piano is here confronted by an orchestra minus all strings except the double bass (retained as fundament for the whole texture). The character of the music is severe and harsh. Stravinsky's imagination had also occupied itself with a texture of wind sounds in the Symphony for Winds in memory of Debussy (1920) and in the 1920 transcription of the "Volga Boatmen's Song." The latter is of little consequence,[6] and it is really only with the texture of the Octet that one can begin to find evidence of procedures that were later to form the basis of the concerto's style.

In the Concerto, the sonority that emerges from brass, winds, and contrabasses is predominantly steel-like in character. Of quite another character are the sonorities of the Symphony for Wind Instruments (strictly speaking, *symphonies,* as in the French title: *Symphonies d'instruments à vent à la mémoire de Claude Debussy*), and I cannot refrain from pausing to say a few words about this work before proceeding to an analysis of the concerto. I consider this one of Stravinsky's outstanding pieces, and I am simply astonished both by how little the work is known and how little has been the attention paid to it. Even in the piano transcription of Arthur Lourié, one can sense the color and the inexplicably deep and affecting fascination of this Russian epitaph, fully worthy of the memory of the composer of the *Six Epigraphes antiques.* Only by familiarity with the score and the sound of the symphony, of course, is it possible to appreciate the richness and freshness of the music, in which irregularity of respiration and originality of rhythm are combined with extraordinary plasticity of design and classical rationality of form. The material is organized like a rondo with a regular recurrence of the basic motto in a vertical arrangement (beautiful, elegiac sequences of chords). The texture is a masterful composition of short instrumental themes, motives, and rhythmic formulae typical of Stravinsky's music of that time. The result is an organic continuum of the most expressive elements, a solidly built mosaic of sounds, whose principal intonational moments are the logical determinants of both the direction and rhythm of the motion, a mosaic whose patterns and timbres are not treated as accessory decoration but are made to serve the dialectical development of the material. I do not have space to quote examples, and it is very difficult to describe in words how the music unfolds, how the full content of the original ideas is gradually disclosed, how the motives grow, move, connect with one another, and how even the "pauses" have an organic function. All this would demand a separate chapter and copious quotation from the score. Here I merely call attention to the work, with the added hope that I may one day be able to deal with it extensively.

The music of the symphony is also impressive because it contains no trace of coarse grief or anguish, of convulsive nervousness, or of intentionally pathetic oratory. In fact, by virtue of its self-control, clarity, and the general moderation of its tone, the work attains something of an antique nobility and elevation of thought. These qualities make themselves evident especially in the concluding section, where the monumentally beautiful and deeply emotional static harmonies replace a rapidly moving passage that had reached the limits of its development. This is pagan music, woven of rural instrumental melodies and doleful wails and laments with characteristic rhythmic punctuations. But, as I have said, the most moving pages are the final ones, pages as affecting as the best of the corresponding passages in Tchaikovsky, passages that assuage grief at the same time that they affirm its irrefragable permanence. These pages could stand with the outstanding models of our pure assuasive lyricism. It is difficult to conceive any music more redolent of vitality, freshness, and clarity than this work, dedicated to Debussy, a composer who reacted with great sensitivity to the brilliance and originality of our musical creations. The Symphony for Wind Instruments is also one of the most brilliant examples of Stravinsky's concise and efficient musical thought, of the formal clarity of his musical language, and the rhythmic flexibility of his compositional technique. The melodic and harmonic material of the symphony is both a transformation of the best features of intonations and rhythms drawn from instrumental works already familiar to us (and the epilogue of *Sacre* is, itself, in many respects, a symphony), as well as an innovation of brilliant new elements. The technique of interweaving two thematic lines with complementary but alien counterpoint is handled with new freedom and facility. In fact, even an ear well accustomed to the basic qualities of Stravinsky's musical language is newly struck by the naturalness and spontaneity and flexibility of this musical speech, by the stylistic economy and the maximal conciseness and accuracy of its expression. To see and understand the complex of these qualities even more clearly—qualities which manifest themselves in the large fresco works as well as in the tracery of the miniatures—it is useful to seek an analogy with the style of old Russian painting, which combines in one organic whole the traditions of antiquity, a feeling for form, mastery of color and line, and rhythmic equilibrium in the presence of unusually flexible and elastic linear movement. The expressive force of the style is precisely the sum of these details. All this now suddenly begins to appear in Stravinsky's music and suggests kinship with the great artistic principles that began to manifest themselves in our fine art as early as the end of the twelfth century.

We can now see clearly why Stravinsky turned to the intonations of the wind orchestra. First and foremost there is the instinct of a great artist: all of our most recent music has striven to break out of the salon and the concert hall into the open air, into the spacious streets and squares, into the city at large. The intonations of winds and percussion are better suited to this then are the intonations of bowed instruments. Besides, the essence of Stravinsky's melodic and rhythmic style is an instrumentalism derived from the dance tune and improvisation and colored by the grotesque nuances of native buffoonery, an instrumentalism that bespeaks constant experimentation with pipes and all manner of percussive sounds. The intonations of Stravinsky's music almost effortlessly reveal traces of our native open-air music (the show-booth, the fair, streets and boulevards, city parks and country lanes). He is a *symphonist* of the plein-air, and his penchant for "wind music" is both a natural channel for his artistic energies and a manifestation of an unconscious but imperious need.

In this respect also, *Soldat* is a work of special significance, not only in its treatment of winds, but particularly in its use of the improvisatory violin. The work shows Stravinsky's exceptional faculty for incorporating the sonorous riches of the "plein-air" violin style into his compositional plan. This style differs radically from that of the conventional orchestral string ensemble, and the Suite for solo violin drawn from *Pulcinella* illustrates a similar differentiation. In the latter work, the essence of the ballet music finds itself being conveyed solely by the intonations of the violin. It is as if somewhere, in Italy at a carnival, a highly gifted improviser had invited the crowd to listen to his violin relate the whole tale of *Pulcinella* in the intonations and rhythms of the commedia dell'arte. The music of the ballet is so naturally conveyed that it seems to have been written only for violin solo. The use of the cimbalum and the frequent treatment of the piano as an instrument of percussion also point to the affinity of Stravinsky's musical temperament for a dynamically "extensive" (as against "intensive") musical style based on the cultural traditions of society, a style directed not inward toward itself but radiating outward, a style, as I have already emphasized, closely related to the gaiety of the festival, a style whose intonations are the distillate of the sounds of life lived by the masses. Therefore, his music shows few traces of that passive, private contemplativeness which characterizes the musical culture of the salon. Neither the early songs on Verlaine texts nor the first piano etudes are as typical of Stravinsky (however beautiful they may be) as those works motivated by extra-personal considerations.

Passing now to Stravinsky's piano concerto, I should like first to remark that in the concerto there inheres, both as principle and as particularity of form, a musical "extensiveness" that is by nature attractive to any composer. This quality derives from the dialectical nature of the species. Plasticity of motivic design, the apposition of contrasting and competitive sonorities, improvisational resourcefulness in the development of material, and incisiveness of thematic ideas for ease of perception are primary requirements, to which one may add the need for constantly careful calculation of the sounds. All these considerations are of far greater importance here than in any other kind of music. The writing of a concerto demands the composer's utter concentration on the act of performance. If the composer cannot perform himself, he must nevertheless be as sensitive to the art as if he could. Symphonies may be written without particular regard for where or when they may be actually played, but not so the concerto. The concerto is music for here and now. It has a lot in common with the theater, and with the feuilleton—or, more exactly, with the art of discussion.

All this taken together can serve as a hypothesis adequate for establishing a rationale of Stravinsky's concerto style. And the fact that this piano concerto is not a virtuoso piece (and deliberately so) is not a hindrance, but an advantage. Contact with the public can also be made without pure virtuosity, and contact has always been a prime consideration of Stravinsky.

Stravinsky's concerto (written 1923-24) has three movements (fast, slow, fast), each with subdivisions. The first movement is preceded by an introductory largo whose imposing ceremonial pace is reminiscent of the Italian Handelian style, and whose thematic and organizational importance for the rest of the piece give it primary significance. Besides opening the concerto, the largo terminates the first and last movements, and the opening theme of the first allegro bursts forth from it, like water out of a rock. The slow majesty of the opening idea, or music of like character, is found here and there throughout the piece and serves each time to recall the severity and impassive grandeur of the opening ceremonial material [see ex. 229].

Example 229

My first impression of the work was that its composer had lost his way and become becalmed in a sea of stylization. But after having given closer attention to the style of Handel and other Italian sources which might have served as models for Stravinsky, I became persuaded that this initial impression was in fact false. Though there is, of course, a superficial similarity of intonations, rhythms, and general procedure, Stravinsky's syntax and rhetoric are deeply contemporary. There are in European music a few basic formal principles and a few rhythmic and intonational formulae that serve as *Urkräfte* and *Urtexten*.

The fact that the composer may lean heavily on them or may use them as points of departure, still does not mean that his music is quotation, imitation, or stylization. For the primary sources of his sound material, Stravinsky returns to the style of the late Renaissance or the Baroque, but the emotional stamp of this music is no longer palpable to us. It is, in fact, precisely the effacing distance between us and the originals that renders old rhythms and intonations suitable as a basis for composition in which the dynamic of the older style, falling on new ears, begets a fresh emotional context.

The largo occupies thirty-two measures. After a characteristic breathing pause (which also serves as a kind of rhythmic springboard), the opening material of the allegro bursts forth. This material is in essence a development of the theme of the largo [see ex. 230].

Example 230

The music moves on with cheerful and easy confidence, its character astringent and angular, but clear and virile. After the joint presentation of the opening argument, the piano is left alone for a short while to continue the development of its position in the following passage, which has great formal and intonational importance later on [see ex. 231].

This is followed by the second leading idea (the new theme appears in the orchestra) [see ex. 232].

Example 231

Example 232

These two themes, with a few additional elements—especially an ascending scale with chromatics—form the basis of a dialectical musical development notable for its heated intensity and for the extraordinary interest generated by the playful confrontations and combinations of ideas. Because of the repeated presence in its texture of short ascending lines, the development is a gradual accumulation of numerous little climactic passages, through which the song-like phrase [ex. 232] twice shines as an integral melodic idea, as a point of support amid the whirl of rhythms and spinning lines. The tension eventually becomes so great that Stravinsky must revert to the opening thesis—he uses the reprise as a means of release and repeats the statement of the thematic material almost in its entirety. Just before the final cadenza, he lifts the pitch-level of the ascending line by one half-step and thereby strengthens the pull of the final cadential resolution. This solo passage is constructed of vertical clusters whose chromatic relationships are embellished by octave dislocations, all of which contributes to the mounting restlessness of the motion. The tension finally resolves, as might have been expected, into the opening largo, which also acts as a synthesis of the whole development. As it enters the broad majesty of this familiar channel, the stormy course of the music subsides, and its flow becomes smooth and regular. Thus, the opening ideas are enriched by final restatement in a new but appropriate context, the terminal largo absorbing and assimilating the allegro motion.

As if to intensify the gravity and severity of the music, Stravinsky moves into the second section of the concerto with music similar in character to that with which the first section concluded—but built out of new material. The flow of the larghetto's main idea is calm and smooth, a line which makes its winding way over steady and heavy pulsations to form harmonies that are simple and austere [see ex. 233].

Example 233

The orchestra takes up this material, while the piano accompanies it in sonorous chords. Following up a pp subito, the color of the music grows more somber. The music "chromaticizes itself." The regular rhythm is interrupted by a cadenza that acts as a powerful leaven whose effects are dissipated by a sparkling staccato passage and a short lyric phrase that burns itself out in a brilliant display. Again the music rises, again the brilliant fireworks. At this point there is preparation for new material: a gradually descending chromatic passage leads to the introduction of a second lyric theme larghetto [see ex. 234].

Example 234

The development is pursued with remarkable rigor, and it is also interesting from a polyphonic point of view, because the countersubject that is introduced is a wholly different melodic idea with a wholly different melodic configuration [see ex. 235].

Example 235

The result—against a background of broken chords in the piano—is a conflict of "thematic interests" that forms itself into a labyrinth of rhythms and intonations out of which, one suspects, it may be difficult to find the way back to the original idea. But the style of the whole design is bold and clear, and the exit from the labyrinth is accomplished naturally by a return via a cadenza to the first theme. After two subsidiary climaxes (cadenza, poco rubato) have been dispersed by a descending scale passage staccato, the opening theme returns; but instead of being garbed in the rich sonorities of the opening, it is now a faded pattern from which much of the detail has been washed out and forgotten. The line of the melody curves gradually and gently downward: from a^2 it descends ultimately to c^1. The concluding mood of the larghetto is thus a conciliatory and quiet one. By introducing into the middle of the movement the agitated improvisatory episodes (reminiscent of Liszt), Stravinsky is enabled to set off more strikingly the severity and virile diatonicism of the principal melody, a melody which has much in common with the concerto's opening idea and whose character "confirms" this affinity.

The third part of the concerto begins with the same phrase that terminated the second part, but is a new and incisive rhythmic configuration. Here are the two versions of the phrase [see ex. 236].

Example 236

The pair of descending and ascending seconds (d^1-c^1, $f\sharp^1$-g^1) acts as the "premise," as the stimulus for the whole final movement, with the important assistance of this characteristic and incisive motive, which is utilized for imitative purposes [see ex. 237].

Example 237

The first stage of the development, or "deduction" of content from the given premises, consists, for the most part, of a process of differentiation, wherein the given motives are splintered, dislocated, and transformed over a steady background of piano "sixteenths." The second stage is more nervous, more agitated. The theme in the piano is as follows [see ex. 238].

Example 238

forte assai

After this moment of more obvious coherence, the material is again subjected to zigzag dismemberment, although the general pace of the music remains brisk and full of energy. The theme of ex. 238 is played again, but with a different accompaniment [see ex. 239]. It then passes into the orchestra, where it is played in augmentation [see ex. 240].

Example 239

Example 240

Here there is also a continuous background of sixteenths, but instead of being rhythmically undifferentiated, they are given a pulsation by accent, sforzando, and syncopation. The movement rushes headlong like a mountain stream past the collisions and jolts of the rocky rhythms, flashing fragments of lines and absorbing intonational shocks as it labors to give birth to the musico-dynamic "content" of the thematic material. Amid the three final stages of the development, which attain a maximal intensity and impetuosity, there is a brilliant passage of concentrated energy. First the A$\flat$ major episode (maestoso), which presents this motive in canonic stretto [see ex. 241]; then, joined to it, a new statement of a few melodic turns whose rhythmic elasticity is typical of the movement as a whole; and finally (constituting a reprise) the last appearance of the principal theme, a marvel of concentrated strength despite the pseudo-whimsical nature of its setting. In this piece, the term "zigzag" defines the dominant character of all the movements and emerges as the logical

Example 241

"consequent" of all the thematic transformations. The "zigzags" of rhythms and intonations, abetted by accents, sforzandi, and syncopation, point up the caustic restlessness (something quite different from mere nervous agitation) of the music's flow. In the third movement, the restlessness reaches a degree of excitement higher than in the first part, where both the material itself and the treatment it undergoes, though no less gripping and intense, contribute a somewhat weaker propulsion to the impetuosity of the flow. The shock of the first movement's opening, for example, is mitigated by the presence in the texture of an element (almost resembling a cadential formula) that encumbers and inhibits each forward thrust [see ex. 242]. On the other hand, neither the opening of the third movement nor any of the subsequent appearances of the opening themes has any such impediment. That [see ex. 243] is the outline of the last appearance of the theme, for instance. (One must also not forget that the original form of this theme grew out of the final motive of the larghetto.) Thus, any "trifling" difference in the intonational premises of the first and third movements may in fact have enormous importance in the plan of the linear development, because our hearing can become extremely sensitive to all such "subtleties" and changes in linear formation.

Example 242

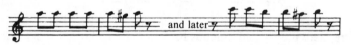

Example 243

As of now, among the instrumental works of Stravinsky's last period, this concerto is the most powerful and ambitious, exhibiting the most significant application of the Renaissance principles of musical dynamic and the dialectical development ("working-out") of the rhythmo-intonational implications of the musical theses.

The pieces for solo instruments form another area in which these same principles were applied. In such a work, of course, as Stravinsky's own arrangement of the three-movement piano suite from *Petrushka* (Russian Dance, Petrushka's Dance, Carnival), we do not have new material, but a new version of old material in which the important rhythms and intonations are conveyed—and marvelously conveyed—through the dynamics and timbres of the piano. But in the Three Pieces for solo clarinet, in the Eight Easy Pieces for piano, and, finally, in the Sonata and Serenade for piano, we have a further development of these same principles. The evidence for this lies in the fact that on hearing any of these pieces, our attention is not drawn to their charms; rather are we completely caught up in the music's flow and in its varying tensions, and it is just this fact that attests to the solidity of the musical construction. The very concept of "construction" terrifies many people, who find in it the frightening negation of precious musical vitality and the haunting spector of "art for art's sake." But music cannot exist without construction. Its strength and endurance, the ease with which it moves, its practicableness—these are all conditions essential for formal clarity. Without them there can be no musical composition, but only a musical debris from which here and there scraps of good material protrude. Even if the listener sets little value by such things as conceptual unity, developmental logic, or the rhythm of expressive force, even if he will experience only individual episodes or even just those parts of individual episodes that he has got into the habit of liking, nevertheless, the force with which these "favorite passages" has impressed him is the result of a conscious ordering that permits them to be identified from among other, dissimilar, moments. Take, for example, an emotional song like *Amid the Din of the Ball* of Tchaikovsky [Op. 38, no. 3 (1878)—Trans.]. It would not produce the one-hundredth part of the impression it does if the composer had not adopted the slow waltz movement as a unifying intonational formula. This formula is the agent of the song's expressive force because it is a distillate of intonations whose emotional connotations are intimately understood and cherished by the public at large. The piece is therefore valuable both as a document of the technique of construction and as evidence of emotional power. The most difficult problem for the contemporary composer, spoiled as he is by an embarrassment of technical riches, is to obtain coherence of construction in a *simple* melodic line without accompaniment. In folk music—"music of the oral tradition"—the working out of a monophonic melody was the labor of generations, and any piece of extended length was the result of the efforts of many people. The best folk melodies, therefore, survive a long time without losing their effect on the psyches of succeeding generations. They have withstood the long process of selection and refinement, and they are the concentrate of the energy of song that has been accumulated and tested through the centuries. I shall go even further and assert that a real composer can be recognized by his ability to invent a melodic line that, without benefit of accompaniment, and without being a stylized folksong, is nevertheless in every way complete unto itself—a self-contained melos. Even Wagner's significance as a composer would be greatly diminished had he not written the celebrated violin solo in *Siegfried* (the ascent of the rock) and the shepherd's melody (English horn) in *Tristan*. Writing for unaccompanied chorus is a test of the same kind of skill.

There are two reasons why a completely self-sufficient melody is difficult to compose. First of all, the fact that the motion must be maintained, and monotony avoided, demands a certain diversity of material, but by the same token, care must be taken not to lose the impression of a unified whole. One must therefore utilize special "reminders" to gain coherence. The pitches may be grouped around one or two tones that are often repeated. Several pitches may form themselves into units that have a specific rhythmic shape, and the units may come to typify given contexts and assume the status of "themes." There may be rhythmic formulae that are being constantly repeated, changing shape, or even entering into new relationships with other such units. I shall not take the space to elaborate further the already familiar methods of linear development. The second difficulty in melodic invention (particularly at the present time) is the need to be acutely aware of the intimate relationship between breath tension and linear rhythm. This means that the compass of a melody must be combined with its durations in such a way that the particular disposition of the rise and fall of the melodic waves may be recognized as determining whether at any given moment the intensity of the musical flow is being increased or diminished, and thus the character of the melody itself will depend on how the particular patterns of breath tension are arranged.[7]

If melodic composition is to convey vital freshness and intensity, if it is to be more than mere head work and avoid sounding like the rustling of dead pages, then the basic considerations that must be complied with are those that have been mentioned. Stravinsky's Three Pieces for clarinet solo satisfy all these demands. There are three "movements:" calm (sempre piano e molto tranquillo, quarter note-52); a lively caprice woven of interlaced triplets (eighth note-168); and a grotesque fantasy, again lively, but more accented and more "collected" (eighth note-160). The opening of the first movement, which exploits the full range of the sounds of the entire lower register, takes the following form (clarinet in A). Note the characteristically wide and "empty" intervals [see ex. 244]. As the movement of the line is varied and extended, the line tends to pass into and define new areas; but each time it does so, it returns to a previous starting point—as if it wished thereby to "establish" a point of reference in the memory and maintain contact between this point and the newly explored area. The lower limit of the opening compass is e (sounding c#), and its upper limit extends to g#^{1} (and once touches a^1). The melodic line fills in the

Example 244

notes between these two extremes almost completely—only the g¹ is avoided. The melodic elements are frequently joined to one another by grace notes that strengthen the continuity of the line (a device used by the clavecinists and lutenists). The last section of the movement draws on its entire compass, and concludes with an expressive coda. The following fragment shows the end of the movement, beginning with the last appearance of the pitch e [see ex. 245].

Example 245

The starting line of the second piece is quite different [see ex. 246]. As a foil to this thematic "ribbon" (whose range extends from d¹ to g³), Stravinsky introduces a wholly different idea, whose character is derived from the qualities of the clarinet's lower register [see ex. 247].

Example 246

Example 247

After this idea has been briefly developed, the first "ribbon" gradually winds out of it and finally shoots up into the air like a "Roman candle" (a device frequently encountered in Stravinsky). This piece runs the gamut of both the lower and the upper registers of the clarinet and concisely but concretely exposes the peculiar qualities of each. Again the lowest e (sounding c♯) forms the bottom of the line, which reaches up to g^3. The full chromatic range is used except for $d\flat^2$ and $f\sharp^3$. The line is bright with fantasy.

The third piece ("third movement") is a rich grotesque, with a typical "ready" humor, and intonations that suggest amusing parodies of gestures (the teasing grimace and the perpetual nod). The whole movement is virtually an improvisation on its original idea (and particularly on the rhythm of the first measure [see ex. 248].

Example 248

Clarinetto in B
♪ = 160

The music has much in common with the Ragtime of *Soldat*. As a whole the pieces constitute a beautifully organized and exemplary "experiment" in making a musical construction that utilizes the riches of clarinet intonations and their idiomatic locutions and rhythmic configurations, giving them a typically contemporary expression and "dynamicization."

The eight easy little pieces for piano (for five fingers) are built on exactly the same principle. The "thesis" of each of these pieces is equally unpretentious: a short thematic element or melody (No. 4), a rhythmic turn (No. 2), or an harmonic complex (No. 8). Brief, concise musical ideas with a very narrow range are the subjects of No. 1 (andantino), No. 4 (larghetto), and No. 3 (allegretto) [see ex. 249].

Out of any given "thesis" or "premise" are developed the formal patterns, dynamic "resources," and motivic impulses inherent in the original idea, but here the whole is accomplished graphically, concisely, ascetically, in a brief span of time. The pieces, of course, have their serious, didactic side, which is to train the ears and the fingers to "feel" musical dimension and the almost imperceptible changes in the direction and pace of the elements that make up the line.[8] The technique of rhythmic variation is particularly prominent: motives are displaced and foreshortened, augmented and diminished, synco-

Example 249

pated, etc. In the sixth piece, lento, there is a very interesting use of the cross-relation that adds its harmonic twinkle to the chiaroscuro of this particular passage [see ex. 250].

Example 250

A study of each of these little pieces (or movements, actually) will provide a great deal of interesting evidence relative to musical construction, how the principles of linear composition are applied, and how the forces of musical inertia are overcome. The idyllic andantino, the jolly allegro, the amusing "Kamarinsky" allegretto, the beautiful siciliano (larghetto), the fragile moderato (whose tender melancholy derives from the archaic blemish on its otherwise limpid diatonicism), the lento with its short recurring phrases that produce alternations of major and minor, the characteristic dance melody vivo, and the astringent severity of the final pesante: these eight fascinating musical moments compose a string of musical pearls, each a gem of inventive genius, and yet the whole so unassuming as to be almost Schubertian in character.

This is a practical age, an age of organization and discipline, an age of grandiose projects, of mechanical rhythms and the dynamic of noise, an age typified by the illuminated advertisements of our city streets and the flashing movements of tramways, motors, and faces passing and repassing in and out of the glare of electric lights, an age whose perceptions are all under the colossal influence of cinematography. It would have been singular indeed if music had failed to reflect the whole reality of our life, if it had withdrawn into a closely shuttered room where it could go on dreaming, afloat on the clouds of poetic fantasy of its romantic past. Is the realm of music only contemplation? Only personal feeling? Can music not dare to shine into all the corners of life and reflect all that it sees? I do not mean at all that music cannot thrive on emotional materials. I only defend the right of music to take its materials from any source. Suppose a music—for example, the *Piano Rag-Music* of Stravinsky—that has no smooth melodic line, but only "fragmentary" melodies that come and go over the steady rhythm of astringent harmonies. Suppose only short melodic ideas, zig-zagging motives, brittle melodic lines that come abruptly into view and just as abruptly vanish, that flash and scurry back and forth, that twinkle and jingle—and suddenly compose themselves into something very much like a familiar tune. And suppose further that all this seeming chaos of sonorities is in fact severely and coherently organized, so that each note and each duration has its place and fulfills its function. Is music of this kind really just a bad dream? Why cannot music have the directness typical of a poster? Why may it not dare to "show" people and events in a steady rhythmic pulsation, like cinematography, as Prokofiev so often does in the *Love for Three Oranges?* Why should its rhythms and intonations not be broken up, like the fractured "dissonances" of the streets? Why should it not have the right to convey the uproarious noise of the contemporary city? Whence, if not from the plenitude of life's sounds, may its materials come? People say that the sound of music is an echo of our inner world, and that such is its sphere and its purpose. I don't think so, at least not absolutely. This view fails to realize that the well of music—even if it echoes the sounds of this inner world—must seek replenishment from the sounds that surround it, or run the risk of going dry. For good or for ill, to live life is to be alert to one's surroundings, and contemporary composers cannot insulate themselves from the effects of the seething activity around them. Many of them, indeed, go beyond the expression of inner experience, contemplation, memories—they build their music expressly out of the movements of life itself. Of this group, Stravinsky is the leader, and he has been its leader ever since *Petrushka.* Whether he will eventually compose a musical inditement of contemporary life in which the color and movement of the city and streets are the real motive force, and not just a background for lyricism, it is difficult to foretell. But there are elements in his music that anticipate such a possibility. That is why I like and esteem the *Piano Rag-Music* (1919) with its wonderful rhythmic irregularities, conflicts of accent, and glittering cinematographic style, in which figures of sound appear and vanish in continuous alternation. The piece exhibits at one and the same time mechanization, spontaneity, the dynamic of dance (the extraordinary flexibility of rhythmic movement utterly overpowers any tendency toward mechanical alternation of sound complexes), hammered rhythm, and a gay and almost casual arrangement of the various musical elements. A trivial dance piece, as many believe it, it is not, nor does any of them have the wit to compose it. On the other hand, we need only look at the numerous imitations of Stravinsky's ideas in the music of a few foreign composers who are in hot pursuit of him, to appreciate his intellect, his temperament, and the force of his imagination. Even the Piano Sonata, which seems somewhat abstract at first acquaintance, is actually heavily saturated with contemporary "urban" impressions—especially, for example, the mechanical revolutions of the first movement that proceed almost without respite. The effect of cinematographic glimmer can be heard in the rondoletto of the Serenade for piano.

These works for piano solo that I have just mentioned—the Sonata (1924) in three "movements," and the Serenade en La (1925) in four "movements"— call attention to the composer's experiments in the field of musical dynamics and kinetics, experiments whose implications are not yet fully known. Both works are strong and practical in design, both extremely ascetic and economical in the use of material (no superfluous digressions, no long lingering lyric moments), both sound indisputably and exhaustively complete, both convey intellectual conviction and force and masculine strength of will. The pieces are beautifully proportioned and beautifully discreet. They exhibit a mature musical sensibility under full control, yet they do not lack vitality, nor is that vitality factitious. On the one hand, they are flawless monoliths of intensely concentrated energy; on the other, models of the mechanization of musical movement, and of an original and new system of expressing thought in sound. These, at the very least, are the fundamental impressions made by these two works. Despite their character, however, they agitate the imagination, they compel attention to themselves—even though the "dryness" of the composer's disciplined thought may surprise and even frighten some of the less adventurous. The material of which Stravinsky disposes has been "neutralized" in every respect, as if to avoid burdening the mechanical flow of the ideas with extramusical associations. Obviously, the composer consciously rejects the use of folk material and any essence of "Russianism" that may trail an ethnographic perfume. All emotional coloration is specifically avoided—first, by precluding any romantic or pathetic nuance or spontaneous fluctuation of tempo, so that the motion is absolutely exact, and second, by stripping the material of every possible mark of emotionalism or sensibility, by rejecting any allusion to experience or sensuality or the conventions of melodic utterance. Conceptually, the music is neutral with respect to feeling and imagery, a conjunction of sounds freed of association with conventional emotional states. That is my analysis of the important qualities of the music of the Sonata and Serenade. I consider both these to be transitional works. The artistic asceticism is so extreme, the dynamics and kinetics of the piano are locked into such a narrow frame, there is such scrupulous avoidance of any emotional tone to the material: are these not the indicators of an inner concentration and preparation, of a period during which processes of thought are being sharpened and new means of expression forged? Who knows? Such concentration might lead directly to an explosion like *Sacre,* as a reaction against the fetters of asceticism—or to an austere classicism, a monumental symphonic style, a synthesis of Raphael and Mozart. After such a period, trust Stravinsky to have a surprise in store.

The Serenade (1925), of course, is no ordinary serenade, and it has nothing in common with works of the type we think of when we hear the term. Or, to put it another way, what (and all) it does have in common, is a common impulse. Stravinsky, starting from what to him are typical aspects of the lyricism of "Serenade-ness," proceeds to develop these aspects within the limitations of the piano dyanamic, and he gives them the following names: Hymn (first movement, quarter note-58), Romance (second movement, eighth note-96), rondoletto (third movement, quarter note-92), and a concluding movement (cadenza finale, quarter note-84). The quality of lyricism is most clearly conveyed in the Romance.[9] The plan of the little rondo is charming: a lively and witty round dance, whose motives and accents, despite displacements and transpositions of all kinds, inevitably lead back to the recurring refrain, and whose frantic and capricious irregularities are all controlled by a steady and undeviating rhythmic pulse. The four phases of the cycle, taken as a whole, convey the substance (dynamics, timbre, rhythm, and melody) of the serenade style, and the result is something like the old dance suites, each of whose movements drew on the rhythmic interplay and dynamic inherent in a real dance (the individual movements of these suites are not actual dance pieces) to form a conception of the dance that was free of all practical associations. The French clavecinists acted in exactly the same manner. Their pieces were not just vulgar program pieces. Behind all the fanciful titles, one discovers a serious attempt to convey in sound the dynamic and agogic musical essence of those ideas, to illustrate them, to embody them in sound, sound that must necessarily be in a state of motion because of the nature of music itself. One of the favorite occupations of the great masters of the eighteenth century was to extract the musical essences of ideas originally poetical or pictoral, and to compose these elements into a series of charming musical episodes. I believe that in his Serenade, Stravinsky draws close to their attitudes and their principles of musical formulation, though he decisively renounces all descriptive, symbolic, or emotional particularity. Despite the poetical "individualism" of the romance, with its improvisations, cadences, fragile lyric melody, guitar and lute intonations, and elegance of ornament, the Serenade as a whole is a work of graphic abstractness. The "idea" of the piece is the movement of clean lines and achromatic timbres. This is a new piano chamber style, a new world of sonorities whose principles are clarity of timbre, percussive "dryness," and the individualization of each sound. There is no pedal (almost without exception, and then only when Stravinsky wants the particular sonorities that result), and no emotional intensification (crescendo or diminuendo). The pace of the music observes an absolutely mechanical exactness and evenness, as if ruled by the setting of a metronome, and there is no accessory designation of the character of the motion. The dynamic indications and nuances derive from percussion: forte, piano, legato, détaché, staccato, with an occasional sharp and dry sforzando. The texture of the Serenade is completely linear. It is the exact opposite of impressionistic texture, with its "timbres of harmonies," indeterminate, unstable, its airy sfumato, its static concentration on complexes of sound as isolated entities. The sound of the Serenade, I repeat, is predominantly a dry piano sound, "pedal-less," and its technique makes extensive use of accentual displacements in a context of steady movement (especially in the rondoletto, where the accentual pattern of a single motive may be changed simply by transposing it to a different part of the measure.)

The Piano Sonata, written a year earlier then the Serenade (that is, in 1924), in many respects also serves as a study for it. The Sonata uses similar methods of formulation, and similar qualities of sound. It, too, is ascetic in thought and dry in language. Its construction is severely classical. The sonata has three parts, or three phases (something like a chain with three links), the central one of which is a comparatively static moment, adagietto.

The material of the sonata, like that of the Serenade, has been "neutralized" to an extreme degree, and the character of the movement has been mechanized. The form of the first movement (quarter note-112) is symmetrical, the opening and closing measures being identical. There is an exposition and a recapitulation, but both are terse, compressed, lacking obvious sectional articulation, caught up in the continuousness of the musical flow. The tonal relationships are clear: c minor, C major, D major, e minor, and a minor (I select only the important points) in the exposition, and in the recapitulations C major, d minor, G major, and c minor. The opening measures (that set the pace and character of the whole "movement") and the closing ones (the coda) are in c minor. Unity is achieved by the reintroduction of these initial measures at intervals throughout the movement (in the "development" they are used to articulate the various sections) and by their reappearance at the conclusion. Here are the first measures, that give unity to the whole sonata [see ex. 251].

These measures are the agent of the motion, its prime mover and constant stimulus. All the other elements are ranged one after the other with the exactness and inevitability of "predetermined harmonies," like the terms of a formula. The dynamic nuances are distinct, without shadow: forte and piano, pp subito, and meno piano. The tempo is absolutely even. Crescendo is used exceptionally and is purely dynamic, without the slightest accelerando. The contrasts of legato and staccato are carefully counterpointed. The movement

Example 251

of the music is orderly and efficient: there is no development, but only a kind of unwinding in which the unexpected and the unforeseen have no place, in which there is no growth or flowering, but simply the mechanical unrolling of a film. There is no hint of the dialectical struggles of the concerto form—the flow of the music is natural, steady, sufficient unto itself as a dynamic quality. To say that this music has no heart, is to say nothing at all. To view it as a tonal arabesque or an intellectual game, abstract and cold, would also be to play on words to no purpose, and to miss the point. Stravinsky's entire life is such a sensitive response to life, and the sonata is so closely related to his other accomplishments, its sparkling gyrations the reflections of such common qualities of contemporary reality, that it would be absurd to deny the truth of its nature. To be sure, there is no dynamic development, no revelation of truth or unity through the struggles of contradiction or contraposition. There is, instead, the mechanical unwinding of a film, whereby the potentialities of the material are exhibited as a stream of inevitabilities. In sum, such music reveals the mechanics of *things,* the ultimate necessity inherent in every fact. One may be frightened by its lack of humanity, but one cannot say it fails to touch, to excite. And is there really no humanity in it? Or is man here turning away from the inner world and its eternally "nagging" questions to the movements and dynamics that are perceived in the rhythms and phenomena of life itself? It is to this later assumption that I adhere.

The first movement of the sonata is the only one that has these qualities in an absolute degree. The second movement—adagietto—is a static idyll that pauses in admiring contemplation of the beautiful patterns of piano ornamentation. To label this kind of admiration as nonsensical, would be absurd. Can we love the shape of a new leaf, the silvery outlines of trees in frost, the fantasy of winter's designs on glass—in a word, the ornaments of nature, and not take delight in musical ornamentation? Those who do not, I fear, may be disposed to talk too much about the want of soul and sentiment in new music without realizing that they themselves lack the substance of a readiness, a genuine predisposition to accept the real joys of musical art, the refraction of all the phenomena of life through the dynamic of sounds and timbres. The substance of music is often music itself.

The slow "movement" consists of three sections in logical sequence. The substance of the first section is the interplay of graphic ornaments. In the second, there is a lyrical development whose course is determined by the context: a clean melody spun out over a sinuous and halting background. If the musical possibilities seem modest, the result is a surprising richness of sonority [see ex. 252]. The material of the final section is drawn from the opening [see ex. 253]. Thanks to a new, more intensive development of its melodic line, this section sounds like a synthesis of all that has preceded it.

Example 252

Example 253

The third movement (quarter note-112) is a brilliant example of musical dialectic. The basic premise, which unrolls with mechanical inevitability [see ex. 254] generates an action rich in dynamic and rhythmic "conflict." True, the "events" of this action do not have the quality of "Sturm und Drang"—but they are not less attractive for being on an extra-emotional plane. Even if the spirit of the music is not forceful or brilliant in conventional ways, the movement is as rich in "substance" as many of the piano pieces of Bach and Handel that are absolutely extra-emotional but in which the full-blooded pulse of life beats with no less force and amplitude than the throbbings of the inner world of man.

In its last appearance, the opening material is sounded against its own augmentation [see ex. 255].

The whole sonata is original, ingenious, in a class by itself. Also, the fact that among all the other sonatas that have been written in our day, only Stravinsky has known how to create an original masterpiece unconventional in

Example 254

Example 255

both conception and execution—this fact attests to the inventiveness and force of his creative imagination. Like any great artist, Stravinsky continually moves forward. He never sits quietly in a cloud of self-gratification. Each new work is a model for the next, each new work marks a new forward step in his continuing attempt to give back to life the sounds that came from her, but sounds such as other men have never heard. Therefore no book about him—or about any of the problems of contemporary music, for that matter—can ever end conclusively, because the composer is in the full force of his powers. The new graphic instrumental style of Stravinsky will lead him to conceptions and inventions of greater and greater value—his entire career is witness to that. Music whose intellectual health is so striking and expressive force so great will continue to overcome any temptation to deviate from its natural course, just as it refused to be caught by the backward romanticism of the salon or the spineless impressionism that had ceased to participate in the action of life. This music, which is so expressive and dynamic, has yet to reveal the full force of its influence. To imitate it would be prejudicial—and impossible. But learn from it one can. It is not a school, because Stravinsky—or Bach—will never create a school. Schools are created not by thinkers and inventors but by pedagogues and systematizers. But if his music is regarded as a point of departure, much else can be achieved. It seems to me that Stravinsky himself has learned many lessons from his own experiences, and that he is now on the way toward the creation of a monumental musical style.

We are now observing the art of Stravinsky at a moment of crisis. It is clear that, to express his ideas, the composer is searching for a language different from the language he himself has made a currency—that of the musical theater with its predominance of Russian folk intonations, even though these intonations had been stripped of specific ethnographic connotations and had acquired the status of an artistic universal. *Noces* was the culmination of the "old" style. In the "new" there has been nothing to equal *Noces*, but only because the experiments I have described still present themselves to the ear as strange oddities written in a kind of musical "esperanto"—an artificial language itself a hodgepodge of Roman, Gothic, and Slavonic elements. Or, if not "esperanto," perhaps a reversion to a "latin" like the Latin that was used throughout Europe in the Middle Ages and the Renaissance. In the development of music in Western Europe there really were moments when the patterns of intonations and methods of musical expression assumed a "universal" character almost completely free of the blemishes of local dialects. We have already seen one critical moment in Stravinsky's work: after the great leap into the future (*Sacre*, with its completely new sound-ideas that exploded all tradition), one felt that Stravinsky had arrived at a crossroads. The course that he chose led on to *Noces* and *Soldat*. One likes to believe that now, after his work outside the theatrical forms of music, after the laboratory "experiments" and his intensely concentrated search for new ways of defining and combining musical elements—that now Stravinsky will soon present European musicians with an objective and creative synthesis of all his work—and a synthesis, I suspect, of which the theater will be a part.

Notes

1. The words concerto and concertare have a double maning. In Latin, "concertare" means to dispute, to fight. In Italian, "concertare" means to arrange, to settle, and "concerto" means agreement, "di concerto"—"unanimously." In his excellent book *Geschichte des Instrumentalskonzert*, Leipzig, 1905 and later editions, Schering writes: The concept of the concerto is an old one. One can follow its traces way back into history—to the alternating choirs of Greek tragedy and to the Hebrew psalms, which became the *antiphons* of the Catholic rite (my italics—Asaf'yev).

2. The details of these listings are taken from the index of Stravinsky's works made by P.B. Ryazanov in the book *Igor Stravinsky and his Ballets* (Leningrad, Academia, 1926).

3. For example, the choral exclamations *"Rai, rai! Udalyi skomoroshek"* in the first scene (pages 16-18 of the piano score).

4. This is the second suite. The first contains: (I) Andante, (II) Napolitana, (III) Espanola, (IV) Balalaika—all also piano pieces originally.

5. Particularly, I repeat, in *Entführung* [*The Abduction*] and in the *German Dances*.

6. By this I do not mean that it is without value. Stravinsky attains a high degree of expressive force with the simplest of means. The instrumentation: flute and piccolo, two oboes, two clarinets, three bassoons, four horns, three trumpets, three trombones and tuba, kettledrums, bass drum, and tam-tam.

7. It is not only monophonic vocal music, of course, that is affected by such considerations. If it has not always been easy to make a dynamically correct calculation of the bowing, or "breathing," of strings, how much more difficult is it—and how few people really reckon with the difficulty—to write proper phrases for wind instruments. And with reference to vocal music again, the majority of composers do not take into account that performance difficulties in singing are very often caused not by intervallic complexities, but by a discrepancy between what the music demands by way of breathing and what in fact is possible (considering such things as breath supply and distribution, physical strength, articulation, etc.).

8. The Serenade in A for piano—especially the last two movements—is music of a similar character.

9. In the Royal March from *Soldat,* by choosing material typical of street bands and vesting it in the garb of contemporary rhythms and intonations, Stravinsky defined the type to which all these marches relate. So in this Romance, he composes the typical serenade whose features he has gleaned from the characteristic intonations of lute and guitar, and whose image in sound he conveys through the dry, semi-pizzicato style of the piano. The serenade as a whole is a paragon of subtlety, lucidity, and technical skill: the quintessence of the romance.

Postscript: *Oedipus* and the New Ballets

When I was completing this book in December of 1926, I gave very careful thought to the concluding lines of the preceding chapter. At that time I did not know that Stravinsky was at work on *Oedipus,* and I was unaware of the various intellectual, personal, and practical considerations that were to affect the following period of his artistic evolution. But now (the end of 1928), *Oedipus* has appeared and has been followed by two new ballets: *Apollon Musagète* and *Le Baiser da la Fée* (on themes of Tchaikovsky). I therefore find it necessary to append a supplementary chapter on these interesting new offshoots of Stravinsky's growth, works which, like everything that he does, continue to exhibit an intuitively chaste intellectual taste combined with the brilliant heterodoxy of his Russian genius.

Certainly, the opera-oratorio *King Oedipus* (1926-27) is a synthesis of Stravinsky's latest and persistent efforts to create a new style that will be strictly practical and also neutral (that is, uncontaminated by national or subjective emotional connotations)—in short, a kind of musical esperanto. After a number of experiments in the strictly symphonic sphere, Stravinsky makes this synthesis in conjunction with the theater again, though he avoids as far as possible both pure theatricality and musical drama. In a certain sense he rehabilitates the almost forgotten secular cantata, but his cantata is devoid of symbolism, allegory, mysticism, and even mythology. On the contrary, the tragedy of Oedipus is given a Latin interpretation that is extremely concrete and straightforward, that has both the clarity and precision of contemporary photography and the monumentality of classical statuary. The work of Sophocles[1] is greatly compressed and condensed. The authors have taken only what is important and essential, only what will survive the translation into the intensities of musical speech and lend itself to development in that language. The pronouncements of the oracle and the enigmatic intrigues of fate are conveyed with the same tone as that used by Roman historians to describe the events of legend and myth. *Oedipus* has no symphonic episodes with purely emotional functions. Before each important moment or turn of events, the Speaker communicates to the listeners the essence of what is to follow, in a style whose laconic formality reminds one of film titles. Then the music (soloists, chorus, orchestra) "relates" or "presents" these events with a kind of epic grandeur in strokes that suggest the severity and massiveness of the fresco. The work is in principle (and in realization) statuesque—like the prologue to *Prince Igor,* like the mighty painted figures on the pillars of ancient temples—though of course without relation to any religious tradition. If the music is static, it is the static of an Handelian order, an equilibrium of episodes whose succession induces a conflict of energies that propels the events toward their inevitable and fatal termination. In each episode the music strives with the strength of a Michelangelo to break apart the constraints of this schematic simplicity. For this static quality is no passive impotence—it is a restriction consciously imposed, a frame of iron discipline and emotional control designed to produce and contain its own energies and intensities. Stravinsky, like Handel and Beethoven, selects the simplest combinations of sounds, material obvious and universally accessible, out of which he creates a music of great majesty. He has, like them, the faculty of discovering the universe of new artistic possibilities contained in the most ordinary matter. Though his rejection of the language of emotional subjectivity in favor of material of the most ordinary provenance accounts for the absence of a personal emotional tone, it does not diminish the emotional intensity or accessiblity of the tragic aspect of the King. The choral farewell of Oedipus ("Vale, Oedipus, te amabam, te miserior") has a human simplicity completely devoid of the bombast of pathos. It is impossible not to accept the truth of what has occurred, not to accept the pitiless horror of life.

Only a great master could permit himself the audacity of restricting his musical language to the most ordinary locutions at a time when the new generation of composers is everywhere seeking new sound materials. The problem is to use the discipline of restriction as a means of extending and enriching the powers of the language, avoiding both the anemia of stylization and the excessive refinements of archaicism. To follow that course is not only audacious—it is dangerous, and as we shall see later in *Apollon,* by refusing to keep to the straight and narrow, Stravinsky fell into the pitfall of a derivative thematicism. But in *Oedipus* the experiment succeeded—in part, probably, because he had the solid old Baroque operas as models, whereas in *Apollon* his prototypes were the small dance forms of the classical ballet. But the music of *Oedipus* is timely—a strong plea for humanity and the ideas of humanism scorned by contemporary European civilization. Avoiding the subjective musical emotionalism of the nineteenth century as a basis for the expression of his ideas, and choosing instead a musical language that was neutral, free (with almost no exceptions) of a subjective nervous current, and made up of ordinary intonations that had long since established themselves in the subconscious and whose implications had been widely explored—Stravinsky achieves a classically proportioned style and a majestic expression of the tragic catastrophe that is above and beyond all particularity. Of course, there is no new musical culture or aesthetic in *Oedipus*. It is on the threshold of novelty, but who can say how wide that threshold is? However, the work is a great blow to that whole domain of European musical culture that is still ruled by the coarse cliches of verismo and its banal musical ideas.[2] Musicians of both the "left" and the "right" may be perplexed and even put off by superficial acquaintance with the music of *Oedipus:* the former, because the novelty of it is in new uses of old materials (is not that a sign of failing powers?); and the latter, because such new uses and an eagerness to break the old molds whenever necessary, produce results as audacious as those achieved with an original and private language. *Oedipus* actually affirms the right of a great master freely to choose whatever complexes of sound may be needed to give the most intense expression of his ideas and feelings, and to organize them in accordance with their natures. I do not subscribe to the theory, now so fashionable, that Stravinsky has imitated Bach or Handel—that is, that he has sought *deliberately* to create a stylized music. People who know Bach and the qualities of his music can only smile at such assertions. The traces of Bach's musical mentality (in the Octet, for example) and the details of other similarities mean only that Stravinsky has adopted some of Bach's methods, together with other methods used by many other composers of the late seventeenth and early eighteenth centuries. The same pertains to the alleged Handelian influence (for example, again, in the Piano Concerto and in *Oedipus*). One can properly speak of a correspondence of principles of formulation with those found both in Handel and in the music of his epoch, but not of restoration or imitation. The great significance of a work like *Oedipus*—affirming, as it does, the right to free selection of materials and methods—is that it brilliantly asserts the artistic principle that contemporary music can remain contemporary and still declare its association with the whole experiences of European art music, that new music and its representatives need not suffer the reproach of isolation or of a sterile subjectivism.

Before describing the musical materials and the style of their development, I should like to make a few preliminary observations on the general stamp and quality of this opera-oratorio. First of all, it is a composition of vocal forms and timbres.[3] It therefore demands good singers with voices resonant, rich, and strong enough to achieve a maximum total saturation. This pertains especially to the role of Jocasta (mezzo-soprano), and also to Creon, Tiresias, the shepherd, and the messenger. The role of Oedipus makes even greater demands of the artist. Above all, he must have a model declamation—he must be an eloquent practitioner of the technique of verbal expression, and he must be deeply sensitive to all the nuances of the drama. In addition, he must be by temperament brilliant, and he must have perfect control of all his faculties and resources. The role also demands that the most subtle contrasts of mood and experience be communicated with the utmost style and finesse: the role of

Oedipus runs the gamut of mood, from a haughty and boundless self-confidence to the extreme of pitiless irony. The role has no single point of view—only an artist of great experience and equally great intellectual cultivation can begin fully to encompass and contain the image of Oedipus and give it theatrical representation in a way that will be meaningful to people living in the twentieth century.

Musically, *Oedipus* is constructed as a chain of contending episodes, a device so simple as to suggest correspondence with a more primitive form of musico-dramatic organization. Arias, ariosos and duets, dialogues and monologues (arioso and psalmodic in character, but not secco like the "functional" recitative of the opera buffa) together form a chain of vocal scenes that parades before the auditors the austere and majestic masques of classical tragedy. To the chorus is alloted a large and important role—it is both the background and the substructure of the musical action. Through it the statuesque mass of the people comments with pathetic moans and wails, severe entreaties, majestic hymn-like outbursts, salutations, expressions of approval and disapproval and weighty opinions. It is through this deeply compassionate sympathy and watchful concern for the proceedings and analysis of the course of events that the whole action acquires unity and articulation. The episodes using solo voices that sound clear of this choral substructure are equally imposing and majestic. With the exception of a few short lyrical digressions arioso, the solo parts are disposed in a series of well-defined, extensively developed arias and flowing recitatives. The style and coloration of the music are virile and impassive. The pace is restrained, unhurried, majestic. The lines and rhythms bespeak imperious inexorability. The occasional outbursts of passionate agitation and anxiety and emotional confusion are saturated with chromaticism and therefore contrast both in color and in spirit with the beautifully statuesque diatonicism of soloists and chorus. (When all is said, the style of *Oedipus* is the majestic style of the classical relief). Harmonically, the music of *Oedipus* adheres to the contemporary principle that a pitch may be established at the center of a musical grouping without the necessary intervention of the dominant seventh. This is "tonic" music, as distinct from both atonal music and music controlled by strict dominant-tonic relationships. Hence the great use of colonnades of triads supporting the clearly outlined melodic lines. The primitiveness of the sequences of vertical sounds is emphasized by the almost complete absence of the customary resolutions of chords. Seventh chords are employed under the most carefully controlled conditions, and there is even an attempt to revitalize the diminished seventh, which in its time had played such an important stylistic role in operatic dramaturgy. All this bespeaks a taste for simplicity of design and for musical masonry of the simplest kind. Even in the role of Jocasta, where the severity of the style is somewhat mitigated and where the vocal line has a slithering, serpentine character, the music does not forsake its basic qualities—even though the figure of Jocasta introduces the pathos of female impulsiveness as a quality complementing the figure of Oedipus that maintains its simplicity and majestic severity. Jocasta's beautiful, extended aria (beginning of Act II), in my opinion, perpetuates the best traditions of operatic classicism and is a model of vocal writing in the grand style. Except, perhaps, for the female arias of *Rusalka, Judith,* and *Prince Igor,* there has been no such aria in Russian music for a long time.

The melodic lines of *Oedipus,* which are uniformly clear, clean, and smoothly flowing, change character according to the course of the tragedy, the characters of the principal personnages, or the sense of the choral comment. The aim is to elaborate a melodic style that can generalize the particulars of mood or circumstance. For the chorus, for Oedipus, and especially for the shepherd and the messenger, Stravinsky writes psalmodic exclamations and melodies of two or three tones of a type found in ancient ritual both sacred and secular. The part of Creon, on the other hand, is written in the conventions of the heroic-pathetic genre somewhat in the taste of the magnificent style of baroque opera. This is done not without irony. The big C major aria of Creon, which flows out of the fanfare on the C major triad, is self-contained, complete unto itself. The aria proclaims the inexorable decree of the oracle (agent of the entire catastrophe) in a brilliant and authoritative tone—but at the same time in such a way that, though Creon believes he is his own master, to the listener he is made to appear as a plaything (much like the Japanese bird in *Nightingale*) which has been set in motion and will go through its mechanical operations.

In opera of this type there can be no texture of leitmotifs as a basis for musical development.[4] True, the opening "speeches" of the chorus contain a group of simple harmonic progressions and motives of lamentation that are stated over the heavy, steady tread of basses (in eighths, 6/8). This passage, which returns from time to time, and sometimes changes tonality ($b\flat$ minor, b minor) without a change in quality, may serve as a kind of leading motive or theme of lamentation (like a Renaissance lamento). The responses of the chorus unquestionably have a unity of mood that is an important factor in the work's coherence, but this material retains its statuesque quality and never undergoes development. There is a purely vocal motivic development in the line of Jocasta—the first "notes" of her aria (the syncopated motive beginning on g^1) branch out into the sinuous chromatic phrase of her duet with Oedipus [see ex. 256].

A similar development (by shepherd, messenger, and chorus) is fashioned out of an archaic motive [see ex. 257].

Such is the method used to give an extended passage a certain melodic unity. In *Oedipus,* Stravinsky in general avoids a mechanical use of leitmotifs in the instrumental texture. Rather does he seek to delineate character by

Example 256

Example 257

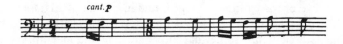

making each person the center of a concentration of music peculiar to him alone—thereby avoiding the need for a symphonic development of motives. The music of *Ruslan* is also constructed in this manner.

Now we can proceed to describe the most obvious features of the plan and sequence of the episodes.

The absence of a symphonic introduction serves to emphasize the vocal and oratorical character of the work. The opera is preceded by a prologue, in which the speaker addresses the public.

"You are about to hear a version in Latin of *King Oedipus*. In order to spare you the need to recall the details of the story, and since the action retains only the principal episodes from the tragedy of Sophocles, I shall describe them to you as the action proceeds.

"Oedipus finds himself the victim of a cruel fate, but of this he has no suspicion. From childhood, his life has been bound by a chain of events whose links are revealed in the drama you are about to witness."

There follows a brief summary of the first episode.

Act I

The opera opens with a lament of the male chorus. The city is ravaged by plague. The people entreat Oedipus to save them. After the commotion and agitation of the opening measures, the movement in eighth notes (dotted quarter note-50) is severe, unflagging, regular as the swings of a pendulum. The intitial tonality is b minor. The supplications relax, then rise again, change into a menacing whisper, and eventually die down in a pattern of exhaustion. Then Oedipus, with a conviction befitting his role as leader and high priest, declares his promise to save the city. He is something of a dithyrambic poet himself. The melody of his monologue resembles the ornamental "jubilation" of ancient ritual. The lament of the chorus returns in more persistent form, and it is led to ask what steps Oedipus has in fact taken to save the city (the voices in stark unison: "Quid fakiendum est, Oedipus, ut liberemur?"). Immediately after Oedipus has replied that Creon, the brother of the queen, has been sent to seek the advice of the oracle of Apollo, Creon appears, hailed by choral exclamations, and in his fanfare-like aria (C major, quarter note-120) declares the inexorable will of the deity: Thebes conceals a patricidal criminal who must be found and driven out—if not, the entire city will be wiped out by the plague. Oedipus replies in an aria with choral responses (opening in c minor, quarter note-60). He still has complete confidence in himself and hopes to penetrate to the sense of this injunction, assuming that it, like the riddle of the sphinx, cannot be taken literally. I call special attention to the beautiful conclusion of this episode, whose E♭ major tonality bears the promise of peace and serenity. It is built out of the ornamental melody of Oedipus's first monologue ("Liberi, vos liberabo"), now softened and made more graceful through chromaticism. Oedipus repeats his promise ("iterum carmen divinabo"). The chorus hails his words.

The speaker proceeds to explain the next group of events. Again we hear the choral supplications, but in b minor (the chorus now addresses itself not to Oedipus but to the deities themselves). Then comes the greeting to the old sage Tiresias. The old man sings an epic and impassive monologue ("I cannot say, it would be a sin to tell; beware Oedipus, my words")[5]. Immediately the drama of the action is intensified, in accordance with the King's growing excitement and the angered Tiresias. From the moment Oedipus interrupts the admonishments of Tiresias with the insolent "Your silence implies that you yourself are at fault," Tiresias spares the feelings of Oedipus no longer. In the terrible intonations of biblical prophecy, he reveals the real meaning of the oracle's words and points to Oedipus as the one responsible for the crime. Oedipus, trying to restrain his anger but little by little losing control of himself, answers the accusation before his people in a marvelous aria. He hurls reproaches at Creon and Tiresias, accusing them of wanting, out of envy with his happy lot, to seize power and drive him, the King, into exile. The aria is a conflict of impulsiveness and restraint. The voice returns twice to the stability of the opening phrase (tranquillo e ben cantabile), but the intermediary passages are filled with nervous, broken lines and pathetic outcries. Having run the gamut of dramatic tension from virtual frenzy down to the expression of submissive surrender to fate, poignant sorrow, and self-reproach (doloroso, piano, "volunt vestram regem perire"), Stravinsky abruptly introduces the bright and festive cries of the people at the appearance of the Queen, Jocasta (C major, half note-69). The first act concludes with the hymn of these greetings. The opening C major fanfares are developed in a strictly diatonic motet-concerto style with imitation, but the tonic chord is always firmly present or implied.

Act II

After the chorus repeats its greetings to Jocasta, the speaker again explains the events to come. The action resumes with the aria of Jocasta to which I have already referred. After an expressive recitative, classic in type, the first part of the aria's melody is developed (g minor, eighth note-84). The Queen rebukes the King and her brother—their personal and internecine quarrels have no place in such distressing times. The second part of the aria (d minor, vivo, half note-84) is a sharp contrast to the first: it is a bold and impassioned "speech" against oracles and against credence in them. The third part is a repetition of the first, melodically though not textually, and with the addition of choral responses which repeat the word *trivium* (drawn from the words of the Queen, and signifying the crossroads where Laius was murdered). At the sound of this word, Oedipus is filled with fear. He has recalled the long forgotten mischance. With horror he admits his guilt before Jocasta. The importunance and anguish of his thoughts are conveyed through a short four-measure phrase that Oedipus states four times with different words, each statement being concluded by relentless and grim timpani triplets. Jocasta tries to calm Oedipus with the assurance the oracles lie (a motive out of the aria developed in a pathetic c minor phrase—tempo agitato, dotted quarter note-144). Oedipus joins his voice to her melody, but he continues to express his suspicion of his own guilt and his horror of it. The duet undergoes an impulsive dramatic development. Despite apparent simplicity of construction, ease of flow, and musical coherence, the interlacements of the two voices are designed to express great tension. To Jocasta's appeal that they return home, Oedipus persists: Volo ("I must have the truth, I must ask the shepherd, who was a witness to the deed").

Here the music is broken off for a moment, and the speaker projects what is to follow.

The shepherd and the messenger enter. The messenger announces the death of Polybus, whom Oedipus had supposed to be his father, and establishes the fact that Oedipus had been only his adopted son. The writing of the whole scene—the dialogue of the messenger and the chorus—conveys a striking feeling for musico-dramatic truth. Out of the archaic-sounding theme of the chorus grows the tale of the messenger, who related how he found Oedipus as a babe in the mountains. The chorus thinks that the birth of Oedipus was miraculous. In a beautiful and tenderly elegiac melody (b minor, 6/8), the shepherd then affirms the messenger's tale of finding the babe who had been abandoned by his father and his mother. The horror of the truth begins to invade the consciousness of Oedipus. Out of the fragment of facts, the tales and recollections that form the dark cloud of accusation suspended over him, remembering that upon hearing the shepherd's tale Jocasta had shamefully crept away, Oedipus reaches his conclusion: as an ironic counterpoint to the pious thoughts of the chorus, he gives expression to the idea that there had in fact been no miracle. The irony continues: he takes up the tale that the shepherd had started and completes it by supplying the missing detail. The ornamental jubilations and flourishes of his arioso monologue are fashioned out of imitations and developments of a sinuous lyric motive from the shepherd's tale, and the end of the arioso gradually slips away like the final hush of a lullaby. This is music of delicate and sympathetic perception. I should call this monologue the work's "ironic scherzo." The tone of irony, which is eccentric to the anticipated mood, moves the pitch of the drama to a new level and adds an intensity of its own. After this, the stark and merciless truth of the babe's discovery is again sounded from the lips of the shepherd and messenger (duet on the archaic-sounding motive already mentioned). Without pity, they now tell all. Oedipus was born of Laius and Jocasta, he killed Laius, his father, and became the husband of his mother. (The shepherd and messenger proclaim these phrases in a kind of psalmody, fortissimo, on the unison d^1. Each phrase is repeated by the chorus on the open fourth d^1-a). There is a moment of silence—the male voices pause: only the nervously agitated orchestra is heard repeating the basic triad. Again the shepherd and the messenger "confess": "How much better it would have been not to relate how Oedipus, abandoned by Jocasta, was found in the mountains." Having declared themselves, they depart. Alone before his people, Oedipus himself now "summarizes" his involuntary crime. His monologue is given the expressive orchestral support of stark progressions of "verticals" which alternate various sequences of triads of d minor, D major, and b minor. The musical invention gives exceptionally brilliant expression to the drama and significance of the moment. From here on, the music begins its quick descent to the horror of the final catastrophe. In terse phrases, punctuated by fanfares of ominous violence, the speaker announces its coming. The messenger then enters and announces the destruction of Jocasta in music that has the majesty and strength of a chorale. Four times he repeats: "Divum Jocastae caput mortuum." The phrase is uttered over violently ascending and descending scales (fortissimo, 3/4, quarter note-132).[6] Between each phrase, the chorus, in a mood of great nervous agitation, excitedly relates the details. After the first—the suicide of Jocasta. After the second—the despair and blinding of Oedipus. After the third—the cursing and howling of Oedipus, and his decision to show himself. The messenger intones for a fourth time: "Divum Jocastae caput mortuum." Then, amid groans of horror from the people (using the opening material of the opera), Oedipus appears. He sings no more. The chorus gazes on the mute Oedipus with pain, with horror, and pity, and bids him farewell (the music of the lamento of the first act, but now in g minor) in doleful, austere phrases that sound over the background of steady eighth notes in the orchestra.

The end of the movement is terse and spare; like a slowing pendulum, the tone of the music gradually subsides to quiet and repose. Foregoing the crudities of violence, shock and agitation, and maintaining a tone of elegiac majesty, Stravinsky has made of the final threnody a moment of stunning and persuasive truthfulness. Stravinsky, composer of the elemental and romantic *Sacre,* inventor of highly original and colorful instrumental works, shrewd master of woodwind intonations *(Noces)* and of jolly and gay intermezzos *(Pulcinella* and *Mavra)*—this same Stravinsky found new artistic resources and impulses within himself to create, within self-imposed limitations, a work in an aesthetically severe "oratorical" style out of materials widely known and utilized, but materials now assembled and formed into original, contemporary, expressive complexes of sound. Throughout almost the whole of *Oedipus* the style is harmonic and homophonic, the exceptions being the few episodes that employ devices of polyphony (imitation, and even canon—though not strict canon).

It is not easy to be contemporary and at the same time confine oneself to a vocabulary of intonations and sound complexes common to all of European music and already familiar to the majority of people. I shall try to explain what this phenomenon means and thus try to get at the aesthetic significance of certain tendencies that have been visible in Stravinsky's most recent music, tendencies that find in *Oedipus* their most brilliant and complete expression. The importance of these tendencies is by no means slight, and even if we may argue about whether the composer did his job well or badly, or whether he was right arbitrarily to restrict himself to the use of materials that are common European property, it is inconceivable that we should object to *Oedipus* on the grounds of novelty of aesthetic principle. The individualism of the nineteenth century and the romantic era of *personal* effort and *personal* achievement in music accustomed people to a method of judging music based on the notion that the primary criteria of aesthetic value could be equated with subjectivity, novelty, originality, and independence of musical invention. The subjective perception and "penetration" of musical phenomena produced in art a distinctively personal emotional tone which ultimately led to the self-opinionated egocentricity of Scriabin. The erotic sensations of life formed the field and the goal of expression. As late as the middle of the eighteenth century (as the works of Handel clearly show), musical creation was under the influence of a philosophy whose aesthetic principles were quite the contrary. Those works were favored which utilized a preponderance of intonational formulae widely known and in general use, and with which expressive force and grace might be achieved. Or, to put it another way, art was considered a collective enterprise whose aim was not the invention of distinctively novel material but the establishment of a technique by which the obvious and the familiar could be converted into something still obvious, still familiar—but new. It was to novelty of texture and refinement of development that the connoisseurs attended, the materials themselves being already widely known. Whereas the modernism of the end of the nineteenth and the beginning of the twentieth centuries demanded absolute novelty of sonority as a token of the discipline and depth of musical thought, the strength, vitality, and grandeur of Mozart's art in his time rested precisely on his ability to give artistic expression to new attitudes while utilizing the most easily intelligible language. The early authors of the Singspiel, and later the Romantics (for example, Weber in *Freischütz* and Schubert in his Lieder), broadened the area of materials to include both folk and urban melodies, but they never abandoned the principle that the material itself should have a maximum accessibility. In every musical master of the nineteenth century, there "coexisted" two basic musical demands: one, to achieve a distinctively personal *expression* of ideas in a new sonorous context; and two (keeping one eye on the compass of society), to aspire toward a traditional language. The *Tristan* and *Meistersinger* of Wagner represent typical thesis and antithesis. Nevertheless, adherence to the principles of aesthetic collectivism in artistic creation and the existence of a concern for public awareness do not, on the whole, characterize the music of the nineteenth and early twentieth centuries.[7]

Now the curtain of subjective expressionism has been torn asunder by constructive realism, and the sounds of objective reality occupy the center of the stage. Everything that I have said in this work on Stravinsky has led toward the appearance of this enormously important phenomenon. But how, then, explain Stravinsky's affinity for Tchaikovsky? Tchaikovsky always worked with the most accessible materials—with the currencies of music that lent themselves to the magic of his powers of conversion. He shunned stylization, and his feelings were those of his era, but these facts were never obstacles to his creating works of great technical and expressive force—just as Scarlatti, Handel, Bach, Haydn, Mozart, and Beethoven had done before him. It is impossible to think of Tchaikovsky as an extreme individualist or an emotional renegade. The secret of his music's continuing effectiveness lies in the intelligibility of its locutions and the directness of its expression. Tchaikovsky had common feelings, but his intellect was that of a master. He therefore selected and produced masterly organizations of intonations. Stravinsky abandoned the school of aesthetic refinement that had held the whole development of Russian music in the grip of one-sided and exclusive canons of voice-leading (Glinka) and style (Liszt). Having done so, he was inevitably attracted to norms and problems of another order in his instinctive pursuit of the spontaneity of the great masters, of a melos that would have the richness of life, and a symphonism that would capture the mass of listeners—in short, in pursuit of a process whereby the musical wealth of the world might again be melted down into a coherent and mature musical style. Or, to put it another way, Stravinsky refused to be concerned with the problems of art in general, and turned his attention toward the sympathy of his listeners and toward the development of a simple vocabulary that might evoke their response. The development of intelligible oratorical speech is the necessary consequence. That, it seems to me, is the way Stravinsky arrived at his conception of *Oedipus.*

Paris was for Stravinsky what it had been for Lully, Gluck, and Cherubini, but the creative element in his work had been steeped in the traditions of his native land, and his earlier prophetic works were stained with the sensitive evocations of Russian life, no matter how European their dress or how deliberately Stravinsky may or may not have tried to remain the Russian artist. Even in *Oedipus,* despite the fact that the intonations had to be so contrived as to fit the patterns of the Latin language, the result is an interpretation of a profound and universal legend of classical antiquity that bears a personal stamp and that at the same time is in the best traditions of artistic realism as practised by Glinka, Dargomyzhsky, Musorgsky, and Tchaikovsky. Of course there is no ethnographic (in the national sense) material in *Oedipus,* but the musical language of the arias, recitatives, and choral laments—for all their "European" melodies, harmonies, and sonorities—continue to sound like a contemporary language that is and remains Russian despite these European-isms. And even if the Latin text of *Oedipus* cannot be understood by everyone (though it is very simple and almost "translates itself" through the music and the general character of the intonations), the music is itself a kind of "Latin," in the sense that it uses a universally felt phraseology of motives, rhythms, and locutions, and concise, clear formal patterns, all of which turn out to have a universal communicability. I think that the manner in which our native artists sing and play would produce a deeply vital interpretation of *Oedipus.* For the deliberate de-nationalization of the musical language and of the plan, style, and character of *Oedipus* do not in the least prevent its expressive qualities from finding a kinship with the traditions of Russian artistic realism which were developed in the music of the masters I have mentioned above, on the basis of materials, textures, and forms of Western European opera-oratorio. The Latin declamation of *Oedipus,* despite the severity of its metrical patterns, is certainly not that of classical literature. But the Latin nevertheless reinforces the oratorical pathos that inheres in the work. And actually this pathos dictates the natural choice of types of intonational locutions (question and answer, doubt, affirmation, etc.) that are appropriate to its expression. All this, moreover, is accomplished with pure melody and (for lyrically important moments) within the framework of tripartite arioso and aria, for Stravinsky does not permit the formal schemes of *Oedipus* to violate the classical canons of musical construction.

To sum up: With *Oedipus,* Stravinsky boldly entered a period of supra-individualistic creation. He tried to express the universal content of a classical tragedy in the simplest formulae of sound, with lines and rhythms common to collective experience, with intonations that represent a new selection and new combinations of the classically common locutions of the European operatic language—a language that is extra-national and extra-romantic but that draws principally on the oratorio forms of the eighteenth century. The musical language of *Oedipus* places a contemporary operatic-oratorio style on an old base, and gives it maximum accessibility. This does not mean vulgarity (for the work has no echoes of boulevard or restaurant music), but a respect for centuries of artistic wisdom. From the point of view of art and society, the work is an experiment in the formulation of an extra-individualistic aesthetic and a possible way out of the blind alley of subjective musical experiments, no matter how beautiful or how profound, and no matter how pregnant their accomplishments may have seemed for the further evolution of music. After *Oedipus,* Stravinsky has written two other theatrical works that I have already named. With them, his creative work enters a phase of still unresolved crisis. In *Apollon,* the process of the Europeanization of the composer's musical language continues. This process had been fruitful in the case of *Oedipus,* and the work did not forfeit a basic organic quality: the subject was of universal applicability—the tragedy of *Oedipus* can deeply affect the contemporary listener—and the simple forms used were those of classical opera. But by refusing to have a coherent extra-musical theme for *Apollon,* Stravinsky breaks with those who expect the musical theater to be a force of aesthetic value. Here he embarks on the dangerous course of recreating the magnificence of the court ballet spectacle for a non-existent aristocratic theater.[8] *Apollon* and *Baiser* mark a break with *Oedipus,* in so far as that work brought the composer back into contact with listeners who were outside the public of aesthetes in the large cities. True, the nature of *Oedipus* made it more an idealistic appeal to humanity in general than an attempt to influence a particular class of people through treatment of a more contemporary and vital subject. But however remote the specific tragedy, the ethos of *Oedipus* alone would justify to a very large degree the composition of the work. *Apollon* and *Baiser,* however, hang in mid-air. Neither ballet can count on a long life outside of the symphonic concert field, and only then if the long since exhausted theatricality of its theme from fairy tale and mythology does not act as a deterrent. The second ballet has a better chance, since there the musical themes of Tchaikovsky revitalize the melos of Stravinsky which, in *Apollon,* is only a dry and lifeless eclectic esperanto.

The period following *Oedipus,* therefore, appears to be a critical one for the creator of *Sacre* and *Noces.* The crisis resides in the process (something that the times demand) whereby the composer's musical materials and language may find their orientation toward the general public. The process in this case is closely related to a movement that has recently arisen in France—a movement toward *simplicity,* toward the suppression of a detached individualism and the narrowing of artistic problems to a concern with one's milieu and its day-to-day affairs. This effort which unquestionably had a certain instrinsic value, rather soon resulted in a stylization of simplicity itself, by concentration on the refined lyricism of certain neglected French melodists (for example, Gounod) and on imitation of their materials, but of course in an adaptation that bore the stamp of contemporary features. *Apollon Musagète* was written in 1927. Its choice of subject follows in the line of certain distinctive developments in recent theatrical music of the West: an affinity for adapting subjects drawn from mythology and classical antiquity. Though there have been many mediocre works, the movement has also produced much of value. Besides the *Oedipus* of Stravinsky, let us cite as examples the *Socrate* of Satie (1920-22), and the *Antigone* of Honegger (1924-27). *Apollon* marks the most recent point on this line, and though it is therefore aligned with *Oedipus* in one sense, in another the two works are notable for their differences. *Oedipus* is a reformulation of the classical opera-oratorio, *Apollon* belongs to the tradition of the suite (a sequence of variations and pas de deux); *Oedipus* is an intense treatment of a tragic theme, *Apollon*—as the composer himself says—is a piece without intrigue, a piece in which the choreographic action develops the theme: "Apollon, leader of the Muses, inspires each of them with his art." The forms of the ballet are small, its melodic style dry. Stravinsky's mastery of the string ensemble enables him to conceal these deficiencies within a score whose distinctively aristocratic and elegant sonorities convey a very special intensiveness. The music of *Apollon* was born of dance—not dance in the basic, direct, motor-muscular sense, but a stylization of dance—dance as it crystallized in lines and forms of classical ballet, and in their accompanying musical and rhythmical formulas and schemes.

The ballet begins with a tripartite prologue (the birth of Apollo): a gracious central Allegro framed by a slow majestic Largo. This is a contemporary version of the Lully overtures. Here the elements of Stravinsky's *classicism* are obvious: an astringent diatonicism, textural motion that is heroicized by the clarity of its classical meter, and—most important—a manner of concealing the simplicity (simple triviality, usually) of progressions and locutions by altering the usual tonal functions and by a very special manner of displacing the expected courses of melodic lines. In *Apollon,* Stravinsky is dealing with second-hand material—reminiscences of old-fashioned motives out of classical court ballet—but he puts this material together by means of a "new syntax" with results that display a wonderful resourcefulness and great delicacy of taste. But the price of such simplification is high: to put it bluntly, Stravinsky appears as the "retrograde of himself" and his melos takes on all the negative features of esperanto—of an artificially contrived language, even to the point of neologisms from Wagner and melodic locutions that might have come from Pugni [Cesare Pugni (1802-70), Italian who went to St. Petersburg in 1851 as ballet composer to the imperial theaters—Trans.]. Almost all the music of *Apollon* bears witness to the annoying attempt to make new cloth out of old thread: the ear is continually drawn to patches of cheap, old material that spot the fabric of the sound. It is impossible not to regard *Apollon* as a marvelous set of ingenious gyrations on a theme of great and annoying musico-choreographic triviality. It takes all of Stravinsky's virtuosity to overcome the inertia of the material, but the result is an hyper-refinement of texture and a simplification that is itself an utter failure.

These general remarks on the music have interrupted my description of the score. The prologue also serves as the first scene of the ballet. The second scene opens with the beautifully elegant variation of Apollon (solo violin). Here the beneficial influence of Tchaikovsky's classicism is operative, not in the sense of any passive borrowing of material, but in the sense that the movement is a further development of his methods of formulation. The method is applied most brilliantly in Stravinsky's latest ballet *(Baiser de la fée)*.

Following Apollon's variation there is the plastic pas d'action—Apollon's dispensation of gifts to the Muses—with a very trivial B♭ major melody. This pas d'action, plus the four following variations, the choreographic duet (the pas d'action of Apollon and Terpsichore) and its typical dance coda (on rather banal material) together form the main substance of the music and dance of the ballet. Here there is a lot of elegant music with piquant melodic and harmonic permutations and surprising alterations of familiar locutions. But even so, much of its moves back and forth between simple artificiality and artificial simplicity. In *Soldat, Renard, Pulcinella,* and *Mavra,* the materials had a robust quality, and the works exploited their potentialities brilliantly. Here, there is a dangerous aesthetic that sanctions the hyper-refinement of a texture that is antiquated in the first place and good for nothing in the second. It is as if we were back in the days of the unforgettable *Roi Candaule,* one of the most trivial of Pugni's ballets. To be sure, Stravinsky is a sensitive artist and a great master, and by bringing the energy of his brilliant intellect to bear on the elements that make up this genre of compositions, he can cleanse and purify them for his own use. But the question nevertheless arises: why occupy oneself with a renaissance of the form of the classical ballet and the images of classical mythology, if the purely musical craftsmanship must exhaust itself struggling with—or, more accurately, juggling with—worthless materials? The composer tries hard: he avoids the vulgarities of "squareness," he shuffles and alters stereotyped cadential formulas, he breaks the metrical monotony that inheres in the variation scheme by inserting measures of varying length, he replaces the usual tonic-dominant bass line with one that is more flexible and mobile, his two-part writing (melody and bass) is tracery of the utmost refinement and weaves an exquisitely calculated pattern—in a word, his score is without peer as a laboratory of the composer's technical skill. Even more: it is an encyclopedia of his technique. By utilizing novelty of function to refresh progressions of the utmost triviality, he craftily constructs new formations out of the most ordinary elements and gives them an air of calculated artlessness. It is interesting, but it becomes tedious, to watch a great master make such exertions. It is something like the entertainment of a shadow play, where the most fanatical images can be projected onto the wall through the simplest motions of the fingers.

All this, of course, cannot detract from the several aspects of the work that are successful. The music that characterizes Apollon Musagète brilliantly reflects the luminosity of his image. Apollon's first variation, melancholy, vacillant, and his second, sunlit, in the spirit of a dithyramb, both afford evidence of the evolution of Stravinsky's classicism. The most brilliant symphonic moment is indisputably the hymn of apotheosis (the ascent to Parnassus), which provides a beautiful conclusion to the whole conception and contains very promising elemments of a new style of majestic simplicity. The hymn is itself justification of the whole work. Listening to it, one forgets the motley mosaic and eclecticism of the other pages of the score. Everything that the rest of the music, with all its antiquated and lifeless formalisms, has implied or tried to say, is concentrated and revealed in this final passage.

Stravinsky's last ballet (*Baiser de la fée,* after a tale of Andersen) is a work of quite another kind. Its musical material is a gleaning of partial or entire musical melodies and phrases from the works of Tchaikovsky. The result is not always to Stravinsky's advantage, because it is just those episodes where the composer risks the appearance of his own melodic constructions that sound dry and listless, despite the fascination of the orchestral apparel. Nevertheless, in comparison with *Apollon,* the whole ballet leaves the impression of stylistic integrity and great freshness.

The principal thematic material of *Baiser* is the popular melody of Tchaikovsky's *Berceuse pendant l'orage.* The ballet begins (an exquisite lyrical prelude) and ends with it. In addition, its last transformation, in the finale, thanks to the exceptional transparency and airiness of the texture, opens up new perspectives—presentiments of a symphonism of atmospheric sonorities. Like the final hymn of *Apollon,* one page of such music makes one forget all the naive and belovedly antiquated theatrical and choreographic dramaturgy of the ballet and permits one to believe that after a critical period of peregrination, the art of Stravinsky will once again resume a steady course.

What does Stravinsky do with the material from Tchaikovsky, and which of its elements does his music refract and develop? Briefly, compared to his handling of the melody of the gracious composer of the eighteenth century, Pergolesi, Stravinsky treats the material borrowed from Tchaikovsky with more originality and boldness. One might even say that he develops Tchaikovsky's sound ideas as hypotheses, as if to suggest how Tchaikovsky would have expressed his thoughts in our own day. When Stravinsky alters the harmonic and melodic locutions of Tchaikovsky, he does so with a view to sharpening their design, giving them a severe and even dryish quality, eliminating any casual traces of a specific epoch, revealing still new qualities of value. The epigones of Tchaikovsky have weakly imitated or repeated in a thousand different ways everything that the master had said better himself before them. Stravinsky, however, with his natural authority and capacity for instinctive calculation, has seen at a glance the most obvious, characteristic, and basic elements of Tchaikovsky's melos and has fashioned them into a contemporary edifice. If he had applied similar technique to the vapid material of *Apollon,* that would have given the work more rigor. Here, the technique combines with the rich and direct emotion of Tchaikovsky's melody to form an organic neo-classic style—neo-classic by virtue of its economy and clarity of texture, the severe simplicity and conciseness of its form, and the restraint of its expression. The impression gleaned from the piano score is confirmed by the testimony of those pages of the full score that I have been able to study. The severe economy of Stravinsky's instrumental style, which admits of no excess whatever, and the calculated strictness and rationality of his music, not only fail to destroy the poetry of the tale but actually enhance it: all flabbiness, all tedious sentimentality, all the little pools of saccharine lyricism, have vanished. To all this, however, there is another side. The "latinization" of Stravinsky's mentality and language (savoir-faire, economy, the exact calculation of every effect) sometimes does violence to Tchaikovsky's melody, by giving it a dry and sober quality at the expense of its characteristic tenderness and plaintiveness. In such cases, Stravinsky finds new and unusual qualities in Tchaikovsky's material, but in doing so he destroys the patina of intellectualized idealism and mannered tearfulness.

In *Baiser,* there are four scenes. In the first scene, the lyrical element is dominant. As I have already pointed out, the principal musical idea is the melody of the *Berceuse pendant l'orage,* which is interspersed with fragments of other Tchaikovsky melodies or new music created in the same style. The delicate transparency of the harmonies, the elegant but precise design of the melody, and the magical fascination of the orchestration combine to make of this scene a charming symphonic episode. This is followed immediately by the animation and buoyancy of the typically rural second scene, and Stravinsky here shows what an outstanding master he is. The theme, drawn from

Tchaikovsky's piquant piano Humoresque (the first part), is converted into rich and colorful orchestral music. The material itself, which is fresh and provocative in its original version, sounds even more so under Stravinsky's witty and inventive treatment. A theme from the *Album pour enfants* is cleverly and unexpectedly woven into the texture *(Le paysan prélude)*, and there is a host of other witty devices. There is a beautiful use of the melody of the *Natha-Valse* which is given a striking pastoral coloration. Among Stravinsky's favorite procedures (also found in *Oedipus, Apollon,* and *Pulcinella*) is a great reduction in the uses of dominant sevenths in cadential formulas, and in the tiresomely predictable expectations that such uses evoke. We might even say that by this procedure, Stravinsky "unveils" the tonic. The result, as applied to Tchaikovsky's material, is a new, somewhat astringent, quality.

The music of the second scene is clear, fluent, simple, bright, cheerful. The music is in the tradition of the *Kamarinskaya* of Glinka, a host of authentic festival scenes in Russian operas and symphonies, Stravinsky's own *Petrushka,* and the vernal dances of *Sacre*. Once again, the composer has revitalized the genre in intonations that are colorful and fresh, without any intrusion of skittishness, or deliberate modernization. If, beside the richly ornate mass scenes of *Petrushka* and *Sacre,* this score has a somewhat modest aspect, as musical painting it is finer, and more intimate.

In the third scene (By the Mill), the listener is submerged in an atmosphere of love, in the playfully affectionate lyricism of maidenly florescence. (The music reminds one of *Firebird*.) Here the predominant fragrance is the fantasy of Tchaikovsky's music, redolent with connotations of fairy tale and dream. Scherzoso elements (the Scherzo humoristique for piano, the "atomized" scherzo of the Third Symphony) are prominent. There is an exquisite use of a delicate melody from the *Album Leaves,* also one of Tchaikovsky's more popular piano pieces. The opening of the scene seems obviously derived from the entr'acte (Dream) of the *Sleeping Beauty,* but the music is Stravinsky's own. The big choreographic duet (pas de deux, variations, coda) and part of the fourth and final scene are episodes of less musical interest. I have already spoken of the ballet's amazing finale. Melodically, the choreographic duet is impoverished, sluggish—once again an artificial musical esperanto. The contrived melody of the adagio makes this passage especially and distressingly uncommunicative. The variation is nice, but many Russian composers have done this kind of thing before, and Stravinsky seems only to be trying again to learn a lesson that he already knows by heart. Unfortunately, the coda does not overcome the fate of all codas of classical ballet: its material is trivial, and so is its form. As in the variations and imposing coda of *Apollon,* the sonorities of the music are elegant, but they cannot compensate for penury of melos and flabbiness of conception. Though this episode (entrée and pas de deux) may be of little interest, one must not therefore fail to acknowledge the fascination and charming lyricism of the rest of the music. It seems probably that this work will attract the sympathies of the entire European and Russian public not in its theatrical version but as symphonic music, to which it accomodates itself much more easily than does the music of *Apollon*. The language of *Baiser* is not based on a motley aggregate of material—*Baiser* is stylistically more coherent, fresher. Here again, as in *Pulcinella,* Stravinsky has brilliantly solved the problem of how completely to objectify the creative act, how to work creatively with materials drawn from outside one's personal experience, how to make a creative transmutation of another's material. The particular significance of this for Stravinsky, a pupil of Rimsky-Korsakov, lies in the fact that though Stravinsky's work developed into something that became the antithesis of Tchaikovsky's (whose music was deeply subjective, wholly personal, occupied with inner experiences), Stravinsky had nevertheless reached the point where he could conceive of taking Tchaikovsky's material into the inner circle of his creative musical conceptions and, by changing a few intonational functions, converting the material into contemporary fabric. The question now presents itself: might not such a thing be premature? Much of the music of Tchaikovsky lives on as it was first heard by human beings still alive. Much of it is still perceived emotionally, as an emotional event, as an inner experience. Is it not too soon to regard it merely as building material, as a subject of research and experiment? The music of Pergolesi is so far from us that the very thing we fail to perceive in *Pulcinella* is precisely what sounds strange to us in *Baiser*—the functional changes in elements of a music that is still alive. At present there can be no answer to this question. One can only have faith in the infallibility of Stravinsky's instinct, in his sensitiveness, in his presentiments of historical necessity—in the qualities, in short, that prompt him to do what he does when he does it. The art of Stravinsky is a musical outpost, and *Petrushka, Sacre, Noces, Soldat,* and *Oedipus* mark the boundaries of newer and newer claims. The immediate fate of the music of *Baiser* will show how opportune this experiment was. But in any case it will stand as a first experiment—first with respect to the music of Tchaikovsky (if one does not count Stravinsky's arrangements at the time of Diaghilev's London performances of the *Sleeping Beauty*), but not the first in Stravinsky's works.

This brings me to the conclusion that I want to draw from my book of observations about the music of this great master—a conclusion that must be tentative and not final, because we are dealing with a living person whose creative life has not ended. My conclusion is that Stravinsky has an almost barometrically sensitive capacity to foresee the course of musical change, and that the creative element in his works (like the creative element in objective experience) expresses itself in his ceaseless aspiration to contribute to the evolution of musical language through a constant renovation of its materials. Our critical epoch has been enriched by the achievements of historical musicology, by the widened expanse and deepened perspective of our knowledge and attitude toward the past, and by our optimistic anticipations of future possibilities. In addition it has faced squarely the problem of how the whole corpus of the intonational experience of past epochs can be utilized as material for new creation. At its own level, jazz has been a brilliant agent in the revitalization of improvisation. In music at the highest intellectual level, as in musicology, the problem of materials and their relation to current language have a primary importance. So, in this respect, do Stravinsky's works.

The influence of the body of these works is still difficult to determine. The fact that the superficialities of his style are inspiring certain imitations in Western European music is, so far, a promise of nothing. It is more or less simple for foreigners to pick out those elements of Stravinsky's art which brilliantly reflect the urban, constructionist tendencies of our time, elements that are echos of the contemporary European city, whose rhythms and dynamics control the movement of the music. But even so, can these imitators penetrate to the organic basis, the womb, of these extraordinary works, which are the products of Stravinsky's sensitiveness to the spontaneous music of life and nature in his great fatherland? Moreover, we must not forget that even in the works that seem to be wholly urban and European, Stravinsky cannot, despite himself, help being a Russian observer, a Russian spectator of "another" life and culture, no matter how much he may have tried to submerge his identity and reincarnate himself as a complete Westerner. It is possible that a radical assimilation of his art and an understanding of its real nature will come from the critical analyses of his music that are beginning to be made by composers of our country, analyses that are at a far remove from what one hears about Stravinsky in the West. Stravinsky's "masks," his European finery, the discussion of the cultural importance of his work as if he were just one more great foreign musician who had acclimated himself to Paris—none of this confuses us. However alien their subjects may be to us *Oedipus* and *Apollon*— not to mention *Baiser*—are profound and mature works. Perhaps Stravinsky erred here and there in his choice of certain simple, "common" intonations whose expressive connotations were familiar and "accessible" to a great many people, but the idea of regenerating the musical language through a creative transmutation of material out of the past seems to me absolutely and faultlessly contemporary, because the whole of the creative musical activity of our epoch is reaching out toward a new classicism (in a constructionist, not in an historical and stylistic, sense) which will match the public's new artistic consciousness.

Notes

1.   *Oedipus Rex,* opera-oratorio in 2 acts after Sophocles, by I. Stravinsky and J. Cocteau.

2.   I have in mind certain bourgeois musical trends. At the same time, however, there is such a brilliant model of the psychological musical drama as the *Wozzeck* of Alban Berg, a work of great aesthetic and social significance, and of outstanding importance by virtue of the way it combines severe logic of design with musical vitality and displays an extraordinarily rich and spontaneous flow of lyric emotion. Both *Wozzeck* and the *Fiery Angel* of Prokofiev show that the hot lava of romanticism has not yet cooled. *Oedipus,* of course, is at the opposite pole.

3.   *Pulcinella* in part, and *Mavra* in its entirety, are earlier examples of Stravinsky's use of strictly vocal forms.

4.   If one wants to relate *Oedipus* to the evolution of Russian opera, then it represents a continuation of the line of *Ruslan*—and in this respect it is a deeply traditional work.

5.   The orchestral accompaniment makes one thick of Pimen in *Boris Godunov.*

6.   The cumulative repetition of these scales has the effect of continually heightening the tension. The result is sheer terror.

7.   Naturally, I do not speak about criteria of artistic collectivity in the naive belief that music is created only by a communal effort, but in the sense that the composer thinks and works not as an isolated, personal, and irresponsible "dictator of taste," but in consonance with the highest norms of public artistic standards of his epoch.

     I think in this connection of Verdi, who in an era of subjective tendencies, was known for his "peasant temperament," but who never forgot what it meant to control a mass taste.

8.   Musically, the luxuriant writing of *Apollon* (despite its being scored for strings alone) on the one hand suggests a contemporary adaptation of the "vingt-quartre violons du roi," and on the other appears to be a brilliant solution of stylistic problems set by Tchaikovsky in his classically modest Serenade for string orchestra. In these respects, both are precursors of *Apollon.*

Index